Creative Bible Teaching

LAWRENCE O. RICHARDS

MOODY PRESS • CHICAGO

DEDICATION
To my parents,
Vivian and Charlotte Richards,
whose quiet living of God's Word
has proven to be His creative
force in my life

Copyright © 1970 by
THE MOODY BIBLE INSTITUTE OF CHICAGO

Ninth Printing, 1975

Library of Congress Catalog Card Number: 74-104830

ISBN: 0-8024-1640-3

Unless otherwise noted, Old Testament quotations are
taken from the Authorized Version, New Testament
quotations from the New American Standard Version.

Printed in the United States of America

CONTENTS

104167

A PERSONAL WORD BEFORE YOU READ ON, PLEASE!

What are you looking for as you open this book? If you're a layman, teaching a weekly Sunday school class or home Bible class, you're probably looking for practical ways to improve your teaching. If you're a Christian educator or a student, you're looking for more —for insights into the theory as well as practice of Bible teaching. How will this book fit your expectations? What will you find here?

Part I, The Bible We Teach (chaps. 1-5), looks at the theology of Bible teaching. It sketches the dominant contemporary view of the Bible and then discusses the conservative view in more detail. A professional or student will be deeply concerned about the issues raised here. A layman may want to move immediately to the more practical and come back at leisure to this section. So I suggest most Sunday school teachers begin to read at Part II. What will they find there?

Part II, Teaching the Bible Creatively (chaps. 6-12), applies theological and educational principles to develop a distinctively evangelical approach to Bible teaching. Here the *why* and the *how* of creative Bible teaching are analyzed and explained, with a definite emphasis on the practical. This section, developing a framework for Bible teaching, is the heart of the book. It's this section that will be of most interest and help to the lay teacher. So, if you teach Sunday school and are looking for helpful ideas, I suggest you start reading at chapter 6.

Part III, Guidelines to Creative Teaching (chaps. 13-24), shows how the basic approach can be applied by teachers of various age groups. This too is a practical section: its goal is to help teachers of the Bible develop the ability to use a variety of teaching methods well. But because that ability depends so much on the framework of teaching developed in Part II, chapter 6 is really the layman's starting place in this book.

One final word. I write this book from a decidedly conservative and evangelical position. I make no apologies for my conviction that the Bible is God's Word in propositional form, and state that the total structure of teaching developed here rests on this presupposition. At the same time I observe with sorrow that this conviction, although shared by conservatives, has not preserved us from communicating Bible truths inadequately and, at times, wrongly. It is with the sole desire that God's life-changing truth might be taught in a life-changing way that I submit this book.

LAWRENCE O. RICHARDS

PREFACE

To be called to teach is among the highest callings you can receive. The Christian teacher is entrusted with the sacred responsibility of studying and knowing the Word of God, then carefully sharing this Word in such a way that the pupil "shall be able to teach others also." (II Tim. 2:2)

Teaching is an art—a skill that must be developed through regular practice. While there are some basic "rules" or "laws" to guide, knowing the laws of pedagogy doesn't make one a teacher. One could memorize and recite all the traffic laws applicable in his city and never acquire the necessary skills to drive an automobile.

This book deals with the mastery of the art of teaching. The theories and laws are here—but in sound, practical form. While it is not a "how-to-do-it" book in that it doesn't propose "five easy steps to success," the book abounds in examples to be adopted and followed.

Such a book on teaching is long overdue in Christian education. However, after reading the manuscript two different times, I can assure you that this book has been worth waiting for. Mr. Richards has combined the genius of teaching with the gift of writing to provide us with a most helpful volume; you'll not only be instructed, but spiritually inspired as you study these pages.

WAYNE E. BUCHANAN, JR.

PART I

THE BIBLE WE TEACH

THIS
BIBLE

"It's a great book, this Bible we teach!"

That's what Chuck thought as he taught the Bible to his high school class. A great book. God's book! A book that God would use to lead his lively, noisy bunch of guys into a vital, exciting walk with Christ.

That's what Chuck thought. And he couldn't understand why his faithful, week-by-week Bible teaching didn't seem to touch his teens. Chuck taught. He taught the Bible. But the Bible just didn't seem to work.

There are many teachers like Chuck in our churches. Teaching the Bible—but without effect.

And we'd better begin this book by asking why.

MIRROR OF GOD'S WORD

I ONCE VISITED a church that helps to bring Chuck's problem, and perhaps yours, into clearer focus. I remember it as a very disturbing church. Oh, it was fundamental—and conservative—and evangelical. What disturbed me wasn't what was said in the pulpit or taught in the classes. What disturbed me was the people.

For one thing, they repulsed "outsiders." One of the farmers went into a feedstore and overheard the tail end of a questionable joke. With a grim and condemning glare at the laughing pair, he turned on his heel and stomped out. Another church family turned down invitation after invitation from neighbors, until the neighbors stopped asking them over. To the folk of the area, the people in this church were a peculiar, forbidding clan with unknown beliefs, but with many known don'ts.

And if you had seen them, you too might have wondered why. Why, when the Bible was believed and known, weren't these people more like those in the early church. Why weren't they men and women marked by their *love*, not their lists; men and women who were far more concerned with communicating Christ to their neighbors than with condemning them for their sins?

Now, I'm not creating a mythical "fundamentalist" and criticizing all believers by clubbing him. I'm describing an actual church. It may or may not be like your church. But it does exist. And the fact that it exists forces us to ask an important question: *How can people who believe the Bible, and who know the Bible, become spiritually warped?*

If we're honest, we can all think of individuals who are warped. Like the youth from a Christian home, brought up through the Sunday school, taught the Bible from toddlerhood, who goes off to college and immediately "loses" his faith. Or the businessman I know who, after training in a famous Bible institute, took a mistress while his wife was carrying their second child. Or the cantankerous old saint who can correct the pastor on any biblical topic, but who can't get along with anyone, and actively feuds with church leaders. Every church has people like these: people who know the Bible, but whose lives are warped out of its pattern. And we wonder, *Why should this be?*

One easy answer is this: "Of course! We're all sinners." No Christian is freed from the warping presence of sin, even though the Bible says we can be free from sin's power. While this is true, it's no solution. When we turn to sin for the explanation, we're really saying that we don't *expect* Christians to be Christlike! That, after all, if we're all sinners, it's only natural that we behave like sinners.

But conservatives do expect Christians to be different. We don't expect *natural* behavior of those whom Christ has touched; we expect *supernatural* behavior. We expect those who know Christ and His Word to be transformed.

That's why people like Chuck and you and me teach the Bible. We believe that men who are by nature sinners and lost can discover themselves in the mirror of the Scriptures. We believe that there they can hear the gospel. We believe that they can learn the good news that God loves us sinners and forgives all who put their trust in His Son Jesus Christ, who became Man and died to bear our sins. A person who receives this message from God and trusts himself to Christ is changed inside. And we believe that through the Word of God, applied by the Spirit of God, this new life within a person can become progressively more dominant, until experience is transformed and the very life of Christ overflows and controls the believer.

We believe this. And this is our problem.

The people in the church I described believe the Bible. They claimed Christ. The youth at one time professed to believe, as did the adulterer and the old critic. And each had gone on to learn more and more Bible. *But the Bible they learned did not transform.* And again we're forced to ask, Why?

How is it that a book, given by God to transform, seems so unproductive when taught in the very churches where it is most honored and best known? And unproductive it seems to have been. Our Christian education has often produced warped personalities; our teaching has often failed to straighten twisted lives. Warping is so common that we've become used to it! Used to shaking our heads about "lost faith" in college and dropouts in high school. Used to congregations and individuals without vitality or dedication or reality in their walk with Christ. Used to an exploding population and a sputtering evangelism. Used to living day after day with men and women who need the Saviour, and used to saying nothing to them about Him. Used to reading and studying and teaching the

Bible without seeing God use it to transform. Are we successful in reproducing the biblical faith in our twentieth century world? Have we "turned the world upside down" as did the early church? Are our churches filled with spiritual giants?

Hardly! Teaching the Bible as we teach it has not transformed men as our theology says the Word of God should. But why not? Is it possible that we haven't really understood the nature of the Bible we teach? Is it possible that we haven't been teaching the Bible in a way that harmonizes with God's purposes in giving it?

VIEWS OF SCRIPTURE

The conservative view. What we call a conservative view of Scripture—that it is God's revealed and authoritative written Word—dominated Protestantism after the Reformation. The conservative has always believed that in the Bible God communicates with man. He communicates information, truth, which we could not otherwise know. Because God has communicated His viewpoint to us in words, we need not guess what He is like or what He gives us in Christ. God has communicated with us in words, in just the way we communicate with other people.

For this speaking, God chose certain men and superintended their writing by His Holy Spirit, so that the product, our Bible, is His message. Its accuracy and infallibility are guaranteed. Of course, God didn't blank out the mind of the writer and use his hands as we would a puppet's. He didn't simply dictate. He worked through the consciousness and personality of each writer, through his feelings and patterns of expression. Yet the end result is God's message, His truth, His Word. So the conservative believes.

But in this century other approaches to the Bible have become dominant and popular. Men have suggested entirely new understandings of the nature of Scripture, and new understandings of the place the Bible has in our relationship with God. These new views have led to new approaches to teaching, to Christian nurture, and to Christian education.

The old liberal view. This view dominated the thinking of religious educators of the denominations from the twenties through the thirties. Men like George A. Coe and William C. Bower drew from the liberal theology and the progressive school of education and proposed a new approach to Christian training. And they modified completely the role of the Bible in Christian teaching.

Briefly, men of this school viewed God as One who acts in our world of today just as He acted in the biblical world. God, therefore, should not be sought in a book, but in life. To these men, however, God's activity was not supernatural in the sense of miraculous. It was natural. God worked through the natural processes of individual and societal life.

What then about the Bible? In a basic sense, the Bible was considered not needed. It did not, to these men, contain truth about God or truth from God. Instead it recorded human experience. It was the story of men and women who looked for God in the normal events of their lives and times, and who believed that they had found Him. Today, they said, we are to look for God not in the events of the past but in the events of our own society. "God is at work today!" was their exciting cry. "Let's leap into life and meet Him."

And so the Bible was discarded as a source book of truth and values and authority, and human values and relationships moved onto center stage. The goal of Christian training became the enrichment of human life, the process one of guiding people to discover the "higher Christian meanings" of their experiences. It was only in living life that God could be found, and found to be meaningful.

So religious educators and church leaders turned to the development of ways in which experiences could be guided and learners helped to grow in their ability to live meaningfully as individuals and in groups.

The new orthodox response. "Not Christian" was the charge raised against liberal religious education by H. S. Smith in his *Faith and Nurture.* The Christian faith, said Smith, is rooted in something deeper than "growing values." It is rooted in a Christian revelation. It is rooted in a sovereign God, who stands outside of history, yet who disclosed Himself in a historical Christ. Liberal religious education, without a God who discloses Himself and encounters individuals supernaturally, cannot claim to be Christian.

In a short time the neoorthodox viewpoint dominated theologically and educationally. Paul Vieth's *Church and Christian Education* reflects the changing climate. Soon Christian educators like James D. Smart, Lewis J. Sherrill and Randolph Crump Miller appeared. They attempted to develop a philosophy of Christian teaching based on neoorthodox theology. Today their influence is seen in the curricula of the major denominations, and the basic concepts they developed are reflected in most books on Christian education and in religious education publications.

The neoorthodox influence was a healthy corrective to the old liberal viewpoint. The new religious educator saw man's state as sinful (though this was variously defined). Man needs to know God, and in this process God is sovereign. There are no buttons to push to produce Him. God's revelation is channeled through the Bible, these men believed, and so the Bible did have a place in Christian training. Roy Zuck, Executive Director of the Scripture Press Foundation, pointed out six commendable emphases in neoorthodox religious education:

1. There is a great concern that Christian education theory and practice be based on theological foundations.
2. Neoorthodoxy is interested in pupils coming to know God, not just to know about God.
3. There is dissatisfaction with pupils learning Bible facts only. Bible information is not to be presented for the sake of information.
4. In neoorthodoxy the purpose of Christian education is to help pupils be responsive to God's revelation.
5. There is a growing distrust in the effectiveness of simply moralizing about the Bible or making easy applications of principles to conduct.
6. There is more stress on man's sinful condition and God's sovereignty.[1]

The theology of neoorthodoxy has now passed from favor in the denominational seminaries. As yet no theology has replaced it as dominant, although the views of Tillich, Bultmann and Altizer have all had their adherents.

But the neoorthodox years did serve to focus the attention of Christian educators on the nature of the Bible. And they led to the development of a new theory of the nature and purpose of Scripture that does dominate Christian education today. This theory rests on a distinctive concept of what revelation is, what the place of the Bible is in revelation, and how the Bible should be taught.

And in this respect we have been done a service. For development of this theory has forced us to examine the new view—and our own. We have been forced to look honestly at our own Bible teaching and to ponder why the teaching of the Bible in our churches has been so unproductive in terms of transformed, dedicated, Christ-centered lives if, as we believe, the Bible *is* the written Word of God. We have been forced to ask *theological* questions about our *teaching* of the Bible.

How we need this. How we need not merely to assert the fact of propositional revelation, but to understand the nature of that revelation and to see its implications for our Bible teaching.

Not long ago one of my students at Wheaton College introduced me to teacher Chuck by describing his experience as a high schooler in Sunday school. Here's what my student wrote:

> In our Sunday school class, Chuck followed the book to the letter and usually read the material. The class was all boys and we were from "good" homes, so we behaved fairly well at first; but when we found how far we could push Chuck and how to get a rise out of him, we really cut loose. Even though we used good material and he was prepared, we had little if any net gain from the class. We began to mock Chuck outside of class, and it wasn't long before the attitude spread to the material he was teaching.
>
> As I look back I see that Chuck was sincere and dedicated, but not prepared to teach six or eight teenage boys. As I grew older and less critical I thought of those class sessions at times, especially when the young people would get together and we would laugh about them. But it was hard to remember a class when there was any attempt to relate current events or link up the lesson to daily life. We had nothing to challenge us when we were beginning to challenge what we had been taught, and to test these "adult" ideas that had been thrown at us. We had no occasion to express our imaginative thoughts or sense of humor in the class situation at all, for Chuck believed in a highly structured, formal teaching situation, and God's Word was serious business. We were told this, but never really given any sound basis for believing it.

We can't dismiss Chuck as simply another bad teacher—though he certainly was that. We can't charge Chuck with liberalism or with being a "neo." Chuck held firmly to a conservative view of Scripture. To him teaching the Bible and learning it was "serious business."

But Chuck could and did teach the Bible without challenge, without relationship to life, without relevance. Taught the way Chuck taught it, the Bible did not promote spiritual growth; it stunted it!

That's what I meant earlier. Perhaps the Bible hasn't proven effective because we haven't understood how to teach it. Spiritual warping may be the fault of the teacher. The Book of God, given to transform, may be ineffective in the churches where it is most honored because it has been taught wrongly.

You see, God never intended the Bible to be taught as the Chucks among us teach it. And, *if they truly understood the nature of Scripture, they could never teach the Bible as they do!*

As conservative, evangelical Christians, we believe firmly that God uses His Word to transform. Let's make sure we know *how* He uses it before we dare to teach.

Research and assignment
> for the student

1. Write out your personal view of the nature of Scripture, and explain in detail implications of your view for the Bible teacher.
2. For discussion: Think of several people you know who have learned much about the Bible but aren't changed by it. How do *you* explain this?
3. Do you agree or disagree with the author that the failure of the Bible to prove productive in many situations may be traced to the way it's taught? Why? Be prepared to defend your position.
4. Collateral reading: Kendig B. Cully, *The Search for a Christian Education—Since 1940.*
5. Collateral reading: H. S. Smith, *Faith and Nurture.*

Exploration
> for the lay teacher

1. Write out your personal view of the nature of Scripture and explain in detail implications of your view for Bible teaching.
2. Look over the description of Chuck's Sunday school class. Can you see any parallels to your own teaching?

2

PERSON
TO
PERSON

"Yes sir, I would like to join the church. I think I'd make a good member. I got the highest grade in church membership class."

"But do you know God?"

"I took a test on Bible, and knew 93 percent of the answers. The national average for that test is only 38 percent."

"But do you know God?"

"When I was growing up I memorized Scripture daily. I review the verses even now. I can quote over two thousand verses."

"But do you know God?"

"Right now I'm working on memorizing whole books of the Bible. I'm just finishing Romans, and the next book I plan to start on is Ephesians."

"But do you know God?"

This is a fair question. Those who know the Bible do not necessarily know God. To the contemporary Christian educator this is an extremely significant fact.

THE CONTEMPORARY VIEW OF REVELATION

IF YOU OR I pick up a Bible, we believe that we hold in our hands the revelation of God. This is not what the contemporary* Christian educator believes. *Revelation* to him is not something recorded in the Bible.

At the time neoorthodoxy appeared, there were two basic ideas about the nature of Scripture. One (the conservative) held that "the Bible is a series of infallible propositions or verbally inspired truths." The other (the liberal) that it "is a 'resource' written by men who, in their search for reality, have discovered and recorded insights from their own experiences." Both these ideas have been largely discarded. A new idea of the nature of revelation has changed the majority thinking about the Bible.

What is this new concept of revelation? A theologian like Barth will talk about revelation as "the whole of the existential relationship in which man is confronted by God." Christian educators put it in simpler language. Sara Little says, "Revelation is essentially the self-disclosure of God."[1]

SELF-DISCLOSURE

For those used to thinking of revelation in the conservative way, this idea is hard to grasp. But go back a minute to the dialogue leading into this chapter. The speaker kept bringing up his mastery of the Bible. The questionner kept asking for testimony of personal relationship with Christ. A conservative might conclude that the person knew God's revelation, but did not know God. To the contemporary theologian this distinction is nonsense. The *Bible* isn't viewed as God's revelation. God's revelation is a personal experience of God.

Lewis Sherrill explains this in detail. "To speak of revelation as God's *self*-disclosure implies that *what* is revealed in the encounter between God and man is not information *about* God, but God *him-*

---

* In this book *contemporary* is used to designate those holding the view of revelation described in this chapter. While this view of revelation is definitely rooted in neoorthodoxy, it would be inaccurate to describe those who hold it today as neoorthodox.

self as a personal being." "Revelation takes place in the meeting between God as a Person and man as a person. Revelation is not information about God; it is what happens in the encounter between God as a Self and man as a self."[2]

Take, for instance, the time of the exodus. Remember the miracles recorded in the Bible? Well, that Bible record is *not* revelation. The miracles themselves were not revelation. *Revelation was the subjective awareness of the Israelites that they were encountering God.*

Look at a common example. A young girl is sitting in the choir. Down in the auditorium is a young man, obviously interested in the girl. You watch with some amusement as she carefully studies her music, avoiding but feeling his gaze. Then, finally, she glances up and their eyes meet. She flushes slightly and looks away. But in that intense instant each communicated something of himself to the other.

In this situation no words were spoken. No information was passed. If you describe the incident, you can only say that the third girl from the end of the first row of the choir looked up, flushed slightly and looked down again. You might say she happened to look toward the left of the auditorium at the same time a young man in that section was looking toward the choir loft, but you couldn't even say (for sure) that their eyes met.

But what about the two? Each of them is sure something exciting and tremendous has happened. Each of them *knows* that he shared something of himself, the intensity of his feelings, with the other. How? He knows because he experienced. It was real. He "knew" her and she "knew" him, in a way no mere words could express.

Something like this happened to the people in the exodus. Somehow they experienced God. And they knew that He shared Himself with them. They met Him, Person to person.

It's important to understand that to the contemporary Christian educator subjective experience is the *whole* of revelation. Iris Cully suggests that "the only revelation that has a unique character is the revelation of a self to another person."[3] She is asserting that revelation is *not* both experiential and informational; it is *only* experiential. Sherrill develops this idea. "The reports of revelation may be cast in terms that contain information, or that attempt to describe what was perceived in the encounter. But in the encounter itself what is disclosed is some aspect of infinite, perfect Selfhood, being unveiled in some form of relationship with finite, imperfect selves."[4]

What are they saying? Simply this. We may have real encounters with God, but in those encounters *we gain no information*. God does not communicate ideas. He communicates Himself.

Here our analogy of the boy and girl breaks down. After all, when she glanced at him the girl may at least have seen the color of his eyes, the shape of his jaw, the way he combed his hair. So the experience was *accompanied by* the opportunity to gain information. But who, in meeting God, sees the color of His eyes? Who sees the shape of His jaw? God is infinite, perfect Selfhood. And we; we are finite, imperfect. He is simply too vast for us to grasp, too different for the categories we use to pigeonhole our ideas. We can experience Him, but we cannot limit Him; we cannot squeeze Him into finite terms or capture His soaring thoughts in our crawling minds.

And that's it. That's revelation to the contemporary Christian educator: experiencing God without the communication of information about God.

CAN I HAVE A REVELATION?

Revelation experiences are not limited to those in Bible days. A person today needs to know God, not just to know about Him.

Contemporary Christian educators are strong on this point. The purpose of Christian education is to bring learners to direct experience with God. "Revelation as understood in the Bible," says Sherrill, "thus has the double quality of being rooted in the events of history and yet of being prolonged in history in such a way that the revelatory events of the past continue to disclose not a fixed and dead meaning, but a living God who still speaks freshly through what he has already said."[5]

Broken down, this sentence shares several vital ideas. The events of the exodus comprised a context in which God revealed Himself to Israel. While these events occurred once, in past history, the revelation experience that accompanied them isn't necessarily over. We can meet and know God in the way the Israelites did. We can hear God speak freshly to us today, even though the context of events will never recur.

And it's the fresh word that counts. The writer of Exodus didn't capture a revelation, freeze it, and slice it up into lines and paragraphs to be pasted into a book of "fixed and dead meaning." He described as best he could the experience and the events. And some-how, as we through the Bible project ourselves into that past, God reveals Himself to us today. Not that what He says is summed up in the words of the Bible. Remember, revelation communicates God, not information. What happens is that the Bible itself becomes a context (as did the original events) in which God reveals Himself.

And this leads up to the Bible. What about *it?* If revelation is *self-*disclosure, not information disclosure, what role does the Bible play in revelation? And how do you teach it to provide a context for personal experience with God, rather than a mastery of facts?

THE CONTEMPORARY VIEW OF THE BIBLE

When the neoorthodox abandoned the traditional doctrine of rev-elation in favor of the one we've just described, they were forced to rethink the nature of the Bible. If revelation (now viewed as an immediate experience which does not provide truths about God) cannot be communicated, what is communicated in the Bible? Let's look at the ideas about the Bible which the neoorthodox held.

WHAT IS THE BIBLE?

"The Bible is a witness to revelation in that it contains the record of the original revelation by which the church was called into being and to which it owes its continued existence. It is not the revelation itself, but points to it. It is the written record of the revelation."[6] "The Bible is a record of the historic source of the Christian community and the Christian faith—a medium of revelation to this community."[7] "The Bible, as witness to and participant in the events of revelation, is of unique significance to the church and in the life of man."[8] The Bible as "a report of revelation is the attempt to give account of such an experience, in words which will so far as are possible com-municate to others what one has perceived when he was so con-fronted."[9] "What the Bible does for men is to witness to what God has done and the ways in which he has shown himself to His people."[10]

In words like these the contemporary Christian educators express their understanding of the Bible. It's a witness. It's a report. It's a channel of revelation. But it's not revelation itself.

The pattern is illustrated in figure 1, Event and Report. For instance: during the exodus period the Israelites lived through several great events. Within the context of these events they had a revelation experience. They were aware that God revealed Himself to them. The revelation was *not* the events themselves (although some speak of "God's mighty acts" as though the acts constituted the revelation); the revelation was *associated with* the events.

The writer of the exodus experience couldn't communicate the revelation. (Remember? Revelation is experiential, not informational.) What could he communicate? A report of the experience.

That's what he did. He wrote down a report of the events, and he attempted to describe what his people experienced. He gave the best description he could, limited by his understandings in that prescientific age, limited also by the fact that one cannot describe God. And this *report of revelation* is what we have as the Bible. Not words inspired by God, but a human being's attempt to share with others the fact and meaning of his personal experience with God.

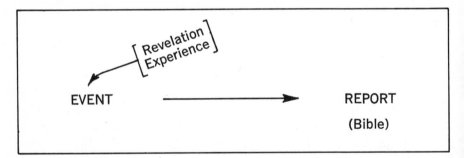

Fig. 1. WHAT IS THE BIBLE? A REPORT OF REVELATION

The report attempts to describe the revelation experience and the events accompanying it, and to interpret its meaning for those who experienced it.

This view of the Bible as a human attempt to express something inexpressible is another jolt to the conservative Christian. It implies a fallible book, one not necessarily containing "true" information about God, and one whose teachings need to be reinterpreted to fit new understandings. And this is just what the contemporary asserts.

"The words record in human, fallible words God's revelatory acts," claims Sara Little, and "the message is not to be identified with specific words of the Bible." Sherrill comes out clearly and says that "reports of the original experiences are [to be] examined critically in the effort to determine whether the original experiences and the reports of them are authentic; and if so, to determine what they reveal."[11] In this way the literal meaning of the Bible is denied, not so much by claiming that it is not "true," but that its "truth" is irrelevant. What counts is the experience with God the writer had, which he is trying to express in his archaic patterns of thought. This we can discover by going beyond and behind the literal.

And so contemporary Christian education views the Bible as a human book, fallible and open to critical examination. As Butler says of the Sermon on the Mount and Paul's epistles, "Some discernment and judgment is to be used in determining how much of this precept is derived from the Faith, and therefore necessarily follows from it, and how much of it is an expression of the limited cultural background of the person writing it."[12]

WHAT IS THE ROLE OF THE BIBLE TODAY?

Just because the contemporary view of the Bible differs so significantly from the conservative, don't feel the Bible has no role in that system. Sara Little claims the opposite. "The role of the Bible in Christian education has undergone crucial changes in recent years, and is now moving toward a point of at least relative stability. The new vitality and depth of concern generally evident . . . seem closely related to the resurgence of interest in the Bible, in its message, its authority, its relevance."[13] Why has contemporary Christian education emphasized the Bible if it's such a fallible book? Because, in the words of Iris Cully, it is "a participant in the events of revelation."

Let's go back to our diagram of the Bible, and add another dimension. For that same fallible report may, by God's sovereign act, *become* "the Word." It may become a channel, a context in which God reveals Himself to men today.

As an individual reads the writer's account of the exodus and the report of Israel's revelation experience, God may choose to reveal Himself afresh. This is the exciting thing about the Bible. It's God's Book, in the sense that God awaits us there, willing to meet us personally and make Himself known to us.

This idea of the role of the Bible—that it serves as a doorway

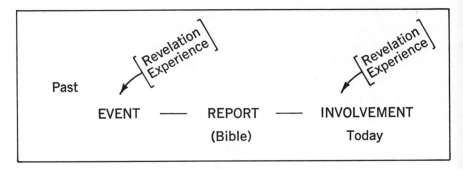

Fig. 2. WHAT IS THE BIBLE? A CHANNEL OF REVELATION

As an individual reads the report of revelation and identifies with the events, God may reveal Himself to him also.

through which God chooses to step into lives today—explains the important place it is given in many contemporary denominational curricula. The Bible is *not* the Word, but it can *become* the Word.

"The Bible," says the Statement of Basic Presuppositions of the Covenant Life Curriculum, "is the spectacles through which a man may see God. Through the pages of Scripture we seek to meet the living Savior of whom the Scriptures testify." This is possible only because "through the Holy Spirit the words may become the Word. Yet the Word is Jesus Christ. . . . The authority of the Bible therefore rests in its content, not in its words."[14]

The Bible's function thus is not informational. Its purpose is to help an individual know and experience God personally. It can help an individual know God because Jesus Christ reveals Himself (not information *about* Himself) there. And it's to this end that the Bible must be taught. "The Bible does not come into its true function in the Christian community," says Butler, "unless it becomes contemporaneous revelation, and not just a record out of the past. The primary content of Christian education is not the Bible, but the message of the Bible, and that message is the Person of Jesus Christ."[15]

WHAT DOES IT ALL MEAN?

The view of revelation and of the Bible that we've sketched has led to a distinctive approach to Bible teaching. It boils down to this.

The content of revelation is God Himself, not information about God. The information in the Bible is not revelation. It is the report of experiences men have had with God. But the Bible is more than a report. It is a channel for present-day experience with God. In it we can find not truth about God, but God Himself. Thus the Bible teacher *must teach the Bible so that the learner meets God, not so that he learns information about God!*

This is one possible solution to the problems we raised in chapter 1. The members of the loveless church knew the Bible. The immoral man, the old Bible student with the critical spirit, had Bible information. But did they know God? No! And the contemporary theologian might say it was because they took a literal approach to Scripture! Because they confused words and ideas about God with God Himself. They thought they had arrived when they mastered doctrines. But they hadn't even started. For the "climax of the Biblical revelation [is] not to be found primarily in a body of material, but in the confrontation of a Person."[16]

We all recognize the fact that many who know biblical truths never seem able to go on to knowing God. But why? One reason that neoorthodox thinkers put forth is that "conscious literalism" is the enemy of true theology. That is, if you consciously take the Bible literally, you're not likely to see beyond it to Christ. Sherrill says that "when we refer to the symbols* in the Bible and assert that they are literally true, we convert symbols into signs. This is one of the grave errors of fundamentalism: it has taken symbolic literature in the Bible and by rationalistic fiat has made it literal description or formula."[17] It's dangerous to take literally what wasn't meant literally! You're likely to miss the whole meaning. You're likely to miss the Person.

Contemporary Christian educators are working hard on ways to teach the Bible so that students don't miss the Person. They don't believe that they've arrived. "Education today within the Church," says Hunter in *Christian Education as Engagement*, "is not focused on immediate encounter with God; . . . it is centered, rather, on instruction, on teaching about someone else's encounter."[18]

Yet people like Iris Cully and Thomas K. Dendry have presented

---

*Ideas that are meant to point beyond themselves. To Sherrill this is *most* of Scripture.

ideas on how to focus on encounter. They go something like this: First you involve the learner as vitally as possible in the biblical situation. This may mean playing out the Red Sea story for younger children; or, with adults, identifying issues in today's world which are like the issues that Amos prophetically condemned and becoming involved in these issues. When the identification is as real as possible, the context for encounter is created.

Contemporary Christian education doesn't stop here, of course. With encounter comes insight—not knowledge, but awareness of new dimensions and Christian meanings of life situations. With this insight comes awareness of the need to respond, to *do* as God seems to direct. For with each fresh encounter, the one who has met God is to change. A final step in the process, as suggested by some, is expressing (putting into words, being able to explain) the meaning of the experience.

By this process of encounter with God and response to God truly Christian personalities are produced. And by this process, with its new understanding and use of the Bible, the errors of "literalistic fundamentalism" are avoided. So speaks the contemporary voice.

Probably all this leaves you with some questions. It does me! The *end* certainly is desirable. We conservatives want our students to know God, not just to have information about Him. We want them to respond to God, to be transformed by Him. But how does this *really* take place?

Charge the failures of conservatism to a literal approach to Scripture if you will; but how then can you explain its successes? How explain the lives of literalist saints who through the ages have adorned the doctrine of God? It seems hard to believe that abandoning the literal meaning of Scripture provides the solution to our problems. And how can one learn authoritatively from a book that is only a fallible record of God's self-revelation to man?

But right or wrong about revelation and the nature of the Bible, contemporary Christian educators have raised some helpful issues. How *do* you teach the Bible to help students know God? What *is* the relationship between information about God and personal experience with God? How *can* God be known?

And they have done another thing: they have forced us back to the basics we must understand in order to answer these questions.

We must understand revelation. We must understand the nature of the Bible. And we must ask, Is the contemporary view right?

Research and assignment
    for the student
1. Read the article on "Revelation" in the *Westminster Dictionary of Christian Education*. What about this article reflects the neoorthodox view?
2. Look through several Christian education magazines in your school library and locate at least one article in which a contemporary position is expressed. Be prepared to discuss the article in class.
3. Write a letter to a friend in your home church who asks you to explain *neoorthodox*, something he's heard your new curriculum is.
4. Read all the books of at least one contemporary Christian educator. Write a report stressing his view of the nature of the Bible and the influence of this view on his thinking.
5. Be prepared for a quiz. Prepare by studying the Exploration assignment, below.
6. Visit a pastor or DCE who holds the contemporary view and ask him to explain revelation and the role of the Bible as he understands it.
7. How would you go about seeking a revelation of God if you were neoorthodox? Describe in detail.
8. How would you *know* you had a revelation? Explain.
9. Explain as well as you can how *you* teach the Bible to lead your students to personal experience of God.

Exploration
    for the lay teacher
Test your understanding of the position discussed in this chapter by writing down your answers to the following. Then check them by reviewing what you've read.
1. What is revelation to the neoorthodox?
2. What is the Bible?
3. How is the Bible related to revelation?
4. Why should the Bible be used in Christian teaching? What to the contemporary Christian educator might be *wrong* reasons for its use?

CONTEMPORARY CRITIQUE

What happens when Bible statements are no longer regarded as revealed truths? When "experience behind the words" is seen as valid and true, but not the ideas the words express? Randolph Crump Miller in *Education for Christian Living* writes that "with this dynamic view of revelation . . . we are not bound by fixed words or by historic formulations of the faith."

"Not bound." We no longer have to believe what the Bible says.

This doesn't mean that all contemporary Christian educators reject all historic doctrines. But it does mean that they feel free to reject old meanings of such terms as *sin*, resurrection, justification by faith, conversion, etc., in favor of new meanings. It's instructive to take a look at some of the meanings contemporary writers have suggested for historic Christian doctrines. Such a look helps us see where "freedom" from fixed words and meanings has led.

A NEW FAITH

WE'VE SEEN that the contemporary Christian educator doesn't understand the Bible as others throughout church history have. He views the Bible as communicating Christ, but not communicating information about Christ. Biblical statements reflect the experience of the writer with Christ, but do not convey truths about Him.

This raises a question about all the statements the Bible makes. For instance, the Bible does say "All have sinned"; "Christ died for the ungodly"; "By grace are you saved through faith." And events are described in the Bible: the creation, the resurrection, the miracles of Christ. If these aren't to be understood as true information, how should the Christian take them?

The contemporary answer seems to be that such statements and descriptions must be understood as expressions of religious understandings. They speak to us today, although we do not take them in any literal sense. The surprising thing is, though, that when contemporary Christian educators restate these "religious understandings" for today, *the restatement often seems to be in complete contradiction to the literal meaning!* Here are a few quotes, taken from a variety of sources, to illustrate what I mean.

MYTHICAL EVENTS

The idea of myth is important to contemporary writers who try to understand biblical events. "Biblical myths," says the *Westminster Dictionary of Christian Education,* "are dramatic stories in symbolic language about God and his relation to men and the world, which demand of man a decision and a commitment. Mythology appropriates symbolic language. The believer who uses mythological language knows that it is symbolic, that it does not denote exactly, that it does not describe (as, e.g., scientific language does) but points beyond itself to truth apprehensible in faith."[1]

What are these mythical events, which are not "real" in the sense that phenomena described by science are real? The Westminster dictionary suggests the following are, in some degree, mythical: creation, heaven and hell, angels, Jesus' preexistence, the incarnation and virgin birth, miracles, the crucifixion, the resurrection, the

Antichrist, the second coming, the Holy Spirit, the millennium and the last judgment!

Speaking of the miracles of Christ, Sherrill says that to take them literally "places on faith a burden too grievous to be borne." So he suggests we "treat these stories, or at least many of them, as myths. When this is done the value of the stories lies in their symbolism. Through symbols they communicate meanings which defy any other means of communication."[2]

The writings of Randolph Crump Miller give illustration of the "meanings" such mythical events can communicate.

> The story of Lazarus, for example, seems improbable on the face of it, but if what is being communicated here is the fact that new life can come out of death, it fits into the total scheme of things, not as a fact, but as an acted parable. Certainly the story of the Ascension is in this same category of being an account within the framework of a three-storied universe of a genuine experience of the apostles. The apostles did cease at some point to be aware of the presence of the Risen Lord, and the story is told in terms of what might be called a "flying saucer theology." Literally the story is absurd to adults and children alike, but what is being said thru the story is very important.[3]

To contemporary writers, then, the happening which is described may be absurd and unscientific. But the absurdity isn't important, because we don't have to take the Bible literally! That is, Lazarus wasn't really raised. Christ didn't really ascend. The story is "true" and relevant for us not because it happened, but because it conveys an important religious insight: that new life can come out of death, or that the disciples became suddenly aware that Christ wasn't with them.

And men like Roger L. Shinn (*Educational Mission of the Church*) ask us which is more important: "Is the story of Jonah and the whale meant to be an incredible fish story, or a parable about missionary responsibility?" To them the accuracy of the account just doesn't matter.

DOCTRINAL FORMULATIONS

Van A. Harvey, professor of philosophical theology at the Southern Methodist Perkins School of Theology (in the August 4, 1965, *Christian Century*) says, "All religious doctrines can't be given a 'cash value' [pragmatic validity]. For this reason we find many traditional doctrines, like the doctrine of the Trinity, the belief in a life after death or the language about 'God's mighty acts' not so much false as empty."

What meanings do writers today discover in old and "empty" doctrines? Take, for example, the thinking of contemporaries on sin and salvation.

A "reconstructed liberal," Harold L. DeWolf, thinks of sin more as a societal condition than a personal perversion. He suggests that a baby is not a sinner, but in sin. "He has come into a world rife with injustice, prejudice, hate and jealous fear. . . . The willful self-assertion which raises barriers against God permeates the whole societal atmosphere he breathes. To be born a human being is to be involved in the moral, social, and physical hazard of life in a wretchedly sinful society."[4]

G. C. Schreyer defines sin as "a consciousness that a thought or deed weakens or breaks man's relationship with God. . . . A sinner is one therefore who is living unnaturally without a responsive nature to God, trusting in self for life's highest values." To Schreyer man's state of lostness means that he is "occupied with material things and technical skills, to the neglect of the moral and spiritual discipline within his being. This condition has left him vague and uncertain over purposes, values, and destiny. He is moving toward meaninglessness, inner conflict, and basic frustrations that will tend to call into question all moral and spiritual aspirations."[5]

If this is being lost, what is salvation? Schreyer, commenting on Romans 3:23, notes that "man has a capacity for sin, but he also has the capacity for goodness." Because of this, Christian education must "guide man toward a growing response to God, to cause him to see his helpless state in sin without God, and to show him that he does not know God if he does not feel his own unworthiness and the need for forgiveness." Randolph Miller comments on regeneration and forgiveness this way: "Men are transformed and become new creatures, reborn in the Spirit. But such a relationship is never stable because men fall from grace and stand in need of further forgiveness. Regeneration is not a once-for-all conversion but is a continuing process throughout all of life."[6]

There are some good, biblical terms used here: forgiveness, regeneration. *But these terms are not used in the traditional way.* This is seen clearly in Sara Little's explanation of the essential place of "conversion" in Christian education. Conversion, she says, has a place in Christian education, but the term must not be interpreted too narrowly. "This does not mean that one is first a child of sin and then, by a sudden conversion, becomes a child of God." No matter how deeply a man has fallen into sin, "beneath it all he is a child of God. We do not make a person a child of God by telling him that God is his Father. He has been a child of God from the beginning and our words do no more than make him aware of who he is."[7] What then does "conversion" describe? "The transformation which takes place in our human lives with each fresh inbreaking of God upon us."

And so sin today is an upset perspective on life; conversion is the transformation that comes when God breaks in on us. And salvation? Salvation seems to be a turning of man "from his secular motivations to the realization that the only way out of his dilemma is to seek a Power beyond himself who can give new direction to daily life." Just daily life? No eternity? James D. Smart writes,

> The only immortality that man can know is life in God and God's life in him. To be cut off from God is death, not just in eternity, but in time. . . . Not many generations ago it was characteristic of evangelical Christianity to define salvation as salvation from a hell of torment with assurance of a blessed life in heaven. . . . With the recognition that . . . salvation is the deliverance of man primarily from present evils, there has been a powerful reaction from the otherworldliness of the earlier time. Salvation is interpreted in terms of transformation of personal and social life; . . . in some quarters it would be regarded as most unhealthy and neurotic for anyone to be concerned about what will happen to him after death.[8]

THE PERSON AND WORK OF CHRIST

We've seen how contemporary writers view the events recorded in Scripture, and the doctrines presented there. But what about the most crucial area of teaching? What is the view of Jesus Christ? Is He the preexistent God, the second Person of the Trinity, who became man, lived, died on the cross for our sins, was raised, ascended to heaven to sit on the right hand of the Father, and will return and put all enemies under His feet and judge the living and the dead?

We've seen that the *Westminster Dictionary of Christian Education* has classified most of these ideas as mythical and that Miller looks on a literal ascension as "absurd," an example of "flying saucer theology." Two quotes from James Smart, one on the virgin birth and one on the ascension, show what happens when men are "freed" from literalism.

> Jesus was from the beginning responsive and obedient to the Spirit. Where our relation to God is a broken one long before we are conscious of it since we are born into a humanity that is estranged from God, his relation to God is one unbroken oneness. . . . Conceived by the Holy Spirit asserts that this was the nature of his being from the first moment of his early existence.

Biological ideas were never involved!

> The ascension marks the end of one stage in God's redemption of mankind, begins another, and points forward to a consummation at the end of history. In this context, we can understand why Christians would speak of an ascension.

> We shall not try to visualize an "ascent" into heaven in which he who had been known among men as Jesus of Nazareth was exalted to the right hand of the Father to be worshiped henceforth as King of kings and Lord of lords. The ascension, then, is . . . going from one form of manifestation to another. . . . The ascension is the early church's way of saying that the time of direct knowledge of Jesus came to an end, and the time of indirect knowledge of him began.[9]

In short, freedom from fixed words and historic formulations has meant the development of a new faith.

In 1940 Smith criticized the old liberalism as "not Christian." It's rather difficult to understand how a contemporary religion which takes out of biblical terms and historic doctrines the very meanings that have for twenty centuries set Christianity apart dare call *itself* Christian!*

All this, of course, does not *prove* that the neoorthodox view of the Bible and revelation is wrong. But certainly leaving the orthodox view of Scripture has had peculiar results. Suddenly, in the past twenty years, we've discovered that the Bible isn't really saying what believers have thought it's been saying for twenty centuries. Thus the contemporary reinterpretation of the Christian faith highlights an important question. If the words of Scripture aren't meant to be taken literally, how do we know what they mean? How can we tell what religious meanings they convey? How can anyone know his doctrines are right?

A PROBLEM OF INTERPRETATION

Whenever anyone suggests, as Butler does, that "discernment and judgment is to be used in determining how much [biblical] precept is derived from the Faith, and therefore necessarily follows from it, and how much of it is an expression of the limited cultural background of the person writing it,"[10] he implies that some standard of judgment exists by which we can make this distinction. When neo-orthodox writers speak of biblical myths and presume to interpret their religious meaning, they implicitly claim to have a key that unlocks that meaning.

The conservative feels the key to meaning is to be found in the normal approach to language. He takes the Bible literally. This does not mean, of course, that the conservative fails to recognize poetic expression ("The mountains saw thee, and they trembled: the overflowing of the water passed by: the deep uttered his voice, and lifted up his hands on high" [Hab. 3:10]) or symbolism ("The LORD is my shepherd") or other forms of nonstatemental communication. It does mean that when the Bible makes a statement such as "Behold, a virgin shall be with child, and shall bring forth a son" (Matt. 1:23), the conservative understands the statement in its normal linguistic sense. A virgin will have a son. This, of course, is biologically im-

---

*The above quotes aren't meant to prove, or to suggest, that no one who holds a contemporary view of revelation is a Christian. Many would not go so far from the literal meaning as those quoted have.

possible. And so the reader has two options. He can believe that God accomplished a biological impossibility or he can reject the statement as untrue. *If you take the Bible in a literal way, these are the only options you have.* But you have no doubt as to *meaning!*

With the contemporary concept of revelation another option is opened. You can refuse to believe this statement in its normal biological sense and still try to find a religious "truth" behind the literally false. This is what James Smart does when he claims that "conceived by the Holy Spirit asserts that this [a relation with God of unbroken oneness] was the nature of his being from the first moment of his early existence."

Now, if I take a literal approach to Scripture, I know what the biblical statement means. But if I don't take this approach, *how do I know whether Smart's interpretation is right or wrong?* Why can't the "virgin birth" assert that no normal human being can become as spiritual as Jesus? Or that intimate experience with God is only possible when He breaks in on us from outside our world, and is never attained by our efforts? Or even that Christ seemed to His disciples so superior and "other" that they couldn't bring themselves to think of Him as human? In a very real way, you can *never* know the "religious meaning" if you separate it from the literal.

Various contemporary writers have suggested keys to enable interpretation of biblical myths and "empty" terms. Shinn presents a common view. "One way," he writes, "to describe the key to Christian understanding of the Bible is to use a traditional phrase, important in the Bible and reemphasized by the Protestant Reformation, the *Word of God.* This Word was made flesh in Christ. The deed of God in Christ, therefore, determines the Christian interpretation of the Bible and its authority." Shinn goes on to point out that to understand Christ we need both the Old Testament and the New Testament, but at the same time must not "justify sub-Christian conduct by the 'authority' of passages in Scripture that report lower standards of conduct." To understand Scripture we need to understand "God's revealing work in Christ."[11]

But whose Christ does Shinn mean? The virgin-born, preexistent God of literal interpretation or Smart's human Jesus who lived a life of unbroken oneness with God? Or perhaps yet another?

Sara Little also speaks of Christ as "God's direct authority," and Harry C. Monroe wants to evaluate Scripture by the historic Jesus.

But in point of fact, each interprets Scripture not by Christ, but by *his own idea of Christ.*

What I mean is this. If the only way you can understand Christ is through Scripture, as Shinn says, *you have to give meaning* to the passages that speak of Christ *before* you can conceive of Him. So the "Christ" you find depends on how you approach the Bible in the first place. If you take any nonliteral approach, your own idea of Christ *must* be read into the Scriptures in which you claim to discover Him. Such a Christ of personal invention can hardly serve as an objective standard by which to guarantee the accuracy of further interpretation!

Other writers suggest different keys. Randolph Miller sees the Bible as a drama, in which relationships (separation, reconciliation, etc.) are expressed. Sherrill thinks the key to interpretation is found in major biblical themes that correspond with our human predicament: creation, vocation, judgment, etc. Each of these keys shares the difficulty of the first. Each "key" is as much a human invention, in the sense that it is not revealed, as is a "Christ" who is not God, not raised from the dead, not ascended into heaven, not waiting to appear a second time. There is no way to be sure of the meaning of the Bible if its words are not to be understood in their normal, literal sense.

AN APPROACH

While the conservative can express appreciation to the contemporary Christian educator for raising the question of the nature of the Bible and for reemphasizing the importance of personal experience with God, he can't agree with the contemporary answer. The new view of revelation has led to a faith which is not historic Christianity. And this view offers no means of verifying its reinterpretations.

But the questions it raises must still be answered. What *is* the nature of the Bible? How *does* a person find reality in personal experience with God? And how *can* the Bible be taught to promote spiritual growth?

We're going to take a simple approach in search of answers. We'll see what the Bible—taken in its literal sense—says about itself. What does the Bible say about revelation? About how God intends Scripture to function in bringing men to know Him? When we take this direct approach, some clear (and condemning!) answers are found.

Research and assignment
for the student

1. Look through several Christian education magazines or books by contemporary Christian educators for more examples of what happens when people are "not bound by fixed words or historic formulations."

2. The author says that contemporary "restatement" of biblical ideas "often seems to be in complete contradiction to the original biblical expression." What's the significance of this fact?

3. Read in the *Westminster Dictionary of Christian Education* the article on "Myth." Be prepared to explain what *myth* means, and the relationship between myth and truth. Can you see how this concept removes all possible conflict between Scripture and science?

4. Do you agree with the author that the religion expressed in the quotes in this chapter is not Christian? Why, or why not?

5. What does "literal interpretation" mean? Look through hermeneutics books (such as Bernard Ramm, *Protestant Biblical Interpretation*) and develop a clear picture of the major tenets and approach of literal interpretation.

6. Express in your own words the author's meaning when he says, "You can *never* know the 'religious meaning' [of Scripture] if you separate it from the literal." Do you agree or disagree? Why?

7. Express in your own words why the author thinks that those who say that "Christ" is the key to understanding the Bible are not really speaking of Christ, but of their own idea of Christ.

8. Write a defense of, or attack on, the following statement: "There is no way to be sure of the meaning of the Bible if its words are not to be understood in their normal, literal sense."

Exploration
for the lay teacher

1. Look over the above assignments and check yourself to see if you understand the ideas questioned.

THE NATURE OF
REVELATION

It's fun to make up words that have their own private meaning. One word used around our house just now is "skronk." We use it of our three children, and its meaning depends on our tone of voice. Spoken in a light tone, it's a term of mild affection. Spoken with displeasure it expresses the common irritation of parents who find offspring both annoying and amusing.

Someday I may change the meaning, maybe have it mean "potato bug" or something else.

That's my privilege. It's my private word.

But I have no right to change the meaning of words that aren't private. Their meaning is determined by the way people commonly use them.

That's why to find out what revelation is, we need to find out how the writers of the Bible used the word, what they meant by it, and what the people who read the Bible understood by it. It certainly did not mean "noninformational personal encounter"!

JUST GLANCE through the Bible and it strikes you that the writers were not only sure they knew God; they were sure they knew a lot about Him.

They thought they knew what God had done in human history; they labeled events as His acts, like His overshadowing Mary so that her child was truly man and truly God (Luke 1:35; Matt. 1:18). They said God caused the flood, that He led Israel out of Egypt. They said national emergencies, the invasions of Israel by pagan nations, were God's chastising acts (Isa. 10:5 f.; Hab. 1:6). Peter said that God caused, in the sense of ordaining, Christ's crucifixion (Acts 2:23).

And the writers went beyond events. They claimed to know God's motives, and outcomes of events that simply could not be observed. They tell, for example, *why* Christ died, and what His death accomplished. Christ died for our sins (Rom. 15:3) to reconcile us to God (II Cor. 5:18) in order that we might have God's forgiveness (Eph. 1:6) and be given immortality (II Tim. 1:10) and eternal life (Titus 1:2). Christ's death means other things, too, and the writers thought they knew what the meaning was for the entire universe (Rom. 8:19 f.) and for Satan (Heb. 2:14).

The Bible writers even dare to talk about what God will do in the future, giving details of Christ's physical return (I Thess. 4:14 f.), of the end of the earth (II Peter 3:7), of man's final rebellion under the "man of sin" (II Thess. 2) and of the final judgment on unbelievers (II Thess. 1:7 f.). And of God's plans for the future, Bible writers dare to say "the Spirit speaketh expressly" (I Tim. 4:1)!

No one can read things like this without being sure that these writers felt that they had—and were communicating—information about God and from God.

INFORMATION—PASSED FROM GOD TO MAN

THE PLACE OF WORDS

Obviously, if information (as distinct from raw data) is going to be communicated, words play a part. Words have a relation to revelation in neoorthodox thinking, too. To the contemporary, words may describe a revelation experience or events men perceived as

God's activity. But words cannot communicate true information, for no information is passed in revelation.

Paul, writing in I Corinthians 2, gives a strikingly different picture. In this passage, particularly 2:9-13 (see fig. 3), he portrays both a divine source of information and a verbal means of communication. Let's note the most significant ideas.

Information, not secured in human experience. All of us draw conclusions from our experiences. We watch another person for a time, and we get ideas of why he acts as he does. We assign motives and even predict behavior. This much we deduce from experience.

In this passage Paul is talking about something a little different. He's talking about God's plans, "the hidden wisdom, which God ordained before the world" (2:7). It's information about these plans which Paul says is now revealed.

Now, in what possible way could men discover God's hidden plans? Paul quotes the Old Testament to nail down the fact that no source of such information exists in the realm of human experience. No eye saw it. No ear heard it. No one imaginatively figured it out. These ideas did not develop as a human interpretation of a "revelation experience." Such information had to be directly revealed by God.

The Spirit reveals. It's one thing to deduce from observed behavior, and another entirely to know by revelation. No one on the outside can get down into another person's mind and know his thoughts. The person has to share his thoughts if they are to be known.

Paul points out that the Holy Spirit *is* God. So He can comprehend the thoughts of God, "even the depths of God." Revelation to Paul is a work of the Spirit by which He communicates information from God to men. And the initial purpose of this communication isn't said to be "to bring men to encounter." It's that we might *understand* God's gifts to us.

Communication is by words. After all, God wants us to understand, to know, not to guess. And so He communicates to us in the way that we communicate, in a way that we can understand, by words.

In the passage Paul says we impart (communicate) God's revelation in "words . . . taught by the Spirit" (2:13).

What view of revelation does Paul present? Boiled down, the passage looks at revelation like this:

The source of revelation is the Spirit.

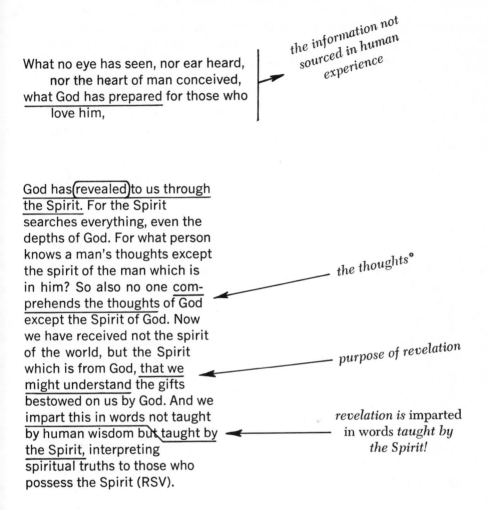

What no eye has seen, nor ear heard, nor the heart of man conceived, what God has prepared for those who love him,

→ *the information not sourced in human experience*

God has (revealed) to us through the Spirit. For the Spirit searches everything, even the depths of God. For what person knows a man's thoughts except the spirit of the man which is in him? So also no one comprehends the thoughts of God except the Spirit of God. Now we have received not the spirit of the world, but the Spirit which is from God, that we might understand the gifts bestowed on us by God. And we impart this in words not taught by human wisdom but taught by the Spirit, interpreting spiritual truths to those who possess the Spirit (RSV).

*the thoughts**

purpose of revelation

revelation is imparted in words *taught by the Spirit!*

Fig. 3. CONTRIBUTION OF I CORINTHIANS 2:9-13 TO OUR UNDERSTANDING OF REVELATION

*Literally *ta tou theou*, defined by context.

The content of revelation is information (not God's "Self").

The medium of revelation is language (not existential encounter).

The idea that God speaks to us in words isn't peculiar to Paul. The Old Testament prophets spoke words they claimed were God's, not theirs. Jesus viewed words spoken of Adam and Eve and recorded in Genesis as the words of Him "which made them" (Matt. 19:4-5). The writer to the Hebrews talks constantly of the Old Testament as what "God said" or "the Holy Spirit says" (1:5-14; 4:7; etc.).

The consistent biblical picture then is that information is communicated to us by God in human language, in words. And "revelation" is a label for that information.

VARIETY IN REVELATIONAL EXPRESSION

In suggesting that revelation is a label for information communicated to us in words, do we mean revelation is limited to biblical statements expressing information? Is truth communicated *only* by propositional assertions?

No, not at all. The Bible shows that God has spoken to men in more than words. How? In events, like the plagues of the exodus period. In things, like the tabernacle and its furnishings. In experiences, like the sacrifices ordained in the law. *But the meaning of these nonverbal forms is interpretable only because of other revelations in words.*

God showed His power overwhelmingly in the plagues. But the Bible doesn't simply record the events; it offers information as to why God acted as He did. Exodus assigns three reasons for the plagues: (1) that Israel should see and know "that I am [Jehovah] your God" (6:1, 7), (2) that the Egyptians should "know that I am [Jehovah]" (7:5), and (3) that judgment might be executed on Egypt's gods (12:12).

But an even larger context is needed for understanding. Why did God act this way for Israel? Why did He choose Israel? What were and are His purposes? And here the whole pattern of Old Testament revelation is relevant. God made a covenant with Abraham; He honored that covenant. God set His love on Israel by sovereign choice, not because they were better or more holy than others. In them God determined to glorify Himself, to show His power and establish His salvation and rule on the earth. For interpretation, events require more information than they convey!

The same may be said of objects that communicate. According to Hebrews, God used the veil of the temple to signify that the way into the holiest was not yet open. Note the phrase "the Holy Spirit this signifying" (9:7-8). God is communicating by symbol. Yet this too needs a verbal key for interpretation. And the Bible gives it (cf. Heb. 8-9). How about the sacrifices? Leviticus 17:11 explains that "the life of the flesh is in the blood: and I have given it to you upon the altar to make atonement for your souls: for it is the blood that maketh an atonement [by reason of the life]." Thus verbal interpretation makes the meaning of the sacrificial act clear, long before history reveals that the blood of animals shed for sin only pictures the lifeblood of God's Son, poured out in expiation on Calvary.

It is important to realize, then, that while the Bible describes nonverbal revelations, it retains the right to interpret them. When you look for the meaning of an act or symbol, you will find that meaning in Scripture. Revelation is not left open to careless or subjective explanation.

WHAT ABOUT THE BIBLE?

Probably the simplest thing to say about the Bible is that the words imparting God's revelation are written there. Because the revelation is in words, Evangelicals often say that the Bible itself is God's revelation. They claim that it does not contain the Word of God; it is the Word of God.

THE BIBLE, THE WORD OF GOD

"The Word" often refers to Jesus Christ. He is God's revelation, incarnate in human flesh. And the Bible is "the Word," for it is God's revelation, incarnate in human language.

We've already noted how the writers of Scripture regarded it. Two incidents in Christ's life show how fully He shared their evaluation. Once He warned His listeners, "Do not think that I came to abolish [lit., annul, repeal] the Law or the Prophets: I did not come to abolish, but to fulfill. For truly I say to you, until heaven and earth pass away, not the smallest letter or stroke shall pass away from the Law, until all is accomplished" (Matt. 5:17-18). Christ was talking about the Old Testament, using the common Jewish designation of the law and the prophets. In His view, the Old Testament communication was sure and unchangeable. God has said what He means, and that settles it. The Bible isn't open to reinterpretation.

Another time Christ rebuked some Sadducees, Jewish religious leaders who denied resurrection. He quoted God as saying in the Old Testament, "I am the God of Abraham, and the God of Isaac, and the God of Jacob." His rebuke hinged on the *tense* of a verb: *am*. God did not say "was." Therefore, "God is not the God of the dead but of the living" (Matt. 22:32).

What kind of book is unchangeable, so reliable that proof of a vital doctrine can be advanced by pointing out the tense of a verb? Only a book in which the words are God's words, not man's.

No wonder, then, that emphasis is made in the epistles and elsewhere on remaining true to the words! Believers are to "agree with sound words, those of our Lord Jesus Christ, and with the doctrine conforming to godliness" (I Tim. 6:3). They are to "retain the standard of sound words" (II Tim. 1:13), "holding fast the faithful word . . . in accordance with the teaching" (Titus 1:9), holding "firmly to the traditions [*paradosis*, teachings] . . . delivered" (I Cor. 11:2). The teachings are God's words!

How were God's words given in the first place? The Bible doesn't explain the mechanics. Second Peter 1:21 gives the clearest picture of the process. "No prophecy [expression of a divine revelation][1] was ever made by an act of human will, but men moved by the Holy Spirit spoke from God."

Because the authors of Scripture were "moved by the Holy Spirit," Peter finds Scripture more convincing than his eyewitness experience of Christ's glorification (1:16-18), or the fact that he himself heard a voice from heaven identify Christ as God's Son! Experiences can lack objective reality. God's Word cannot.

Moved is commonly translated "inspired." The Greek word pictures a boat, with sails filled by the wind, being borne along over the seas. So the writers, filled with the Spirit, were borne along. The result: the words and thoughts recorded are guaranteed to be God's. The writings are true and accurate, and the information authoritative beyond question. And, according to Paul, all Scripture is inspired by God (II Tim. 3:16).

Biblically and theologically, then, *inspiration* refers to the influence God exerted over the human writers of Scripture. By inspiration He guarantees that the product accurately expresses that which He intends to communicate.

Of course, inspiration guarantees only the accuracy of the original writings, not of later copies or modern translations. But the science of textual criticism has proven what we would expect: that the degree of accuracy with which the biblical text has been transmitted is fantastic!

We can be confident that in the Bible we have the Word, and the words, of God.

THE WORDS OF THE BIBLE

A while ago I asked a question: Is revelation limited to biblical statements expressing information? Is truth communicated only by propositional assertion?

Nonverbal revelation is only part of the problem. As any reader of the Bible knows, the Bible isn't all statements or all assertions. Not every sentence gives hidden information, or even definitive information.

I'm talking of course about things like poetry and description.

Poetry in the Bible often expresses human emotions. In the Psalms we read of and feel worship, fear, love, anger, doubt, trust—the full range of emotions that torment us and yet raise life to the sublime. In what sense are such psalms revelation, or inspired? How are they the words of God?

Or look at the extended description of lives and national histories. Chapter after chapter tells incidents in the lives of Abraham and Isaac and Jacob. Whole books describe the life of Christ on earth, and great sections of these books share no revelation, communicate no hidden information. They simply record what men observed, what Jesus did and said, how His friends and enemies reacted. Yet this is part of the Bible and is called God's Word. What does it all mean?

First, the form does not change the fact of inspiration. The writing of poems and description too was superintended by the Holy Spirit, and these are God's Word.

Second, when we call the *whole* Bible revelation,* we're not using revelation in its specific sense of making known that which was secret and hidden. We mean that in every word of the Word, God speaks to us.

This speaking need not be wholly informational. After all, we're not disembodied minds—cerebral computers designed to sift and store facts. We're human in the fullest sense of the word. Our capacity to understand is matched by our capacity to feel. The Bible speaks to this capacity too; to every aspect of our personality, that in every way we might know and respond to God. Inspiration, relating to forms like poetry, guarantees both that the feelings are accurately portrayed and that God included them in His Word for a purpose.

The same can be said about description. Inspiration guarantees the events presented as historical to be historical; to really have happened, and in the way described. Inspiration also guarantees that God included them for a purpose.

Third, the reason for which God inspired such forms is discoverable. The key to interpretation is found in the Bible, and by taking the words in their normal usage in the form.

Take a phrase from a poem, such as this one in Habakkuk 3:6 (RSV):

> He stood and measured the earth;
>   he looked and shook the nations;
> then the eternal mountains were scattered,
>   the everlasting hills sank low.
>   His ways were as of old.

Does this verse say that at a particular point in time God stood and looked at the earth in such a way as to cause earthquakes that shook nations and broke up and scattered mountains? Not at all. This is poetry. The words have *poetic* meaning. In the context of Habakkuk's vision of coming judgment, in which he sees God as the awful judge, poetry conveys the sense of terror and majesty far better than any statemental assertion. After all, this is the way we use words in poetry. God uses words as we do, and their meaning is determined by the literary form in which they're used.

*This is actually a theological usage which is in harmony with, but not specifically the same as, the biblical usage.

Or take the description of events recorded in John's gospel. How are these to be understood? How are we to learn from them? John provides the key to interpretation himself (20:30-31). The book was written that men might believe that Jesus is the Christ, the Son of God. Events from Christ's life are carefully selected to demonstrate this theme (about 92% of the material is unique to John), and much material is omitted. From the opening verses the demonstration of Christ's deity is focal.

Within the framework of this purpose, told plainly and simply, the reader can draw conclusions and make applications which are not specifically stated in the text. And this is clearly God's intention, for all Scripture is profitable to equip the man of God (II Tim. 3:16).

The Bible says that the experiences of individuals and peoples "happened to them as an example, and they were written for our instruction" (I Cor. 10:11). And abundant New Testament interpretations of Old Testament experiences give us clear guidelines as to how to draw out the intended lessons (cf. I Cor. 10:6; Heb. 3:7—4:6).

Needless to say, no major doctrine rests on this indirect form of expression for its communication. Events may illustrate, but God has taken care that the basic tenets of our faith are clearly and plainly *stated* in His Word.

AND SO?

What can we say, then? First, that the Bible communicates that which is objectively and historically true. It describes accurately events which really happened. It shares feelings men of God really had. It communicates in words revealed information about God and from God to which we have no other access.

And the words in which all this is communicated do have "cash value"! They mean what they say; they say what they mean. They're to be taken and understood as all human speech, and are interpretable literally in the context of the grammatical and historical situation. And so they must be taught.

It's clear, then, that the Bible teacher does communicate information. We can't say that the failure of men to be transformed by the truth of God stems from communicating information as literally true. To teach the Bible as truth and as fact, to share with students information about God, is exactly what the Bible is designed to do.

Failure of that information to transform *must* lie somewhere other than in literal interpretation. For so the Bible is to be understood. We are to take God at His word.

Research and assignment
> for the student

1. Restate and evaluate the validity of the argument the author illustrates by his reference to his private word, "skronk."
2. Choose *one* New Testament book and make a list of the concepts for which there could be no source of sure information except God Himself. Does the writer seem in doubt about these ideas? Do you see any evidence that he doubts their authority in his and others' lives?
3. What is the difference between information and raw data?
4. The passage charted in figure 3 (I Cor. 2:9-13) does not say that every word in the Bible imparts a revelation. What does it assert? Explain, without looking at the chapter, the implications of this assertion.
5. Develop a chart contrasting the neoorthodox and scriptural ideas of revelation.
6. Write a summary of the sections discussing revelation and inspiration in two or more theology books. What arguments are advanced to support the inspiration of the New Testament as well as of the Old?

Exploration
> for the lay teacher

1. Look at your next week's Sunday school lesson. What information are you to teach which, if you are to teach with assurance, *must* have been revealed? What does confidence in the veracity and authority of Scripture mean to you as a Bible teacher?
2. Add to your library a good book on revelation and inspiration, such as John Walvoord (ed.), *Inspiration and Interpretation.*

5

BEYOND
INFORMATION

While it's reassuring to slip back into our old pattern of thinking about the Bible, we haven't come much closer to solving the problems raised earlier. Why doesn't the Bible, taught as the words of God communicating truth from God, have greater effect in our churches? Why do we have that contradiction, the sinning saint? Why aren't believers more dynamic? Why do young people rebel against the truth? Why doesn't the Bible, taught as the truth it is, consistently transform?

To discover the answer, we have to look at the Bible from a slightly different angle and ask, How does the Bible *work*? How does it function in our lives? Turn the pages of a Bible and the words rest there, sharing quietly God's thoughts. But how does God share *Himself*? How do the words become a live, dynamic power wielded by the Holy Spirit to shape and to consume? When we know *how* God meets us in His Word, then and only then will we know how to teach.

"To Know About" vs. "To Know"

IT IS CHARACTERISTIC of contemporary thinking to set these two at odds, to build up the contrast between them. The Bible, too, makes distinctions between knowing about God and knowing Him in a personal way. But you won't find the *versus* emphasized. In fact, there's a rather striking relationship suggested between knowing information about God and personal experience with God.

AN AMAZING PASSAGE

In the early chapters of Romans, Paul charges all mankind with sin. The overall argument develops like this:

"You Gentiles are sinners and lost; your acts show it [Rom. 1:16-32]. You Jews, too. You have the law, but you are sinners and lost. Your behavior shows it [Rom. 2:1—3:8]. You want proof? Here's Scripture. It states flatly that there is no one righteous, no not one [Rom. 3:9-20]."

With the charge made and substantiated, Paul goes on to present God's answer for man in sin: a salvation that offers a God-kind of righteousness to those who believe, made possible by Christ's sacrifice on the cross.

It's not until chapter 5 that Paul goes beyond the *fact* of sin to explain *why* men are lost. To do this he turns back to Adam and points out that in Adam all died. All men are born lost, separated from God, sinners by nature and by choice (cf. Eph. 2:1-3).

In Romans 1, then, Paul isn't giving an exposition on knowing God and knowing about Him. He's not explaining how revelation works in human lives. But in the course of his argument about man's sin and lostness, he makes an amazing statement that opens our eyes to the secret of a transforming Word. He states an unexpected relationship between knowing information about God and knowing Him.

Information communicated in revelation. In Romans 1:16-32 (see fig. 4) Paul is clearly thinking of revelation in an informational sense. He mentions truth revealed through the gospel: that God offers men righteousness, and that God reserves wrath for men who hold down His truth in unrighteousness.

Paul goes on to point out that men have always had *some* information about God. Although they have not always had an inscripturated revelation, God has shown Himself in other ways. "The knowable about God," says Paul, "is evident." God's invisible nature—the fact that He is and that He is Creator—is clearly perceived in the things that are made. Evidence of His existence, communication about Him in this evident form, has stood from the creation.

From the fact of confrontation with information about God Paul makes a startling jump. "They are without excuse," he writes, "because, *knowing God,* they did not glorify Him as God" (1:21, free trans.). *Paul has seemingly equated knowing truth about God with knowing God!* Paul has seemingly asserted that God reveals Himself in information about Himself.

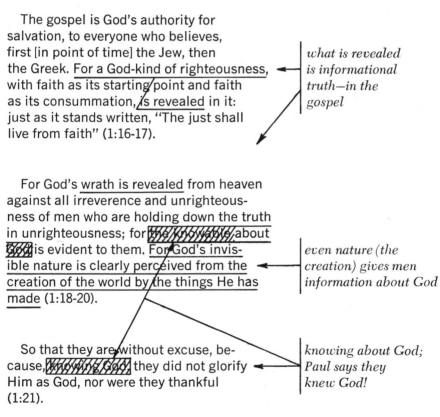

The gospel is God's authority for salvation, to everyone who believes, first [in point of time] the Jew, then the Greek. For a God-kind of righteousness, with faith as its starting point and faith as its consummation, is revealed in it: just as it stands written, "The just shall live from faith" (1:16-17).

what is revealed is informational truth—in the gospel

For God's wrath is revealed from heaven against all irreverence and unrighteousness of men who are holding down the truth in unrighteousness; for the knowable about God is evident to them. For God's invisible nature is clearly perceived from the creation of the world by the things He has made (1:18-20).

even nature (the creation) gives men information about God

So that they are without excuse, because, knowing God, they did not glorify Him as God, nor were they thankful (1:21).

knowing about God; Paul says they knew God!

Fig. 4. GOD IS KNOWN AT THE POINT OF REVELATION
(Romans 1:16-32, free trans.)

To know God. This is a particularly difficult jump for the Evangelical, who tends to use the word *know* in a restricted sense. Thus knowing God is equated with trusting Christ as personal Saviour. It's "saving knowledge." And we have scriptural warrant for this usage. After all, Christ said, "This is eternal life, that they may know Thee the only true God, and Jesus Christ whom Thou hast sent" (John 17:3). And Paul uses the same Greek word in this sense in Galatians 4:9 when he writes about the saints who "have come to know God."

But the Greek word itself (*gnontes*) isn't exhausted by this meaning. It comes from a root with a broad range of uses. It is used in the Bible in the sense of coming to know information, of coming to know a person, of finding out something, of comprehending, realizing; it is even used as a euphemism of sex relations. Basic to its thought seems to be the dimension of experience: this is knowledge that involves experience. In a way Paul seems to say that the people he describes had direct experience with God.

Several lines of evidence indicate that the experience was *not* the saving faith the Evangelical speaks of when he talks of knowing God. In the first place, the men described are gross sinners, who did not see fit to acknowledge God (1:28); who "exchanged the truth of God for a lie" (1:25). Second, Paul in this passage limits the information that they had about God to that conveyed in natural revelation. They knew that He existed, that He was Creator, but they had no gospel. It's not *this* truth by which God mediates His salvation.

Some have become confused here and thought that the passage teaches that men *could* be saved through natural revelation. This isn't Paul's argument. Paul, remember, is charging men with sin. He's pointing out that their reaction to contact with God was to turn away from Him. What greater proof is there of man's depravity than the fact that when confronted with the living, loving God, men are repelled!

But this is the point. They *were* confronted. When they had information about God, they were confronted by God. *God is known [contacted, experienced] at the point of revelation.* And revelation is informational.

This, then, is the biblical relationship between knowing about God and knowing God. Men come to know God through information about Him, because it is in information about Himself that God confronts us. Here we brush up against Him: revelation is our point of contact.

At confrontation. So far we've seen the Romans 1 passage contribute a basic idea: that while revelation *is* the communication of true information about God, human beings are confronted by God Himself in His revealed truth. These two are so intimately connected that it's true to say that in gaining information about God we experience Him: we brush up against God, and in the sense of that experience we "know" Him.

How does it happen, then, that men thus meeting God remain unchanged? Here too the Romans passage contributes. *In each confrontation, man responds.* And that response determines whether we are to be farther from God or drawn nearer to Him.

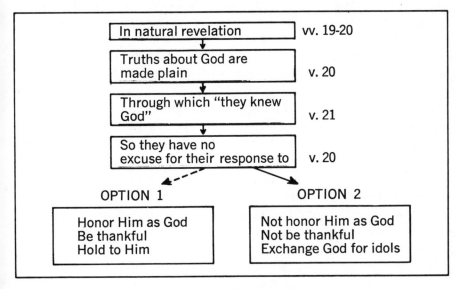

Fig. 5. REVELATION DEMANDS RESPONSE
(Romans 1:19-21)

Look at the chart (fig. 5) that outlines the development of Romans 1:19-21. Men were given truth about God in which they contacted God Himself. In that contact they had two options: they could respond appropriately and honor Him as God, or they could refuse to honor Him and not be thankful. The men that Paul describes are "without excuse" because they chose the second option. They rejected God.

When men reject the God they meet in His revelation, their experience with God cannot go beyond the initial brush. No personal relationship can develop; no transformation can take place.

Put these ideas together, and you begin to see how the Bible works in human lives. In the Bible God presents truth, true information, from and about Himself. But God does more. He presents Himself in the information. God Himself confronts us in His truth.

When a person meets God, a response is always called for. That response varies with the information in which God shows Himself. When God meets us in the gospel, the appropriate response is to put our trust in Christ as Saviour. When God says, "Believe in the Lord Jesus, and you shall be saved" (Acts 16:31), the response called for is belief, trust. When James writes to believers undergoing "various trials," he assures them that God has a good purpose in trial. "Knowing that the testing of your faith produces endurance. And let endurance have its perfect result, that you may be perfect and complete, lacking in nothing" (1:3-4). And the response? "Consider it all joy," for you *know* a personal, caring God ministers to you through suffering and trial.

In every truth God Himself meets and speaks to us. And to every truth there is a fitting response, made to the Lord Himself. It's interesting to note in Scripture some of the response-implications of truths presented as information.

The Lord is Judge; therefore we are not to judge others, or even ourselves. The saints will judge the world; therefore we are to settle disputes between church members. Our bodies are members of Christ; therefore we are not to join them to a prostitute. We are bought with a price; therefore we are to glorify God in our bodies. The events of the Old Testament are given to instruct us; therefore we are to take heed and be warned by them. The resurrection is a glorious fact, for Christ and for us; therefore we are to be steadfast and abound in every good work. Christ is present with us; therefore we are not to lose heart. We died with Christ; therefore we are to be of good courage. The judgment seat awaits in our future; therefore we are to aim to please Him, and seek to persuade men. We have God's promises; therefore we are to cleanse ourselves. We know our eternal destiny; therefore we are to encourage one another in the faith.

These are just a few spelled-out responses. The Bible doesn't spell out in this way the response appropriate for every truth. But the great fact is that in every truth of His Word, God reveals Himself in a new and wonderful way. To each truth there is a fitting response that goes beyond obedience to the Word as law and *can be made as a response to Him.*

This is one of the basic problems of the Evangelical. We see the Word of God as revealed, as true information from God. And so it is. But we tend to see it as information *only!* We neglect the personal dimension.

And when a person tries to obey the Bible as pure information, as rules for living or standards to live up to, he slips into an unconscious and fruitless legalism.

When the Bible is understood and taught as information in which we meet God, when our goal in teaching and reading is to be responsive to the One who speaks to us, then we move beyond information and beyond law into the realm of personal relationship. And it is only this—personal relationship with God—that can transform.

RESPONSE AND FAITH

RESPONSE ESSENTIAL

No reader of the Bible can escape it. Response *is* essential. It is never enough just to have information about God. James ridicules the person who claims to have a faith that isn't responsive. He says, "The demons also believe, and shudder" (2:19).

Intellectual assent to true information, even absolute confidence that the information is truth, is useless in itself. There must be response.

Response to God as an initial commitment in saving faith is the beginning of relationship with God. Abraham had a faith that was responsive in this way. It led to complete commitment. "He did not waver in unbelief, but grew strong in faith, giving glory to God, and being fully assured that what He had promised, He was able also to perform. Therefore also it was reckoned to him as righteousness" (Rom. 4:20-22). This saving response is always the beginning of life with God. But it's only the beginning. Believers are to go on growing in Him. God is concerned with transformation, with making us something we're not. And continued response to God is *necessary* for growth.

The whole idea of response to God is related not to works but to faith. It's important to understand this. The response God wants is not *legal*. We aren't to obey Him the way we obey a law. Outward conformity with inward grumbling is not acceptable response to God.

Christ spoke of responsiveness as the pathway to deepening our relationship with God. He noted that responsiveness *results* in obedience, but it's *sourced* in love. "He who has my commandments and keeps them," He said, "he it is who loves me."

Love for God necessarily expresses itself. "If a man loves me, he will keep my word." Love, and only love, can issue in a spontaneous response that conforms to God's will. And the result of a dynamic responsive love is that "My Father will love him, and We will come to him, and make Our abode with him" (John 14:21-24).

Responsiveness, then, springs from love for God and can never be confused with a mechanical, forced conformity to rules or standards. Being responsive is not doing "works of the law." Being responsive is exercising faith. It was by faith that Abel responded to offer an acceptable sacrifice to God. It was by faith that Enoch pleased God, for "without faith it is impossible to please him." It was by faith that Noah responded to construct an ark. It was by faith that Abraham responded to obey when called to leave Ur; by faith he sojourned in the land of promise, living in tents (Heb. 11:1-12). Responsiveness is inseparable from faith, and faith cannot be faith unless it is responsive to God.

WHO THEN CAN RESPOND?

No one. This kind of response to God is impossible, completely contrary to the nature and character of mankind.

This is the point Paul makes in Romans 1. The men he describes are not lost because they fail to respond. They fail to respond because they are lost.

Perhaps you've seen something like this. A young fellow and his girl friend are walking across a campus. As they walk, their fingers brush and soon twine together. Then, in a moment, each is holding tightly to the other's hand. It's a familiar scene and a natural one.

Somehow the hands of such young people seem to have an affinity for each other! Just a touch, and they want to get closer.

But watch what happens when the same girl's hand brushes against a hot iron. It's repelled. The contact hurts. And the hand is pulled away. In the first case, contact was pleasant and closer contact was sought. In the second, contact was painful and quickly broken.

This is Paul's point in Romans 1. If there were an affinity in man for God, man would respond and seek God. But men who met God in His revelation weren't attracted—they were repelled. They "did not like to retain God in their knowledge." Man naturally rejects, not responds to, God.

Paul expresses this as a fact in the first few chapters of Romans. He explains it later. He points out that when Adam sinned, a great warping happened inside his personality. He was twisted inside; so twisted that where there had been a natural affinity for God there was now a fear, a hatred. This warp has been inherited by the whole human race. We are *not* "all God's children," though we are His creatures. Christ said of men who rejected Him that if they were of God, they would have believed in Him. Instead they are of their "father, the devil." They are Satan's children, for they bear the family traits.

The biblical picture of men isn't pleasant. Responsive to God? Men are "dead in trespasses and sins, . . . [walking] according to the course of this world, according to the prince of the power of the air, . . . fulfilling the desires of the flesh and of the mind; and [are] by nature the children of wrath" (Eph. 2:1-3, AV). This is mankind. Responsive to God? The natural mind is hostile to God (Rom. 8:7). Responsive to God? "While we were *enemies*, we were reconciled to God by the death of His Son" (Rom. 5:10).

Men who are spiritually dead, who follow a trail blazed by Satan, who are enemies of God, certainly are not and cannot be responsive when responsiveness is tied, as Scripture ties it, to love for God and joyous confidence in Him.

Men, unaided, can never and will never choose to respond to God who meets them in His revelation.

And so we're faced with the sovereignty of God, who chooses as He will to work in the lives of men He confronts. As God chooses He creates response to the gospel and makes men His children. "By grace you have been saved through faith; and that not of yourselves, it is the gift of God" (Eph. 2:8). And God in grace moves in our lives beyond the point of conversion. "I will send you the Holy Spirit," Christ said. And, with Christ, He comes into our lives that we who cannot respond may "walk according to the Spirit" and by His power spontaneously do those things which God wills (Rom. 8:4) as He produces His fruit in our lives (Gal. 5:22-23).

Response cannot be law. Response is always of faith, and always produced by God working in us, not by any efforts of our own.

HUMAN RESPONSIBILITY?

We seem to have ruled it out. Am I suggesting that failures in our churches, sins among the saints, and rejection of God's truth by those who know it, are God's fault? In the sense that God *can* over-rule our failures and work even when we cloud issues and confuse His teachings, yes.

At the same time God has chosen to use us as a means. He's made us ministers. And if we teach the Bible in such a way that our students fail to understand it, we're at fault. If we teach the Bible in such a way that God's truth becomes a wall instead of a window, we have to bear the responsibility.

But really, is it as serious as all that? Yes, I believe so. Think back over the picture of the Bible that we've developed.

The Bible is God's Word in God's words. God communicates truth to us in words, and this truth must be communicated and understood as information. But the Bible is more. It is also God's point of contact with men. He Himself confronts us in truth about Himself. When we pick up a Bible and read it, we aren't simply gaining information from God; we're confronting God Himself.

In each such confrontation, we make a response. The response may be wrong. It may be to turn away. It may be to ignore God, while mentally filing away information about Him. Or it may be a response that fits the truth in which God meets us: a response of trust, of worship, of praise, of obedience. But note this: Christian growth, as Christian conversion, *is dependent on response*. We cannot grow spiritually unless we are living responsively to God as He speaks in His Word.

And so to "teach the Bible" involves more than parroting its information. *It involves leading our students to understand the Word*

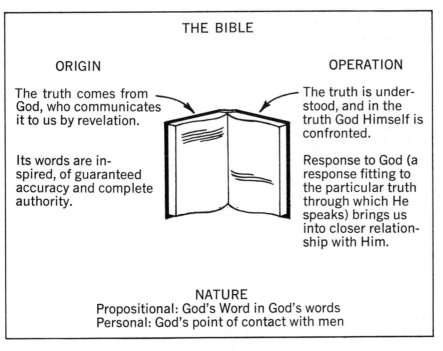

THE BIBLE

ORIGIN

The truth comes from God, who communicates it to us by revelation.

Its words are inspired, of guaranteed accuracy and complete authority.

OPERATION

The truth is understood, and in the truth God Himself is confronted.

Response to God (a response fitting to the particular truth through which He speaks) brings us into closer relationship with Him.

NATURE
Propositional: God's Word in God's words
Personal: God's point of contact with men

Fig. 6

in terms of what it says and what response it invites. It involves leading our students to respond, not as obedient to law, but as obedient to the God we love.

AND SO WE TEACH

Bible teaching has to conform, then, to the nature of the Word and to the way God uses it in our lives.

When we get a clear view of how God meets us in the Bible and how we are called by its truths to respond to Him, guidelines for effective teaching appear. What guidelines?

1. *We do "teach the Bible."* The contents of this Book are unique: truth, communicated to man from God. To know God, we *must* know about Him. To know His will, we must understand what He says in His Word.

So the Bible teacher must care about teaching what the Bible says. He must communicate its information clearly, simply, sharply, so that his students will understand the words in which God speaks.

2. *We aim for personal knowledge of God.* We teach information, but our goal is to help students know God—initially in salvation, then more and more deeply in maturing experience. Our purpose in teaching information isn't simply mastery of the Bible as information.

The fact that God uses biblical information as His point of contact with men must dominate our thinking and shape our teaching. This contact is real, no matter what the attitude of the student. Bored high schoolers, indifferent adults, wiggly juniors, all may be unaware of their brush with God. But brush they have! In knowing about God they have known God, and so stand without excuse if they fail to respond.

The dimension of personal contact with God is what makes Bible teaching so thrilling and rewarding. God is here, in each class, speaking to individuals, reaching out to touch and transform lives and to remake them in the image of Christ. And in this task of transformation, the Bible teacher has a part.

3. *We focus on response.* This is essential to transformation, to spiritual growth. Faith is that which expresses itself as a fitting response in each contact with God.

Because response is essential, the Bible teacher *must* focus the thoughts of his class on response. Each class must be structured not just to communicate a particular truth, but to guide students to discover how God wants them to *respond* to that truth.

If we look back at Chuck's class (p.   ), or visit churches in which the Bible is "believed" but somehow ineffective, what will we find? We're most likely to find a pattern of teaching that emphasizes truth, but neglects response.

This doesn't mean that Christian moral principles are neglected. Usually they're stressed: so stressed that young people feel that the Christian life is summed up in lists of standards and dos and don'ts. But these moral principles are unconsciously thought of as laws. The focus of thought and life on God, with its outcome of a spontaneous loving response that naturally conforms to His will, has been lost.

The place to correct this situation is the place where the Bible is taught—in the pulpit and in the classroom. And the way to correct it is to teach the Bible in the way God uses it. Not just as information, not just as rules to obey or principles to apply, but to teach it as the truth of God in which we meet a God to whom we must respond. Bible teaching must focus on truth-response.

How do you teach to focus on response? How do you structure a lesson that will help each student determine for himself what God wants *him* to do in response to His truth? How do you help students want to learn, want to respond? You'll learn how in the following chapters.

Research and assignment
    for the student
1. Develop a chart contrasting the neoorthodox and biblical positions on these points: revelation, the Bible, biblical statements.
2. Explain thoroughly what the author means: "God is known (contacted, experienced) at the point of revelation."
3. Define the following terms as used by the author: confrontation, response, appropriate response, faith.
4. Explore faith and response more fully. Use a concordance to locate significant passages on faith and write a paper which defines the relationship of faith to response.
5. Discuss: Why can't obedience to the Bible as law be considered response?
6. Discuss: How will an understanding of the way the Bible works help the Bible teacher teach more effectively?
7. How can our teaching of the Bible make God's truth "a wall instead of a window"? Do you agree with the author that this is possible, or do you disagree? Defend your view.
8. *Without reading beyond this point*, plan and write a lesson which you believe meets the three criteria expressed on pages 67-68.

Exploration
    for the lay teacher
1. Did your last lesson focus on response? In what way?
2. How did the response you tried to encourage *differ* from conformity to law?
3. What *evidence* do you have that your students *are* responding to God and applying the truths you teach?

PART II

TEACHING THE BIBLE CREATIVELY

6

WHAT IS
CREATIVE
BIBLE TEACHING?

Creative is an exciting word. When we use it, most of us think wistfully of someone else, someone with that gift of freshness and spontaneity we wish we had. Often the laymen and lay women who teach the Bible feel like this. They wish they could teach creatively, but are sure it isn't possible for them. Fortunately, it is possible.

According to *The Random House Dictionary of the English Lan-guage, creative* means "originative, inventive, productive." All of this is true of creative Bible teaching. A creative teacher makes his classes fresh, vital and interesting. And his class is productive. His teaching bears fruit. This kind of creativity is not something the church can afford to leave to the exceptional teacher. It's the heart of the ministry it expects from *every* teacher!

THE LEARNING WE SEEK

"OH, MY, WHAT A CLASS TODAY!" That was Margaret, looking flustered and worn as usual as she and the other primary department teachers hurried to choir. "I can't get them to hold still for a minute! Why, they'll never learn anything if they don't pay attention."

Sue laughed. "I used to think that until I asked my biggest wiggler a question every time I thought he wasn't listening. Why, he knew every word I said!"

"Well, I don't take any chances." That was old Miss Laine, looking sour and disapproving, also as usual. "Learning the Bible is too important to leave to chance. My girls pay strict attention, and I drill them every Sunday. We repeat the memory verse till it's word-perfect. And I make sure they know every detail of the Bible story, too."

"I wish I could control my class like that," Margaret said a little wistfully. "But I guess the Lord knows I can't. I'm just not made that way. It's such a comfort to know that the Word doesn't return void. If I didn't know that, I'd stop teaching today."

"Yes." Sue opened the choir room door. "It's a real comfort. We teach, and God takes care of the rest."

✿   ✿   ✿

Listen in on such a conversation, and you become aware that the idea of learning is a tricky one. It means different things to different people. To Margaret, attention and interest would be evidence of learning. To Sue, learning was somehow summed up in listening and being able to say again what the teacher said. Miss Laine went a little further. To her, learning was a disciplined drilling-in of information, a mastery of Bible content "word-perfect." There are other ideas about learning too, other immediate goals toward which teachers work each Sunday.

For most Evangelicals, there is also a beyond-class vision, a long-range goal of transformation. But, like Margaret, many expect the Word to automatically produce results in pupils' lives. The teachers want pupils to learn, but have failed to come to grips with the *kind of learning* that produces change. They want their pupils to learn, but far too many teach for a kind of learning that is largely sterile in terms of life-changing results.

A LOOK AT LEARNING

Before anyone teaches the Bible, he ought to understand the kind of learning he must aim for. And he ought to realize that there are several levels at which learning can be said to take place. Let's look at five levels that are significant for the Bible teacher.

The rote level. "Ching fou sou." Look at that phrase again: *Ching fou sou.* Now, close your eyes and repeat it from memory: *Ching fou sou.*

You may not realize it, but you've learned something! What? *Ching fou sou.* A meaningless phrase which, nevertheless, you can repeat from memory.

This is rote learning: to repeat something from memory, without thought of the meaning. Unfortunately, much learning in our churches is on this level. Each Sunday we sing hymns, often so familiar our mouths form the words while our minds think other thoughts. We repeat the Lord's Prayer or the Apostles' Creed in the same way. Probably Miss Laine's class will drill and drill and learn their memory verses—by rote. By definition, this kind of learning is largely meaningless.

Some are aware of the dangers of rote learning. Like the speaker who held a bull session after church one night with a local youth group. "What is faith?" he asked during the evening. Immediately one fellow's hand shot up. " 'Faith is the substance of things hoped for, the evidence of things not seen,' Hebrews 11:1." "Fine," the speaker nodded. "Now, what does that mean?" Clearly surprised, the teen stumbled. "Why, it means the substance of things hoped for. And, er, the evidence of things not seen." But the speaker pressed. "Yes. But what does that *mean*?" Finally the teen shrugged. "I don't know," he said. "I just learned that verse a couple years ago to get to go to camp."

Clearly the Bible, taught and learned by rote, is unlikely to change lives!

The recognition level. Go back to *Ching fou sou.* As you repeated it a moment ago, it seemed meaningless. But suppose you're told that *Ching fou sou* in Korean means "God is love." You've moved up the ladder of learning. The phrase is now invested with at least some meaning.

To discover if you really had learned on this level, a teacher might give you a simple test: True or False? *Ching fou sou* means "God is good." Or perhaps a multiple choice question: *Ching fou sou* means (*a*) God is good, (*b*) The day is gone, (*c*) God is love, (*d*) Night is near.

It's not difficult to teach or learn on this level. For all that is required in this kind of learning is the ability to recognize something that's been said or read. This is often what happens in our Sunday schools.

Let's drop in on Miss Laine's class. She's just taught her primary girls a series of lessons on the gospel. Now she wants to make sure they've learned the vital truths. So she's questioning them, one by one.

"Ann, can a person get to heaven by always obeying parents and being kind to friends?" "No," says Ann, shaking her head. (Good!) "Ah, Jan, can a person get to heaven by coming to church and reading the Bible and praying every day?" Jan too thinks and shakes her head. "No." (Wonderful!) "Now, Mary, can a person get to heaven by believing on the Lord Jesus Christ as his Saviour from sin because He died on the cross to take the penalty for our sins?" Mary nods. "Yes." (Terrific! Miss Laine has taught, and her girls have learned! They *know* a person doesn't get to heaven by good works or religious behavior, but only by "believing in the Lord Jesus Christ as their Saviour from sin because He died on the cross to take the penalty for their sin.")

But *what* have the girls learned? *All her teaching and testing have required is the ability to recognize the things she has said in class!*

There's evidence that this is the level at which many Sunday school students learn Bible truths. A Michigan State University survey of religiously oriented college students showed that 74 percent of the group tested agreed with the statement "Christ died for the sins of mankind." Yet on the same survey, only 38 percent agreed that "faith in Christ is necessary for salvation." They recognized and agreed with the most familiar idea. But they did not grasp its meaning! They could not see the relationship between this truth and the lostness of all outside of Christ.

Tragically, the ability to recognize a truth as from the Bible, or as something a Sunday school teacher or parent said, does not imply either a personal response or an integration of the truth recognized with the learners' total understanding of the Bible and life. It's important to recognize biblical concepts, of course, and to recognize their meanings as they have been taught. But this is never sufficient. This kind of learning simply does not lead to transformation.

The restatement level. While Miss Laine was testing her primaries' learning at the recognition level, over in the junior department Mr. Ransom was shooting for something more. He too had just completed a series on the gospel and wanted to test his boys' understanding. So he drew on an experience he'd had that week with a neighborhood boy.

"Fellows," he began, "I was talking with Tommy Lance this week, and he told me that today he's being confirmed in his church. He said that the bishop was going to anoint him with the Holy Spirit, and that with the Holy Spirit to help him, he was sure he could be good enough to get to heaven. If Tom told you that, what would you say that might help him understand how to get to heaven?" And then Mr. Ransom stopped and waited.

What he was shooting for is no easy kind of learning. It's no multiple-choice type, where the answer is laid out for the student to recognize. It demands a grasp of content in terms of relationship to other ideas, and an ability to express the whole without clues, because the ideas have been mastered. *While this level of Bible learning is not sufficient, it is necessary.*

The Bible is God's Word, communicating true information about Himself, about us, about our world. It expresses the fundamental realities on which we have to base our lives. Thus its teachings must be understood. We must know what the Bible teaches, not merely as something we recognize—"Oh yes, that's in the Bible, isn't it?"— but as a mastered system that controls our patterns of thought and our philosophy of life. This kind of mastery comes only when Bible truths are learned on the restatement level. Only when we have the ability to take a Bible truth, relate it to other ideas and values, and express that truth in our own words, have we begun to learn meaningfully. Even children can be led to this kind of learning of the Bible truths that are important for them.

Sadly, learning characterized by this ability is significantly different from that which takes place in most of our Sunday schools. Too many of us are satisfied to check and see if our students recognize the truths we've taught. Too few of us consciously seek to help students achieve mastery of the teachings of God's Word.

The relation level. While it's vital to understand the Bible as content, this in itself is not enough. The Word of God is more than information; it is a point of contact with God Himself. The crucial issue in bringing us beyond information about God to personal experience with God is that of response. To discern the appropriate response to a Bible truth, we must see the relationship between that truth and our lives.

This level of learning presupposes the restatement process. It's when a person, in his own words, thinks through a biblical teaching, that insight into its meaning for life is most likely to come. It's when Mr. Ransom's boys are trying to formulate and express their understanding of the gospel that one of them is most likely to suddenly see a truth. "Say, this means I have to put my trust in Christ as Saviour." "Then my dad isn't a Christian!" "So that's why we talk so much about missionaries. That's why we give and pray."

When a learner discovers such a relationship for himself, when in a flash of insight the parts fit together and he sees meaning in terms of life, then the pathway to personal response stands open.

There is much that a teacher can do to lead his students to meaningful involvement with God's Word, providing opportunities for the Holy Spirit to point out to each student personally the response He wants him to make. It's only when the teacher consciously teaches for learning in terms of identifying the appropriate response that his teaching is in harmony with the nature of God's Word. The Bible, taught in harmony with its nature, transforms. Learning on any lesser level is inadequate.

The realization level. This is the goal of all Bible teaching: realizing, in the sense of making real in experience. Here is truth, applied in life. It's one thing to understand what response to God's Word is appropriate; to actually make that response is another.

Yet it's in the sense of "response made" that the Bible often uses the word *know*. In I Corinthians 6, Paul asks five times, "What, do you not know . . . ?" In each case he asks this about a concept they had heard from him and were familiar with. He asks because their lives were out of harmony with the truth they heard. In the biblical sense they did not *know* these truths, for they were not living them.

This is the level of learning for which every Bible teacher vaguely hopes, but for which he must consciously teach. For, humanly speaking, learning that changes life is a product of a particular kind of teaching. Not teaching for rote, to produce the ability to repeat without thought of meaning. Not teaching for recognition, the ability to recognize biblical ideas. Not even teaching for restatement, the ability to understand Bible content as part of a system. The Bible teacher must teach in such a way that his students, understanding the truth of God, discover and are led to make an appropriate life-response to the God who speaks to them through His Word. Only thus learned can God's Word transform.

LEARNING AND CREATIVE TEACHING

Realizing that students may learn at various levels, we can now more closely define creative teaching as *consciously and effectively focusing on activities that raise the students' learning level.* The weaknesses in our Sunday schools can often be traced to a failure to understand learning on the higher levels, and a resultant failure to help students learn significantly.

What, in practice, distinguishes creative Bible teaching from noncreative teaching? Let's look briefly at three areas of contrast.

Focus on facts v. focus on meaning. Drop around a Sunday school department during the last five or ten minutes of class, and you can quickly separate the creative and noncreative teachers. In most classes you'll hear climaxes like these: "Now, Johnny, will you review the lesson for us? The rest of you raise your hands if he leaves anything out." Or, "Jean, how many fish were there in the great draught of fishes?" Or, "Our time is almost up, and we still haven't quite finished our lesson. So be quiet and let me tell. . . ." These comments —and the teachers who make them—focus on biblical facts. During the last moments an illustration or exhortation may be thrown in, but the hour has been spent mastering facts rather than meaning. When teaching has this focus, the students develop only the ability to repeat or recognize Bible truths. Learning has stalled on the lower levels.

Yet now and then you'll overhear probing questions that force attention to meaning. "How might Christ say that if He were talking to people like us?" "What would John be like if he were a teen going to your high school?" "Is it always right to separate ourselves from unbelievers? What would it mean if all Christians cut themselves off from unsaved friends?" And then you hear students: talking, discussing, testing their ideas, exploring until the meaning of God's words becomes clear and relevant to twentieth century life.

Teaching for meaning isn't easy. Normally the creative teacher knows and uses a variety of methods. He knows how to cover content quickly and clearly. He knows how to stimulate his students to test and relate truth. But the dividing line is not the use or nonuse of methods. The dividing line is focus. The creative teacher finds time for a thorough exploration of the meaning of the truth taught. And learning in his class moves on up to the higher levels, where appropriate response to God's Word can be seen and made.

Student passivity v. student activity. I once saw a primary teacher in Dallas put on a fantastic demonstration. She had a class of eighteen primary-age children, crammed in a little quonset hut out behind the church, all seated uncomfortably on adult-sized folding chairs. Yet she held these children spellbound for forty-five minutes! She used two flannelboards, a chalkboard, puppets, cutout figures, visualized verses and songs, and outstanding storytelling ability. I'm sure that, had I given the boys and girls a test over the content she taught, they could have passed with perfect scores. She was an accomplished teacher—but not a creative one. Her pupils listened and learned, but only on the first two levels.

To move up even to the restatement level of learning, students must be led beyond listening. They must personally think through the meaning of Bible truths. They must toss the ideas around in their own minds to formulate and express them in their own words. For this kind of learning, the students have to participate, to express their own ideas and their own insights.

There are different kinds of class participation. One teacher may give boys and girls crayons and let them color pictures while he talks. Another may ask factual questions or let students take turns reading verses or paragraphs from a lesson manual. But the creative teacher makes sure that his students *take an active part in exploring meaning.*

This is vital. You can tell a class what a Bible truth means. But then the meaning becomes just another piece of information to recognize. For meaning to the student, he needs to discover for himself the relationship of a truth to his life. And this discovery requires an active student. It demands a student's thinking, integrat-

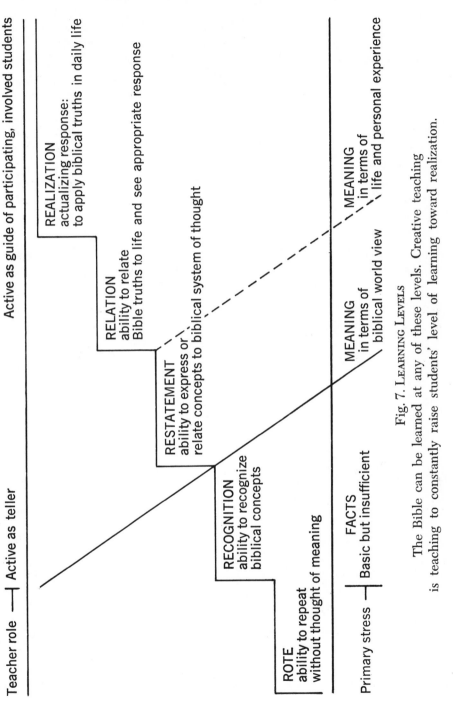

Fig. 7. LEARNING LEVELS

The Bible can be learned at any of these levels. Creative teaching
is teaching to constantly raise students' level of learning toward realization.

ing, relating, reasoning. Listen in on the creative teacher, and this is what you'll hear: his students actively exploring meaning.

Teacher as teller v. teacher as guide. This is the third contrast we want to note in this chapter. When the focus of the lesson is on facts which the students can learn without participating, the teacher serves as a teller. He communicates information, and class activities center on himself. Sometimes noncreative teachers use methods. Remember the Dallas teacher who used a variety? Yet the methods of a noncreative teacher have two characteristics: they are designed to communicate content, and they are primarily teacher activities.

The creative teacher has a different concept of his role. His responsibility is to stimulate his students to discover meaning and to see the response God requires of them personally to His voice. He feels that student activities are more important than his. The class doesn't center on him; it centers on them. The creative teacher serves as a guide to learning, and strives constantly to structure situations which will stimulate his students to discover meaning. The methods he uses are also set apart by two characteristics: they are chosen to focus attention on meaning, and they create student involvement in this process of discovery.

This, then, is creative Bible teaching. It is teaching the Bible in ways that cause learning on the significant levels of restatement, relation and realization. To cause this kind of learning the Bible teacher must (1) focus on the *meaning* of the Bible truth taught, (2) involve his students in active search for meaning, and (3) stimulate and guide his students in this discovery process.

Research and assignment
    for the student
1. Poll several Sunday school teachers: "What did you want your students to learn last Sunday?"
2. Visit a Sunday school department and write a report on the creative or noncreative teaching observed.
3. Evaluate lessons for the same age level from three different publishers. Write on the potential of each for creative teaching.
4. Look up the Greek words translated "learn" in a lexicon. What kinds of learning do they distinguish?
5. Relate James 2:19 to the concept of learning levels suggested in this chapter.

6. Discussion: What does the author mean by "You can tell the class what a Bible truth means. But then the meaning becomes just another piece of information to recognize"?
7. Quiz: Be prepared to give an illustration of learning on each level and to explain the practical distinctions between creative and non-creative teaching.

Experimentation
    for the lay teacher
1. Think through the last lesson you taught. Did you teach creatively?
2. How could your last lesson have been more creatively taught? Revise your lesson plan as you think of ways.
3. As you prepare next Sunday's lesson, test your plan against the three characteristics of creative teaching given in this chapter. Look for ways to strengthen your lesson in each area.
4. Visit a class taught by someone reputed to be a good teacher. If he is a creative teacher, jot down ideas you might use. If he is *not* creative, jot down ways you might improve his lesson.

7

VISIT TO A
CREATIVE CLASS

"I don't know. It *sounds* good, but—well, I don't think I've ever been in a class like that. How can I picture more clearly what you're talking about?"

Unfortunately, we can't all visit a creative class together. Yet it is important to visualize creative Bible teaching in progress. So important that this chapter drops you into an actual class in session and invites you to become the student of a creative Bible teacher.

To help you follow the action with a minimum of description, SENTENCES IN THIS TYPE ARE WORDS OF THE TEACHER. Comments of different students are in this regular type, with paragraph indention usually marking new speakers. Finally, "outside" comments and description are italicized and placed in parentheses *(like this)*.

One final note. The comments are numbered. In later chapters you'll use these numbers to find illustrations of important principles. They're not important to you at this time.

So, for now, imagine you are a member of this class. Take your Bible and follow along. Get involved. And enjoy yourself!

In a Creative Classroom

(It's about time for class to begin. The last few couples, for this is a young adult class, have come in; and the teacher, who has been chatting with several members, moves up to the chalkboard.)

A¹   Before we begin today, I'd like you to do something. Turn to your neighbor, and in thirty seconds come up with a list of what most people think makes them happy.

A²   Do you mean Christians? No, not necessarily. Just most people. What do most think makes a person happy?

(After thirty noisy seconds, class members call out items the teacher records in a column on the left side of the chalkboard.)

A³   Money, security, nice home, success, health, love, friends, leisure, travel, family.

A⁴   Yes, these are what most people think makes them happy. *(He writes* happy *on the board over the list.)* But the book we're going to look at today was written when the author had none of these things. He had no money, but was completely dependent on the charity of others. *(He crosses off each item on which he comments.)* Security? At any moment the writer might be executed by the Roman government. His home was a prison cell, where he sat day after day chained to two guards. Success? Many of the people he'd given his life for doubted his importance. His health was breaking, and at the time he wrote he was about to lose his last Christian companion. He'd never known the love of a wife or family.

Yet over and over in the book, he uses one particular word. Can you tell who the writer is?

A⁵   Paul.

A⁶   The book?

A⁷   Colossians?

A⁸   No, Philippians. *(The teacher nods.)*

A⁹   And the word?

A¹⁰   Joy. Yes, joy, or rejoice. *(He writes* joy *on the chalkboard.)*

A¹¹   Our goal today is to discover what gave Paul joy, when he had nothing that most people need to make them happy.

B¹   To do it, let's divide into groups of three or four. I'll assign each a chapter in Philippians. Your job is first to read the chapter and underline each occurrence of joy or rejoice. Then,

LOOK IN THE VERSES BEFORE AND AFTER, AND SEE IF YOU CAN DISCOVER THE CAUSE OF PAUL'S JOY. *(Teacher divides the class into three large segments.)* OK, GROUPS IN THIS SECTION TAKE CHAPTER 1. OVER HERE, YOU FOLKS TAKE CHAPTER 2. AND YOU TAKE CHAPTER 4. WE'RE LEAVING OUT CHAPTER 3, SINCE PAUL DEVELOPS A SLIGHTLY DIFFERENT THEME THERE.

B² Now, we're to find the joys? YES, UNDERLINE EACH joy AND rejoice YOU FIND. THEN DECIDE WHY PAUL HAS JOY. WHAT'S THE SOURCE OF HIS JOY? AND BE SURE YOU TALK ABOUT IT TOGETHER. SOMETIMES THE SOURCE ISN'T OBVIOUS, AND SHARING YOUR IDEAS WILL HELP. YOU CAN HAVE ABOUT TWELVE MINUTES.

(At first it's quiet. Then someone asks a question. Soon the groups are buzzing with conversation. The teacher circulates, stopping briefly to nod agreement or guide a group with a question.)

* * *

(To get the feel, why don't you take out ten or twelve minutes and trace joy through one of these three chapters?)

* * *

B³ TAKE ABOUT ONE MORE MINUTE.

(The teacher lists the three chapters on the board to serve as a framework for recording each study team's report.)

B⁴ TIME'S UP. LET'S PULL OUR CHAIRS AROUND AND SEE WHAT WE'VE DISCOVERED. *(This takes a while. Some groups are still involved and unwilling to break up.)*

B⁵ ALL RIGHT. LET'S HEAR FROM THOSE WHO STUDIED CHAPTER 1. WHERE DOES joy OCCUR THERE?

HAPPY	JOY
Money	chap. 1
Security	
Nice home	
Success	
Health	chap. 2
Love	
Friends	
Leisure	
Travel	chap. 4
Family	
etc.	

Fig. 8

B⁶ In verse 4. Paul prays for them with joy.

B⁷ Yes, and verse 18.

B⁸ Let's take them one at a time. What's the cause of Paul's joy in verse 4?

B⁹ Well, it seems to be remembering the Philippians.

B¹⁰ He prays for them though. It's more than just remembering them.

B¹¹ Do you see any phrase that tells why he has joy in this particular group?

B¹² It's their fellowship from the first day.

B¹³ Fellowship? You mean the Sunday evening coffee klatch? (*A laugh or two.*)

B¹⁴ No, it's fellowship in the gospel, their sharing together in Christ.

B¹⁵ Yes, that "in the gospel" (1:5) is significant, isn't it. Have any of you ever been on a gospel team? (*Several nod.*) What happens to your relationships when you work together like this?

B¹⁶ You get close to them.

B¹⁷ Yes, the closest Christian friends I have are the quartet I used to team with.

B¹⁸ (*Teacher nods.*) I think this is what Paul is talking about here. From the very first, these Philippians took part with him in getting out the gospel. They shared with him—and "sharing" is what the Greek word here means—in the gospel. It was this mutual concern for others outside of Christ that drew them together. (*Teacher jots down under chapter 1 the heading "sharing in gospel."*) (*See fig. 9.*)

B¹⁹ How about in verse 18?

B²⁰ Well, it's the gospel again. Paul is full of joy because it's being preached.

B²¹ Did you see any reason why he might not be joyful?

B²² Well, it says some people had the wrong motives.

B²³ They weren't doing it from love. It says they were doing it from envy and factiousness. They thought it would bother Paul.

B²⁴ Did you discuss why this might bother Paul?

B²⁵ I suppose because he was concerned about motive. Yes. And note that other phrase too. They were "supposing to add affliction" to Paul's imprisonment. Have you ever seen a man who's just retired? How does he feel at first?

B²⁶ Relieved! (*This draws several laughs.*)

B²⁷ YES, I SUPPOSE SO. *(Teacher laughs too.)* BUT HOW DOES HE FEEL ABOUT BEING CUT OFF FROM HIS WORK?

B²⁸ When my dad retired he had a terrible time. He hadn't prepared for it and just didn't know what to do with himself.

B²⁹ One of the men who retired from our office comes back every once in a while. He just wanders around, like he's looking for a place to fit in again. He's almost tragic.

B³⁰ Is that what Paul's talking about? I THINK SO. FOR YEARS HE'D GIVEN HIS LIFE TO PREACHING THE GOSPEL. NOW HE WAS "RETIRED" BY THE ROMAN GOVERNMENT. AND SOME PEOPLE WHO WERE ENVIOUS SAID, "THIS IS OUR CHANCE. NOW, PAUL, WE'LL PROVE WE DON'T NEED YOU. YOU'RE JUST AN OLD HAS-BEEN." BUT PAUL'S REACTION WAS "I DON'T CARE. THE THING THAT COUNTS IS GETTING OUT THE GOSPEL. PREACH CHRIST, AND I REJOICE."

B³¹ That's quite an attitude. ISN'T IT. *(Teacher writes "Christ preached" on board.)* It shows how important sharing Christ with others was to Paul. IN FACT, WE CAN SUM UP THE THRUST OF THIS FIRST CHAPTER BY SAYING THAT PAUL FOUND JOY IN GETTING OUT THE GOSPEL. AND THE LAST JOY IN THIS CHAPTER, DOWN IN VERSE 25, TALKS OF THE JOY OF THOSE WHO HAVE RECEIVED CHRIST.

B³² HOW ABOUT CHAPTER 2? WHAT SEEMS TO BE THE SOURCE OF THE JOY MENTIONED THERE?

B³³ Well, in verse 2 he talks about joy in their unity. THIS IS THE CHRISTIANS? Yes, he wants them to be "likeminded, having the same love, being of one accord, of one mind." So basically the source of joy here is in the lives of other Christians? THAT'S RIGHT. *(Teacher jots down "other believers" on the board.)*

B³⁴ Do you find other uses of joy here fit this idea?

B³⁵ I don't know about that. In verses 17 and 18 he talks about joy in being a sacrifice. WHAT DOES HE MEAN? Well, I guess he means that he's going to be executed. He was on trial, wasn't he? YES, HE WAS.

B³⁶ Paul talks about dying being far better than living somewhere, doesn't he?

B³⁷ Yes, it's in Corinthians somewhere.

B³⁸ Well, maybe that's what he means here. He's anxious to go to be with Christ.

B³⁹ He doesn't say that, though.

B⁴⁰ But he does say he's glad to be sacrificed, and that they should rejoice with him. HOW DO YOU THINK THE PHILIPPIANS WOULD HAVE

FELT IF PAUL WERE EXECUTED FOR PREACHING THE GOSPEL TO THEM? What do you mean? WELL, SUPPOSE OUR PASTOR WERE TAKEN OUT AND SHOT FOR PREACHING TO US. HOW WOULD WE FEEL? Pretty bad. A LITTLE GUILTY BECAUSE IT WAS ON OUR ACCOUNT HE WAS KILLED? AFTER ALL, IF HE HADN'T PREACHED TO US, HE MIGHT HAVE BEEN SAVED. Yes, but Paul wants them to rejoice with him, too. I THINK THAT'S THE POINT. PAUL SAYS HE REJOICES AT THE CHANCE TO SACRIFICE HIMSELF FOR THEM. PAUL IS JOYFUL BECAUSE HE HAS A CHANCE TO DO SOMETHING—EVEN TO DIE—FOR BELIEVERS HE LOVES.

B⁴¹ DO WE FIND ANYTHING ELSE IN THE CHAPTER THAT SHOWS PAUL FOUND JOY IN SACRIFICING HIMSELF FOR OTHERS?

B⁴² He talks about joy again in verse 28. Yes, and here he's talking about the joy of the Philippians when they see Epaphroditus. ACTUALLY, THIS IS THE INCIDENT I WAS THINKING OF. REMEMBER THAT PAUL WAS ALONE IN PRISON? WELL, THE PHILIPPIANS HAD SENT EPAPHRODITUS WITH A MONEY GIFT. WHEN HE ARRIVED, HE BECAME VERY SICK AND NEARLY DIED. THE PHILIPPIANS HEARD OF HIS ILLNESS, AND ONE OF PAUL'S REASONS FOR WRITING WAS TO LET THEM KNOW EPAPHRODITUS HAD RECOVERED. BUT, APPARENTLY AS PAUL WAS WRITING, HE HAD A SUDDEN THOUGHT. PHILIPPIANS WOULD BE GLAD TO HEAR EPAPHRODITUS WAS WELL, BUT HOW MUCH MORE GLAD THEY'D BE IF THEY COULD SEE HIM! SO PAUL WRITES, "I AM THE MORE EAGER TO SEND HIM, THEREFORE, THAT YOU MAY REJOICE AT SEEING HIM AGAIN" (2:28, RSV). YOU KNOW, IT'S ONE THING TO BE READY TO DIE FOR OTHERS. MARTYRDOM HAPPENS JUST ONCE. PAUL'S SACRIFICIAL LIVING FOR OTHERS WAS A DAILY THING. AND IT WAS A MAJOR SOURCE OF HIS JOY. *(Teacher jots under chapter 2 "sacrifice self for others.")*

B⁴³ *(Chapter 4 is quickly covered. The stress "rejoice in the Lord" [4:4] and "I rejoice in the Lord" [4:14] is clear. Paul's third source of joy is the Lord Himself and his relationship with Him. With Christ his, Paul has learned to be content [4:11]. Under Chapter 4 the teacher writes "the Lord Himself.")*

B⁴⁴ SO WE CAN SUMMARIZE, THEN, AND SAY THAT PHILIPPIANS SHOWS US THREE DISTINCT SOURCES OF CHRISTIAN JOY, AS EXEMPLIFIED IN PAUL. GETTING OUT THE GOSPEL, SACRIFICING OURSELVES FOR OTHERS, AND DEEPENING OUR RELATIONSHIP WITH THE LORD.

C¹ NOW, THINK A MINUTE. WHAT'S THE DIFFERENCE BETWEEN THESE TWO LISTS? *(He points first to the joy side, then the happy side of the board.)*

C² Well, one is spiritual—and the other one's physical.

C³ The happy side is passing. It doesn't last. THAT'S RIGHT. I'M HAPPY IF I HAVE MONEY. BUT I CAN LOSE IT.

C⁴ And the other side is eternal. You can't lose these things.

C⁵ There's another one. The happy side is self-centered. The joy side isn't. THERE'S A REAL KEY, ISN'T IT. IF I HAVE MONEY, IF I HAVE FRIENDS, IF I HAVE SUCCESS, IF I HAVE HEALTH, IF I HAVE—BUT FOR JOY OUR LIFE IS FOCUSED OUTSIDE OURSELVES.

C⁶ BY THE WAY, DON'T ANSWER THIS OUT LOUD, BUT THINK ABOUT IT FOR A MINUTE. HOW MUCH OF YOUR THOUGHTS AND CONVERSATION AND EFFORTS THIS LAST WEEK WERE SPENT ON THE THINGS ON THE JOY SIDE? AND HOW MUCH ON THE THINGS ON THE HAPPY SIDE?

(Take a minute and think about it. Where is your life centered?)

❋ ❋ ❋

C⁷ IT'S A LITTLE TEST, BUT IT TELLS US A LOT, DOESN'T IT. *(Pause.)*

C⁸ BUT NOW LET'S HAVE SOME FUN. LET'S SUPPOSE THAT EVERYONE IN OUR CHURCH WAS TO LIVE CONSTANTLY ON THE JOY SIDE. *(There are a few wry smiles at this.)* IN FACT, LET'S SUPPOSE WE DO, AND THAT OUR LIVES HAVE BECOME SO DISTINCTIVE THAT THE LOCAL TV STATION PLANS TO SEND DOWN A CAMERAMAN TO FOLLOW OUR MEMBERS AROUND AND PHOTOGRAPH THEM FOR A NEWS SPECIAL. NOW, WHAT COULD HE FILM THAT WOULD BE A DISTINCTIVE OF PEOPLE LIVING ON THE JOY SIDE?

C⁹ *(It's quiet for a moment.)* Well, we'd be joyful.

C¹⁰ How could he photograph that?

C¹¹ We'd be smiling. *(Teacher smiles.)* YES, BUT I THINK HE'D WANT MORE THAN SMILING FACES. WHAT WOULD HE SEE US DOING THAT WOULD BE DISTINCTIVE?

C¹² We'd love. ALL RIGHT, BUT HOW DO YOU PHOTOGRAPH LOVE? WHAT WOULD HE SEE? *(It's quiet.)* TAKE A LOOK AT THE AREAS WE'VE LISTED ON THE BOARD. THESE ARE THE THINGS THE BIBLE SAYS CHARACTERIZE CHRISTIANS WHO HAVE REAL JOY. WHAT WOULD CONCENTRATING ON THESE AREAS IN OUR LIVES MEAN? WHAT WOULD WE BE DOING?

C¹³ We might give out tracts. *(Teacher erases board, and begins to jot down ideas suggested.)* ALL RIGHT. TRACTS. Do you think this is the best way to get out the gospel?

C¹⁴ They're pretty impersonal.

C¹⁵ WHAT OPPORTUNITIES DO WE HAVE TO SHARE CHRIST? PERSONAL ONES, I MEAN.

C16   Well, my neighbor drops in for coffee almost every day. Sometimes we talk about spiritual things.

C17   I suppose missions come in here too? Yes, I THINK SO.

C18   And we can bring others out to church.

C19   How about VBS? If everyone would take time to ask neighbor children, we'd probably have thousands out.

C20   Don't forget giving them rides. I was transportation chairman, and we had an awful time getting all the kids in. If it wasn't for Harvey Laine and his vacation coming just then, I don't know what we would have done.

C21   (Teacher nods.) YOU KNOW, THIS NEIGHBOR BUSINESS INTERESTS ME. WHY DON'T WE HAVE MORE IMPACT AS A CHURCH ON OUR UNSAVED NEIGHBORS? WE MUST HAVE MEMBERS LIVING NEAR DOZENS OF UN- CHURCHED FAMILIES.

HAPPY	JOY
Money	chap. 1
Security	sharing in gospel
Nice home	Christ preached
Success	
Health	chap. 2
Love	other believers
Friends	sacrifice self for
Leisure	others
Travel	
Family	chap. 4
etc.	Lord Himself

Fig. 9

C22   Well, for me it's the time. My job keeps me out a lot, and then there are yard work and church meetings.

C23   That's a big one for me. I'm afraid I'm just involved in too many things. WHAT DO YOU MEAN TOO INVOLVED? DO YOU THINK CHURCH ITSELF SOMETIMES KEEPS US AWAY FROM OUR NEIGHBORS? Yes, I know it does.

C24   Well, doesn't church come first? Before socializing, I mean?

C25   Maybe. But I know it's pretty hard to talk about Christ with someone I don't know very well.

C²⁶ Yes, you have to show an interest in people before they're ready to listen. GOOD POINT. HOW MIGHT A JOY-SIDE CHRISTIAN SHOW THAT KIND OF INTEREST?

C²⁷ Well, Helen mentioned coffee.

C²⁸ I think you've just got to be friendly. Talk to them. Find out what they're interested in. Sort of treat them like real people, instead of "souls."

C²⁹ You know, I think we have a lot of opportunities to treat people like human beings, and fail to take them. Take a gas station attendant. Usually people just drive in and sit. The attendant is almost part of the pump. Why not chat with him when we have a chance? Maybe over a period of time we can build a relationship where a tract or a word might really count.

C³⁰ Most of this takes caring, then, doesn't it. YES, IT'S CARING WITH A PURPOSE. PAUL SHARED CHRIST BECAUSE HE REALLY CARED ABOUT OTHERS. I THINK OUR CAMERAMAN WOULD SEE JOY-SIDERS INVOLVED WITH PEOPLE: TALKING, HELPING, SOMETIMES JUST LISTENING.

C³¹ Or maybe even staying home from church some evening to go fishing with the guy next door? MAYBE.

C³² HOW ABOUT THAT POINT SACRIFICING YOURSELF FOR OTHER BELIEVERS? WHAT WOULD A TV MAN FIND THERE?

C³³ A few more in our churchtime program! We're always short because no one's willing to work during the morning service.

C³⁴ Sunday school teachers would prepare.

C³⁵ And committee members would show up—on time.

C³⁶ HOW ABOUT AREAS BESIDES CHURCH PROGRAMMING. WHAT WOULD WE SEE THAT SHOWS CONCERN FOR OTHER CHRISTIANS?

C³⁷ Well, you wouldn't see so much gossip.

C³⁸ We would not be so critical of each other, either. YES, THESE ARE IMPORTANT AREAS.

C³⁹ Isn't it a lot like what we just said? You'd really have an interest in other people and care about them. I THINK SO.

C⁴⁰ I know when my younger brother dropped out of church, no one from the youth group or Sunday school ever called. They didn't seem to care about him.

C⁴¹ CAN YOU THINK OF OTHERS WHO NEED OUR LOVE AND CONCERN?

C⁴² How about shut-ins?

C⁴³ And the hospitals.

3⁴⁴   Yes, my mother knew an old Christian lady in a county home who had no family. For years she went out to visit her every other week or so, and sent out flowers and things. These visits were about all she had to live for.

3⁴⁵   Others get lonely too. FOR INSTANCE? Well, sometimes when my husband is out of town and I'm shut up with my two preschoolers, I get to feeling as if I could climb the wall. *(She laughs a little self-consciously.)* Twos and threes aren't the greatest conversationalists.

3⁴⁶   I know a woman from another church who lost her husband recently. She only knew me slightly, but she's been calling me up almost every day. I think she'd talk for hours if I let her. She must feel pretty lonely. YES, I GUESS SO. HAVE YOU EVER THOUGHT OF THE INCONVENIENCE AS A SOURCE OF JOY? Not exactly. Sometimes *(smiling)* I've had some other thoughts about it though. *(Teacher smiles too.)*

3⁴⁷   WELL, WE'VE GOT A PICTURE OF SOME LONELY CHRISTIANS. WHAT WOULD A PERSON WHO REALLY CARES DO TO HELP?

3⁴⁸   Visit, I suppose.

3⁴⁹   Maybe take a tape recording of a service over and play it?

3⁵⁰   Read to them. Or just talk, and listen.

3⁵¹   YES, I'M SURE WE CAN THINK OF MANY. GO SHOPPING FOR THE SHUT-IN, OR OFFER THE PRESCHOOLER'S MOTHER AN AFTERNOON OF BABY-SITTING. INVITE NEW COUPLES AT CHURCH OVER FOR COFFEE TO GET ACQUAINTED. THAT MEANS MORE THAN WE MIGHT THINK.

WHAT IT BOILS DOWN TO IS BEING SENSITIVE TO OTHER CHRISTIANS' NEEDS AND BEING WILLING TO PUT OURSELVES OUT TO HELP.

3⁵²   LET'S LOOK AT THIS LAST AREA FOR JUST A MINUTE. HOW ABOUT THE JOY-SIDER AND HIS RELATIONSHIP WITH THE LORD? *(The class quickly throws out a number of ideas, which the teacher jots down: daily time for prayer, Bible reading, be at prayer meeting, have family devotions, etc. With about five minutes left, the teacher cuts off discussion, and summarizes.)*

3⁵³   I THINK WE'VE JOTTED DOWN ENOUGH TO GIVE US A PICTURE OF THE JOY-SIDER. YOU KNOW, IT'S EASY FOR US TO GET SO WRAPPED UP IN OUR DAILY LIVES, OUR JOBS AND OUR FAMILIES THAT WE FORGET THE BASIC THINGS THAT GIVE MEANING TO LIFE. IT'S EASY TO SIT IN CHURCH AND NOD AGREEMENT WHEN OUR PASTOR TALKS ABOUT SHARING CHRIST AND SERVING OTHERS AND GROWING IN THE LORD. BUT THIS MORNING WE'VE GOTTEN A PICTURE OF THE PERSON WHO REALLY LIVES THIS KIND OF LIFE, BECAUSE HE CARES MORE ABOUT OTHERS THAN ABOUT HIMSELF.

Sharing Christ:

tracts   missions
coffee   bring to church
VBS transportation
care
spend time
talk
show interest in as people:
   gas attendant

Sacrifice self for others:

workers, church-time, SS
committees
faithful, no gossip or criticism
interest in absentees,
shut-ins, hospitals,
lonely people: lost husband
                        kids little
just listen, shop, etc.

Lord:

prayer, time with Bible,
family devotions, etc.

Fig. 10

D¹   JUST BEFORE WE GO, DO SOMETHING FOR ME. LOOK OVER THE LIST ON THE BOARD. IT'S JUST SUGGESTIVE. THERE ARE MORE THAT FIT.

D²   NOW, JOT DOWN ONE SPECIFIC THING YOU CAN PLAN TO DO THIS WEEK THAT'S DEFINITELY ON THE JOY-SIDE. JUST PINPOINT ONE THING YOU CAN DO. *(It's quiet as the class members think and write.)*

D³   ALL RIGHT. WOULD ANY OF YOU LIKE TO SHARE WHAT YOU PLAN WITH THE REST OF US?

D⁴   Well, I used to do a lot of hospital visitation. I think I'll go out to the hospital this week.

D⁵   GOOD. WHAT DAY? Why, I guess Tuesday. Yes, Tuesday's a good day. WHAT TIME? Oh, the afternoon. About two. WHAT ARE YOU GOING TO DO? Just visit. Maybe take some tracts. HOW ABOUT SOME OF OUR SUNDAY SCHOOL PAPERS? MOST FOLKS LIKE THEIR REAL-LIFE APPROACH. That's a good idea. I'll do it.

D⁶   SOMEONE ELSE?

)⁷ I think I'll find time for regular Bible study. WHEN'S BEST FOR YOU? The evening's bad; the older kids, you know. I guess Sally's naptime is best. AND WHEN ARE YOU GOING TO START? This afternoon.

)⁸ I got a letter from a girl I went to college with this week. She's really mixed up. I put it aside; thought I'd answer it next week when I'm not so busy. AND? Well, I know she's anxious to hear from me. So I guess I'll skip what I'd planned for this afternoon and write it then. GOOD.

)⁹ YOU KNOW, AS WE CONCENTRATE ON THE THINGS THAT ARE IMPORTANT TO THE LORD, HE'LL LEAD US TO OPPORTUNITIES LIKE THESE. AND AS A BY-PRODUCT OF LIVING WITH OUR HEARTS SET ON WHAT'S IMPORTANT TO HIM, WE'LL FIND JOY.

LET'S TAKE THIS LAST MOMENT IN SILENT PRAYER AND ASK THE LORD TO USE US THIS WEEK AND HELP US FOLLOW THROUGH ON THE PLANS WE'VE MADE TO GIVE OF OURSELVES FOR HIM.

Research and assignment
    for the student
1. What percentage of classtime was taken by the teacher? How do you explain the different percentages in parts B and C?
2. Analyze what the teacher said. How much was "telling"? List all the other purposes of his questions or comments you can see.
3. Can you discern attempts to help students reach various learning levels? List and analyze efforts to reach each learning level attempted.
4. Review the concept of meaningful student participation in chapter 7. Select three instances of meaningful participation and be ready to defend your choice.
5. Analyze the role of methods in this class. Are methods important in creative Bible teaching? Why, or why not?
6. Recheck the three lessons you evaluated for assignment 3 of chapter 6. Rewrite one lesson to improve its potential for creative teaching.

Experimentation
    for the lay teacher
1. Study how the teacher in this lesson phrased questions and comments to raise pupil learning levels.
2. Review your own lesson plan for next Sunday's lesson. Plan carefully the phrasing of questions or comments you will use to achieve high learning levels.
3. Reread the chapter and look for ways the teacher kept his students on the subject. Jot down ideas you can use in your class when students begin to stray.

THE PATTERN OF CREATIVE BIBLE TEACHING

How does a creative Bible teacher plan a lesson like the one recorded in the last chapter? Are there basic principles or guidelines he follows? Guidelines we can all use to move toward more productive, life-changing classes?

A glance over the last chapter indicates that this class session *was* patterned by the teacher and carefully planned so that his students might be led, rung by rung, up the ladder of learning.

A patterned class isn't necessarily a routine class. It doesn't involve a rigid framework that has to be followed week after week. But patterning a learning experience does involve awareness of a process which the Bible itself reveals, a process for interaction with Scripture which gives maximum opportunity for impact on life.

In this chapter we're going to discover that biblical pattern and explore its meaning for our Bible teaching.

THE PATTERN OF PRODUCTIVE TEACHING

THE BIBLE ABOUNDS with clues. But perhaps the clearest and most concise statement of the scriptural pattern for fruitful interaction with God's Word is found in Paul's first prayer for the Colossians. Let's look at what he says: "That you may be filled with the knowledge of His will in all spiritual wisdom and understanding, so that you may walk in a manner worthy of the Lord, to please Him in all respects, bearing fruit in every good work and increasing in the knowledge of God" (Col. 1:9b-11).

To understand the educational implications of this prayer we need to know a little of its background, and then to look carefully at each of the ideas these verses express.

THE COLOSSIAN CHURCH

When Paul wrote to the Colossians they were being tempted by teachers who promised a special knowledge of God, higher than Paul's teachings had been able to give. They based this promise on the belief that they had discovered the secret of true spirituality.

This belief can be traced back to their view of good and evil. To them the material universe seemed the source of evil. The good existed only in the immaterial realm of ideas. The idea that the material is essentially evil colored the way they looked at themselves and all human activities. Their bodies, being material, must be evil. Yet they also could think, and thought was on a level beyond the physical. The way they saw it, the good "real me" (the immaterial that thinks and understands) was imprisoned in the bad (the physical body). Now, only the good could be "spiritual," so spirituality must somehow be related to the mind. In fact, if the body were necessarily evil, nothing associated with or done in the body could possibly be spiritual.

Since God is both good and spiritual (that is, nonmaterial), our only contact with God *must* be mental and intellectual. What could the evil body have to do with our relationship with God?

Later two ways of life developed from this kind of thinking. Some asserted the superiority of the mind over the body. They denied themselves food, rest, any enjoyments or activities connected with normal living. They shut themselves away from others, refused to bathe or to marry, and in this way "punished" the physical prison in which the real, nonmaterial personality was held captive.

Others indulged in every carnal appetite. After all, the body was evil anyway. Let it do what it wanted. It couldn't affect the good, spiritual "immaterial me" inside.

Fully aware of this thinking, Paul prays that his converts may come to a true experience with God: that they may learn to know Him better and better. And in this prayer Paul outlines a pathway to spiritual reality that is diametrically opposed to that which others held out to his Colossian converts.

THE PRAYER

There are five aspects of the pathway this prayer presents, suggesting an open cycle of spiritual growth. Each is important, although the first three are crucial in developing our pattern for productive teaching. Let's look at each.

"Filled with the knowledge of His will." We often speak of God's will in the sense of personal guidance. "I wonder if it's God's will for me to go to this college, or that one." But the Greek makes it clear that here "God's will" is used in its absolute sense, as "that which God has willed." The Bible teaches that God has revealed His thoughts and plans and decisions to men. God's very thoughts are communicated in words taught by the Holy Spirit.* We have this information in the Old and New Testaments.

Spiritual growth always begins with knowledge of His Word. It is only as we come to know God's will through the Bible that we have the possibility of personal experience with God.

This is something the creative Bible teacher never neglects. Students must understand clearly just what the Lord is saying in a passage under study. In a given passage God may share truth about Himself or tell us His plans for the future of the world. He may simply speak about the life He expects those to live who are made new through Jesus Christ. Whatever the nature of the content, the creative Bible teacher makes sure that his students thoroughly grasp

---

*This position is developed in chapter 3.

the truth expressed. For mastery of the Bible is required for "understanding what the will of the Lord is" (Eph. 5:17).

"In all spiritual wisdom and understanding." The Greek word Paul chose for *wise* carried the same picture to his readers that our word *wise* does to us. What's the difference between a smart man and a wise one? A smart person may have a quick intelligence and be a good student. But a wise person is able to discern and judge a proper course of action. So too with *understanding*, which in the original portrays an ability to see clearly into the true nature of situations and things.

What then is Paul saying? Simply this. For a knowledge of Bible content to benefit, *that knowledge must be related by us to our daily lives.*

The intellectual approach to Scripture can never transform. The real issue is response to God, not knowledge about Him. And response is only possible when the relationship of God's truth to our human experience is clearly seen.

This was the failing of the Corinthians whom Paul takes to task in chapter 6 of his first letter. They had true information. They knew the saints would judge the world (6:2). They knew the unrighteous would not inherit the kingdom (6:9). They knew their bodies were members of Christ (6:15) and temples of the Holy Spirit (6:19). But they were unable to relate these truths to the lawsuits that shook their church, or to their failures in church discipline, or even to personal morality! Because they had truth but lacked the spiritual wisdom to apply it, Paul addresses them "not as spiritual men, but carnal, as babes in Christ" (3:1).

It's unnecessary for believers to be in this situation. The wisdom to relate God's truth to our lives is promised any who ask Him (James 1:5). And it is the responsibility of the Bible teacher to guide students to see the life-implications of the truths they teach.

"So that you may walk in a manner worthy of the Lord, to please Him in all respects." Seeing life-implications, while important, is not enough. This is merely a prelude to life, not life itself.

Here, in a multitude of daily experiences, is where response to God must be worked out. The Corinthians failed to grow spiritually because they did not relate the truth of God to life. In Hebrews we read of a people who knew fully what God desired, but were rebellious (3:16). Since they did not trust God enough to respond to His wishes, "the word they heard did not profit them, because it was not united by faith in those who heard" (4:2).

To the false teachers in Colosse, daily life was utterly irrelevant to spirituality. To the Bible, if there is no response in daily life, the message is without benefit to us.

The whole of Scripture is in harmony on this point. "Those who do what Christ tells them will learn to love God more and more,"

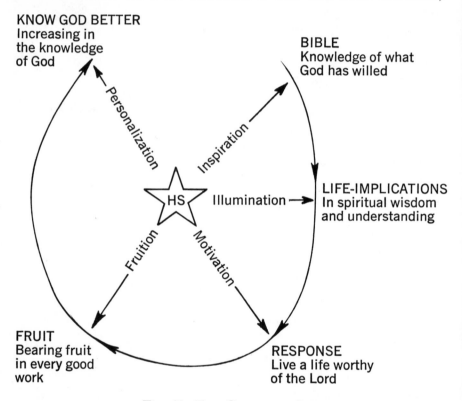

KNOW GOD BETTER
Increasing in
the knowledge
of God

BIBLE
Knowledge of what
God has willed

Personalization

Inspiration

HS   Illumination →

LIFE-IMPLICATIONS
In spiritual wisdom
and understanding

Fruition

Motivation

FRUIT
Bearing fruit
in every good
work

RESPONSE
Live a life worthy
of the Lord

Fig. 11. THE COLOSSIAN CYCLE

Paul's first Colossian prayer shows us the biblical way to personal experience with God. We begin with the Word of God, discern the relationship of Bible truths to life, and respond with a faith that acts on the truth. The result is a fruitful Christian life marked by a deepening personal knowledge of God. At each point the Holy Spirit performs an essential ministry. He inspires the Word, illuminates the believer and motivates him to respond, and produces both the fruit and the awareness of God as a Person.

writes John (I John 2:5, *Living Letters*). And Christ taught, "He who has My commandments, and keeps them, he it is who loves Me; and he who loves Me shall be loved by My Father, and I will love him, and will disclose Myself to him" (John 14:21).

The only way to reality in our life with God is through a believing response to Him as He speaks through His Word.

"Bearing fruit in every good work." Fruit follows knowing, understanding and responding. While the Christian has an active part in studying the Word, in testing his life by it and in responding to it, the fruit is produced without his effort. God produces fruit in the responsive believer (Gal. 5:22-23).

"And increasing in the knowledge of God." This too is a result of responsive living. God, a real and living Person, becomes real to the believer. "I will manifest Myself to him," Christ promised. And He does.

This, then, is the cycle Paul's prayer presents. This is the pathway leading to fruitfulness and personal experience with God.

EDUCATIONAL SIGNIFICANCE OF THE COLOSSIAN PRAYER

In his first letter to Timothy, Paul comments on men who want to be teachers "even though they do not understand either what they are saying or the matters about which they make confident assertions" (I Tim. 1:7). In the same passage he points out that the teaching of true doctrine is to result in changed lives. "The goal of our instruction," he explains, "is love from a pure heart and a good conscience and a faith without hypocrisy" (1:5). Today's Bible teacher must be clear on this: he teaches the Word to change lives.

This is why the Colossian prayer is important to the teacher. It shows him how to teach for changed lives. It isolates four issues that are basic to a spiritually productive ministry.

KNOWING ABOUT GOD, AND KNOWING HIM

In his prayer Paul makes a clear distinction between these two. We Evangelicals are often accused of being bibliolaters, worshipers of the Book. To the extent that we equate knowing what the Bible says with knowing God, the charge is just. The man who can quote the most Scripture in prayer meeting isn't necessarily the most spiritual. He does not necessarily have the closest walk with God. And it's the walk with God that counts.

We all know this is true. Yet too often this knowledge fails to change the way we teach! The Sunday school teacher who concentrates all hour on content is teaching *as if* mastering content is what counts, *as if* life with God is the intellectual exercise the heretics of Paul's day taught!

Where a Sunday school teacher merely teaches the Bible as content, he implies that to know about God and to know God are the same. Far too many young people today leave our churches, rejecting the hypocrisy expressed by one high schooler: "All they want me to do is to say the holy words." Those who teach like this are tragically "without understanding."

But there is an opposite and equal error. It's the idea that a person can know God personally apart from the truth He has revealed in Scripture. A glance at the Colossian cycle (fig. 11) shows us that *the person wishing to know God must begin with truth about God!*

The Colossian prayer also shows us the relationship between knowing about God and knowing God, a relationship over which so many stumble. Information about God and from God, applied to and responded to in daily life, leads to a growing knowledge *of* God. There is a specific route leading from knowledge about God to knowledge of God. For a spiritually productive ministry, the Bible teacher must understand this route and guide his students along it.

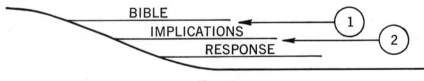

Fig. 12

AREAS OF HUMAN RESPONSIBILITY

The prayer helps us distinguish three responsibilities which are significant to the Bible teacher. The first is, of course, that the Bible must be taught as information. It's necessary to know what God says and, as a teacher, to communicate what God says clearly and accurately.

But the other two responsibilities, indicated by the numbered arrows on figure 12, are commonly overlooked by many Sunday school teachers.

To produce spiritual results, Scripture's implications for human experience must be discovered. Students must cross the gap (arrow 1) between the truth and its relation to every aspect of their lives. The process of moving from truth to implication is one a Bible teacher *cannot* leave to chance. It is his responsibility to guide his students to discover implications. *Time must be taken in class for this process.** Left to themselves, most students do not see the implications of truths they study.

The third area of responsibility (arrow 2) is seen in the gap between seeing implications and responding. Now, no teacher can respond for his students. Each individual must respond to God for himself. So this is primarily a student responsibility. But the teacher *is* responsible to teach to *encourage response.*

Here too Bible teaching in most of our Sunday schools is seriously lacking. Yet for spiritually productive ministry, the teacher must accept and fulfill his responsibility in each of these crucial areas.

A PATTERN OF TEACHING

The Colossian prayer shows us the route from knowing about God to knowing Him, and pinpoints teacher responsibilities. Thus it provides a pattern for the ministry of God's Word. This pattern is as relevant to the preacher as to the teacher. And it's relevant for personal Bible study.

Teaching that changes lives guides the learner from content to implication to response. Preaching that produces results leads the hearer from truth to implication to response. Personal Bible study that is vital and relevant involves us in thinking through meaning, and on to implication and response. This is the pattern of the lesson in chapter 7. The lesson was built to bring each student to an understanding of the passages, then to exploration of implications, and finally to help him toward an appropriate personal response.

This is the pattern of creative Bible teaching. This is the pattern of teaching because it is only this kind of Bible *learning* that transforms lives and brings individuals to ever deepening personal relationship with God.

*The process of successful application is discussed in chapter 10.

THE SUPERNATURAL DIMENSION

It's easy to feel that we've arrived, that from now on success is automatic, when we discover a "system." This is not what the Colossian prayer implies. After all, Paul asks *God* to do this work in the Colossians' lives. He recognizes that we need to be "strengthened with all power, according to His glorious might" (Col. 1:11).

We have the Word, but only because God the Holy Spirit gave it. We can lead students to check their lives against the Word, but only God illumines them and gives the needed wisdom. We can encourage response, but only God fills hearts with love for Christ and "a desire to please Him in all respects" (Col. 1:10). It is God who produces fruit through our weak lives. It is God who sovereignly reaches down into our lives to make Himself known to us.

This truth the Bible teacher dare not forget. He teaches according to a pattern, because that pattern is revealed by God to be in accord with the way His Word works in lives. But as we teach, our trust and confidence are never in the pattern; these are reserved for God.

Research and assignment
    for the student
1. Read up on Gnosticism (the Colossian heresy). Against this background, read Colossians. Do you see other educationally significant passages?
2. Write an analysis of the educational significance of these passages.
3. Study several senior high or adult lessons. Write a report of ways they follow or violate the pattern the author suggests.
4. Study the work of the Holy Spirit. In what ways do His ministries of inspiration, illumination, motivation, fruition and personalization (as the author calls it) have educational significance?
5. Collateral reading: Roy Zuck, *Spiritual Power in Your Teaching.*
6. Review the lesson in chapter 7. Be ready to explain specifically how it follows the Colossian pattern.
7. Think through the gospel using the Colossian pattern.
8. For class discussion: Be prepared to relate the elements of the Colossian cycle to the learning levels of chapter 6.
9. Choose and study two passages of Scripture on the Colossian pattern for your personal devotions. Take notes and bring them to class to share.

Exploration

for the lay teacher

1. Review the last lesson you taught. Did you successfully close the gaps shown on figure 12?
2. Review chapter 7 and observe how the Colossian pattern determines its structure.
3. Before Sunday, think through the Bible portion you are to teach, using the Colossian pattern.
4. As you prepare to teach, pattern your lesson carefully to cover content, explore implications, and encourage response.

BRIDGING
THE
GAPS

The ordinary Bible teacher concentrates on his first responsibility: to communicate clearly and accurately just what the Bible teaches. He may add a word of exhortation or an illustration or two, but his focus nevertheless is on the Bible as information.

The creative Bible teacher, whether in a Sunday school class or in the pulpit, does not neglect the Bible as information. But he goes beyond. *He focuses on helping learners bridge the gaps,* gaps that may cut off its vitalizing power from even those who respect and love God's Word.

It's not easy to bridge the gaps that stand between truth and implication, and between implication and response. A whole complex of ideas and skills enters in. But bridging the gap is necessary, and it can be done. *You* can be a creative Bible teacher.

DEVELOPING A TEACHING AIM

THE BIG AIM of Bible teaching is transformation. This is what the apostle Paul expressed in a verse we looked at in the last chapter: "The goal of our instruction is love from a pure heart and a good conscience and a faith without hypocrisy" (I Tim. 1:5).

You'll find this idea expressed in different ways throughout the New Testament. In Ephesians Paul calls it being "filled up to [with] all the fulness of God" (3:19) and attaining to a "mature man, to the measure of the stature which belongs to the fulness of Christ" (4:13). The writer to the Hebrews speaks of the mature, who "have their senses trained to discern good and evil" (5:14), and urges believers to "press on to maturity" (6:1). The transformed men Paul speaks of in Romans (12:2) he describes in Galatians as led by and living in the Spirit, full of the fruit of "love, joy, peace, patience, kindness, goodness, faithfulness, gentleness, self-control" (Gal. 5:22-23).

FOCUSING ON A TEACHING AIM

The trouble is, transformation is a big aim—too big. We all want this, but the idea of transformation or maturity doesn't give helpful guidelines for constructing a specific lesson. To say, "I want this lesson to bring my students to maturity" may be commendable, but it really isn't meaningful. One lesson simply won't do it.

You see why when you break down the idea of maturity. What's involved? Many, many things. There's relationship with God: prayer, Bible study, worship, meditation, praise, confession, honesty. And then there's relationship with our family: love, patience, guidance, discipline *and* receiving discipline, forgiveness. And how about relationship with non-Christians, and its cluster of concern, witness, separation, exemplary living, consideration, suffering, and so many others. And we can go on and on.

Certainly no single class, no series of lessons, no year of lessons, will bring a student to maturity in Christ. So, while the big aim of transformation is always there, our *teaching aim* has to be more specific.

The question is, what kind of teaching aim is in harmony with the big aim of transformation? How can we direct each lesson to lead our students closer to that maturity which is God's will?

KINDS OF LESSON AIMS

Christian educators have suggested several kinds of aims from which a Bible teacher may choose. One is the *content aim,* in which his purpose is to communicate biblical information. Then there's the *inspiration aim,* in which his purpose is to inspire, or touch the emotions. Finally there is the *action aim,* in which his purpose is to move to action. Each of these aims has a valid but different place in Christian teaching.

Which leads to transformation? In I Corinthians 2:15 Paul claims that the spiritual man "appraises all things." The Greek verb here, *anakrinō,* speaks of a capacity to discern. The believer, in virtue of his salvation and relationship with God, has the capacity for spiritual discernment of "all things." He can look at life the way God does. He can see the implications of God's truth for life situations and can respond in harmony with God's will. But this is only a capacity—one that is not developed in all believers.

The development from capacity to ability is intimately related to maturity. Hebrews 5:14 says that mature men "discern good and evil." The word *discern* is from the same root *(krinō)* as the word *appraises* of I Corinthians. It's set apart by a prefix *(dia)* which indicates that what is a capacity in all believers has become an ability in the mature.

Now, how did the mature move from capacity to ability? How did they become mature? "Because of practice [they] have their senses trained to discern good and evil." *These are people who have seen the implications of truth and responded appropriately.*

This is the educational significance of Hebrews 5:14. Growth comes by experience, by using our capacity to understand and to respond.

What does this mean to the teacher whose goal is spiritual growth? Simply that his teaching aim will be to produce response. For it is those living responsively to God who grow and mature.

The content aim. I suggested a moment ago that content and inspiration aims are valid ones for the Bible teacher.

In seminary I learned much about the Bible as content. I was trained in theology, which is a systematization of the information contained in Scripture. In such classes we did not go deeply into implications. Yet this training is the most valuable I have received.

Why? Because the Bible *should* be mastered as content. With a framework of understanding of the whole, tremendous light is thrown on every passage. Without such a framework, it's possible to misinterpret a passage or verse.

Certainly somewhere in the Christian education of our children, youth, and adults the church should provide for teaching the Word as a whole, as a system of truth. Such teaching is an important framework for more meaningful personal Bible study.

Yet one of the basic weaknesses in our Sunday schools and churches today is that believers are not being taught the Word *for growth*. Most Sunday school teachers hope for spiritual growth, but teach only information. If growth toward maturity is our first purpose, teaching with content aims will not achieve it. To teach for growth we must teach for response.

The inspiration aim. This actually is a type of response aim. After all, to some truths of Scripture the appropriate response is emotional! It's one of praise, or an expression of love for God.

No response to God can be a cold, emotionless performance of actions that are distasteful to us. If a response is truly to God, love must be the underlying motive (cf. I Cor. 13). Anything less is not response to God but response to law. And response to God's Word as law leads only to the frustration of our hopes and of God's purposes for us.

The response aim. For spiritual growth toward maturity, the teaching aim will be framed in terms of response. When the teacher builds his lesson, *he must think in terms of the learner response he hopes to achieve*.

A survey of evangelical Sunday school lessons shows that this principle is overlooked by many editors and writers. Look, for instance, at these aims, drawn at random from materials of several independent and denominational publishers.

1. To teach that Christ is a powerful Person who can change our lives for good.
2. To help primaries realize that God loves them and cares for them in difficult situations.
3. To communicate to high schoolers the length and depth and breadth of the love of Christ, and to help each understand that this love is made available to him today through trust in Christ.

4. To convince each pupil of the importance of looking to Christ for help when in need.
5. To help each student discover why the present ministry of Christ as our High Priest is important to him.
6. To explain clearly and compellingly the necessity of accepting Christ as personal Saviour.
7. To help students dispel any fears that they may have which might prevent them from dedicating their lives to Christ for His service.
8. To discuss the implications of the gospel for our growingly tense national racial situation.
9. To help young teens understand that church membership is an important spiritual responsibility and a vital part in a developing Christian life.

Go back over the list of aims again, and relate them to the partial diagram of the Colossian cycle (fig. 13). To which part of the cycle does each aim direct the teacher?

Does the aim focus on understanding "to know that"? Then the teacher is led to think of his job as one of teaching the Bible for information.

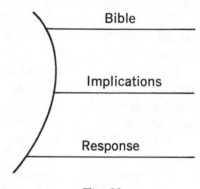

Bible

Implications

Response

Fig. 13

Some aims lead the teacher to think in terms of implications (see 5-9). But none of the aims quoted directs the teacher where he must go if his students are to grow, to respond.

It's important, then, for teachers using curriculum as well as for those few able to teach without aids, to be able to structure response aims. You must understand your goal clearly enough to state it if you hope to build a lesson that will achieve it.

BUILDING A RESPONSE AIM

Understand the passage. This comes first. Any response we seek to evoke must be appropriate to the true meaning of the passage.

Christ said to one man, "Go and sell all you possess, and give it to the poor, and you shall have treasure in heaven; and come, follow Me" (Mark 10:21). Is the appropriate response for us to sell all we have? Not when the context is understood. Not when we see Christ's purpose, which was to forcefully point out to this law-abiding young man that he had unknowingly violated the first and great commandment. He did not love God with his whole heart. He loved his wealth—so much that he chose it and rejected the invitation of Christ, his God.

Rightly understood, the appropriate response to this passage is a careful and honest self-evaluation. Has someone or something displaced God in *my* affections? Only when I examine my life and decisively reject any idol have I made an appropriate response.

So "What does this passage teach?" is the first question that must be asked in building a response aim. The response at which we aim must be appropriate to the Word.

Understanding implications for the learner. This is particularly important when you teach children or youth, or adults whose life situation is different from your own.

Sunday school curriculum writers try to select passages that present truth relevant to each age group. This is one advantage of a departmental or closely graded curriculum. With this curriculum plan a lesson can be geared directly to the characteristics and needs of each age grouping. Other curriculum plans select passages for the whole school, or take a general theme for all with various passages determined by age groupings. These planners must at times choose portions which are not relevant to the life of all.

This is an important concept, this choosing passages which are relevant to the learners' present lives and experiences. In Proverbs 22:6, the familiar command to train up a child in the way he should go, the Hebrew clearly indicates that such training involves teaching the truth needed, in ways it can be used, at each developing stage of life. How clear this should be. If spiritual growth comes through response, we must teach truth to which the learner *can* respond.

To guide this response the teacher needs to know as much of the life and patterns of life of his students as possible. Read up on the characteristics of the age group you teach. Observe the students, visit their homes, talk with them. The better you understand their lives, the better you can tailor your lessons to lead them to response.

When you understand the passage and see its relevance to the lives of your pupils, you're ready to state your aim. Usually several criteria are suggested for constructing aims:

short enough to be remembered
clear enough to be meaningful
specific enough to be achieved

Be careful, though, of the temptation to become too specific.

Remember the different responses recorded in the chapter 7 class? One man planned hospital visitation. A woman determined to make a new start on personal devotions. Another put aside a pleasant activity to write a difficult letter. *No teacher could have stated these responses in his aim!*

Why? For one thing, he simply couldn't know the details of his students' lives. How could he have known of a letter just received, a date with God being missed?

So, when a response aim is written, it is not stated specifically. It's stated *flexibly,* flexibly enough to permit the Holy Spirit freedom to guide each learner to the unique response He chooses for him to make.

What does a short enough, clear enough, flexible enough response aim look like? Well, let's construct one for John 11:17-44. This is the record of the raising of Lazarus. Note the movement of the passage. Christ comes to Bethany and is met by Martha, who tells Him tearfully of her brother's death. In a touching expression of faith, Martha tells Jesus that she knows if He had arrived sooner, her brother would not have died. Jesus responds with a promise that her brother will rise. She agrees. Jesus is the Christ, the resurrection and the life. He will raise Lazarus on the last day. Then Mary arrives and expresses the same confidence as her sister. "Lord, if You had been here, my brother would not have died." And the three move up to visit the tomb. There Jesus shocks everyone by ordering the stone closing it removed. Martha, so full of faith a moment ago, objects. "Lord, by this time there will be a stench; for he has been dead four days."

Martha was convinced that Jesus had power, even to the control of eternal destiny. But she unthinkingly limited His power to act *now.*

As you read you're convicted of the same sin. How many times do you, who trust Christ as Lord and God, unthinkingly leave Him out of your life? How often have you worried and become upset? And what is this but unbelief? Christ isn't limited! He can reach down into your daily life and meet every need. What a thrill to read these words of His: "Did I not say to you, if you believe, you will see the glory of God?"

You're excited. Here is a passage you want to share. So you sit down and begin to work out your aim:

To exalt Christ as a *present* help.

To show that Christ's power is available to meet daily needs.

To help my students see that Christ's power is unlimited.

To show ways we unconsciously limit Christ's power.

To guide my students to tap Christ's power today.

To help each student discover areas in which he may be limiting
  Christ, and to help each begin to trust Him in them.

There! It's not perfect, but it does express your purpose. The first two aims you wrote focus on content. The next focuses on content too, but you began to think in terms of your students. The next two focus even more on the students. But the last one says how you hope each student will respond to the truth you're going to teach.

This last aim makes room for the fact that each student may have a different way in which he limits Christ. So the lesson will need to be structured to help the class explore various areas, so God can pinpoint each student's need. And the aim goes beyond insight. The aim is stated in terms of the response that actually is the goal.

When a teacher reaches this point, where he sees the goal of his teaching in terms of student response, he's ready to construct his lesson plan.

STRUCTURING THE LESSON

The teaching aim is developed from a study of the passage to be taught. It spells out in a flexible way the response for which we're teaching. Thus it gives us a clear idea of where we want to go.

The Colossian cycle shows us how to get there. It suggests a structure that will bring us to the response goal. And what the Colossian cycle suggests is a class structured to a four-step pattern.

FOUR THINGS TO OCCUR

It's best to avoid thinking of these as mechanical steps. They're more like four parts of a continuous, systematic but exciting process. In class the students probably won't even notice passage from one part of the process to another. No part is marked by routine; each is full of opportunity for spontaneity and interaction.

Yet each of these parts in the process has its own—and essential—role. Let's look at the four in sequence.

Hook. This part of the pattern isn't suggested by the Colossians cycle, but by the learner.

Look at it this way. You, the teacher, have prepared the class. You've been gripped by the truth you're to teach. You've seen it work in your life. When you come to class, you're excited about the lesson.

But your students aren't. They haven't had your experiences, and they aren't thinking about your lesson. They have their own problems! One may be worrying about a late income tax. Another about a faucet: *Now did I turn it off, or didn't I?* A teen may be replaying last night's game or nursing the tragedy of a rejected date. All differ, but each comes to class operating on his own wave length. You have to make him want to leave his thoughts and share yours.

And so the hook. Fishermen use it to get the fish out of the lake into the boat. You use it to bring your students into the Word of life.

There are several qualities of a good hook:

1. It gets attention. Remember in chapter 7 how the teacher immediately involved his class? "Turn to your neighbor, and in thirty seconds come up with a list of what most people think makes them happy" (A¹). Here's something everyone can do, a way in which all can take part. And they do. He has their attention. The hook is in.

But getting attention isn't the only task of a good hook.

2. It sets a goal. Preachers call this a "need step." Something to answer the question "Why should I listen to this?" This is a fair question. If this sermon or lesson is going to be about something important to me, I want to pay attention. If it's an irrelevant recounting of dusty data, I don't!

The teacher in chapter 7 quickly gave his students a reason for listening. After he listed their ideas of what most people think makes them happy, he showed that the writer of Philippians spoke of *joy* at a time when he had nothing we associate with happiness. Then he made this statement: "Our goal today is to discover what gave Paul joy, when he had nothing that most people think makes them happy" (A[11]).

By this statement he told his class why they should pay attention. All of us want joy. To discover its source the class would listen. He had earned the right to teach.

When your students have no reason for learning, no reason that is important to them, you'll find it hard to hold them. But set a goal *they* want to reach, and they'll be with you.

3. One more thing. The hook should lead naturally into the Bible study. In the chapter 7 lesson it did. The teacher then turned to Philippians, and the class was under way.

A good hook is one of the secrets of effective Bible teaching. When you capture interest, set a goal, and lead your students into the Word, you have a good start on a creative class.

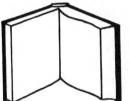
Book. In the chapter 7 lesson this part of the class is set off by the letter *B*. The Book corresponds to the first part of the Colossian cycle. Spiritual growth begins with "a knowledge of that which God has willed."

During this part of the lesson, the teacher tries to clarify the meaning of the passage studied. Look through chapter 7 and you'll notice that this teacher was careful to help his students see meaning (B[8]-B[18], B[20]-B[30], B[40]). In this part of the teaching-learning process the teacher helps his students get—and understand—the biblical information.

A variety of methods are available to the creative teacher for this purpose. He can use a participative one, such as the buzz groups and reports used in the demonstration lesson. Or he can use a teacher-centered method. A good lecture is the fastest way to cover content and make points. Or one can use charts, visuals, and so forth.

Whatever the method, the purpose in this part of the lesson remains constant: to give biblical information and help students understand it.

Look. When the students understand what the Bible says, it's time to move to implications. Their knowledge must be tempered with "spiritual wisdom and understanding."

So the teacher plans this part of the process to guide his class to insight into the relationship of the truth to life.

This process is illustrated in chapter 7. The class discovered that sources of Christian joy are getting out the gospel, sacrificing self for others, and the Lord Himself (B^{44}). But what does this mean for the pattern of our daily lives?

These ideas may provide a test of present spirituality—or lack of it (C^6). But for response, the implications to *me* of getting out the gospel or serving others must be spelled out.

And so the teacher developed the fiction of the TV cameraman. The class *had* to think in terms of life. Members weren't permitted to meaninglessly mutter the "holy words," although some tried (C^9-C^{12}).

Read over the C section of chapter 7 again. Note how the class was led to see what a real concern with evangelism means in lives like theirs (C^{11}-C^{31}), and how they were forced to describe a self-sacrificing love that actually affects behavior (C^{32}-C^{51}). By thus spelling out the *realities* involved in Christian witness and community, *the students opened areas of their own lives to the probing ministry of the Holy Spirit.* This is utterly essential to truly creative —that is, productive—Bible teaching.

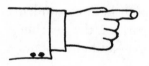

Took. But, like a vaccination, the Word of God is of no effect until we can say it "took." Response is required.

Normally response to teaching will take place outside of class, in weekday life. "Faith without works," the Bible says, "is dead" (James 2:17). For spiritual growth and reality in Christian experience, faith demands response in all the varied situations of human life.

The teacher in chapter 7 encouraged such response. He led his class members to pinpoint personally areas in which they could respond (D^2) and he helped them plan specifically ways they *would* respond (D^5, D^7).

Often we leave church full of good intentions. We'll be more loving that week, more dedicated. But because the resolution is vague, because we haven't gone beyond the generalization to plan *how* we'll change, no change takes place.

The creative teacher helps his students respond by leading them to see God's will and by helping them decide and plan to do it.

STRUCTURING A UNIT

So far we've talked as if the four parts of the creative teaching process must all take place in a single hour. In most cases they will. But it's not necessary.

Figure 14 shows how the process works out in a single class hour. All the parts of the pattern are there. Figure 15 shows how the process might be worked out for a five-week series. So, if you find a lesson that doesn't fit the creative pattern, don't condemn the curriculum too quickly. Look and see if the process isn't carried out over a period of weeks.

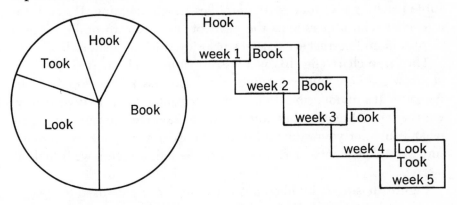

Fig. 14. The Lesson Hour   Fig. 15. The Unit of Lessons

Actually, there's little doubt that of the two, the approach that looks at a series of lessons as a single unit has more advantages than the one that sees each class as a unit.

VALUES OF LESSON STRUCTURE

The ability to handle lesson structure is invaluable to the Bible teacher. The process we've described and the key words (Hook, Book, Look, Took) suggested to characterize its parts are tools for the teacher. These are practical tools with which to develop structuring ability. How can these tools be used?

As a guide to method choice. When you understand the purpose of each part of the teaching process, it's easy to select methods. Most books on methods are rather confusing. They talk of role play, of buzz groups, of brainstorming, of dozens of other techniques, and give rules for their successful use. But what should determine your choice of method is function, the job a method is to do in class.

This is how you should understand method. A method is simply an activity designed to hook students, to communicate information and meaning, to lead to insight, or to encourage response. The last section of this book talks about activities suited to these purposes for various age groups. But the main thing is this. *If you understand what you are trying to accomplish, you can select or invent an activity to accomplish it.* Master the parts of the lesson process, and method skill will follow.

To simplify lesson planning. Breaking down the process of creative Bible teaching into four parts simplifies lesson planning. It's easy for a teacher who understands the parts of the lesson to build a lesson or to find and correct weaknesses in printed lesson material.

The large chart (fig. 16) is a lesson planning chart. It shows how you can use your understanding of the process to develop a teaching plan. It's divided into four areas horizontally and two vertically. On the left, jot down what *you* will do or say. On the right, write in what you want your students to do. (This is a simple way to make sure you plan plenty of student participation, a factor we'll look at later.)

Figure 16 is partially filled out with the lesson plan used for teaching the demonstration lesson of chapter 7. Look it over. Then review chapter 7 and fill out the rest of the plan as you think the teacher originally prepared it.

You can use this form in planning your own lessons (unless you teach preschoolers). Make sure that your Hook gets attention, sets a goal, and leads into the Bible. Plan the Book to communicate both information and meaning. Check the Look to be sure you guide your students to implications. Finally, construct a Took that will aid and encourage response.

And, you're on your way to creative Bible teaching!

	ME	THEM
	ask what most think makes happy lecture: Paul had none (cross off) state goal: to find joy when not happy	thirty-second neighbor buzz, report

Fig. 16. LESSON PLANNING CHART

Research and assignment
      for the student
1. Find a lesson quarterly which does *not* contain good aims, and re-write as response aims.

2. Choose one of the above lessons, and write out an evaluation of what changes the writer might have made had he written the lesson to achieve response.

3. To hand in, rewrite each aim on pages 103-4 for response.

4. Study various curriculum plans (see Lawrence O. Richards, *The Key to Sunday School Achievement*), and be ready to explain the advantages and disadvantages of each.

5. Study Keil and Delitzsch, *Commentary on the Old Testament*, on Proverbs 22:6, and write a two-page statement of the implications of this verse for Christian education.

6. Select one passage of Scripture from the Old Testament and one from the New. Outline briefly its teaching and write an aim to guide you in teaching it.

7. Complete the lesson plan for the chapter 7 lesson (see p. 113).

8. For discussion: Why does the author stress the idea that the class is a process, not a series of steps?

9. Be prepared for a quiz over the four parts of the lesson plan (Hook, Book, Look, Took).

10. Analyze lessons in several curricula at a given age level. Are any parts of the lesson process neglected? Which? Write briefly your estimation of the *significance* of what you find.

11. Visit another Sunday school class and observe for lesson structure. Carefully analyze and report your findings.

12. Plan out how you would teach John 11:11-44 with the aim given in the text. Record your plan on a chart like figure 16.

13. In carrying out assignment 12, did you discover why the author asserts, "If you understand what you are trying to accomplish, you can select or invent an activity to accomplish it"? Be prepared to discuss.

Exploration
    for the lay teacher

1. Rewrite any aims in your teacher's manual which are not stated in terms of response.

2. Complete the analysis of the Philippians lesson on the chart provided (fig. 16).

3. Analyze your last lesson on the same kind of chart.

4. Plan your next lesson using the chart approach, making sure you begin with a response aim.

10

TRUTH
INTO
LIFE

The most difficult task of the Bible teacher is to help students see truth in terms of their own lives. This is particularly difficult, because he *may not know its implications for them.*

What do I mean by this? Let's say you teach a class of primaries. You teach them, but you don't live the life of a six- or seven- or eight-year-old. You don't think as they think or feel as they feel. You don't have this child's problems, or that one's parents, or the other's personality. You may teach high schoolers, but your life is fantastically removed from theirs. The generation gap is real. Teens today

don't think or understand in the same pattern as adults. You may even teach adults, but you do not live another adult's life. You live your own. While God's truth is relevant to everyone, while you can see specific implications of that truth for *your* life, you will not see all its implications for another.

Because each human being is a unique personality, living a life that is distinct, no one outside can determine with assurance all the implications of a truth for another. And certainly no one dare claim to know *the* response another must make, a response which God alone has the right to direct.

APPROACHES TO APPLICATION

NEARLY EVERYONE who teaches the Bible believes that the Word should be put to use. All teach with a purpose, with some thought that the Bible is relevant to life. And most try to make it relevant. They attempt to apply what they teach.

The problem is how to make an application that works. The purpose of application is to make truth usable, to get it into the experience, into the life, of the learner. Yet many Bible teachers "make applications" that do not show up later in the lives of their students. The techniques they use simply do not work.

CONTENT IS ENOUGH

Sometimes we meet a teacher who says, "I teach the Word. It's the Holy Spirit's job to make it relevant." Not many of us would agree. If the Holy Spirit uses us to teach the Bible, He may want to use us to relate it too! Yet even teachers who disagree with this statement, and some curriculum writers, plan lessons as if content *were* enough.

A peculiar picture of people and learning underlies this approach. The student is looked at almost like an IBM machine. The teacher takes a mental file card, punches a few holes (representing the biblical information) and drops it in the machine. Whenever a situation arises in which the truth is needed, the student's mind is automatically supposed to sort through the punched cards, and whirrrr! The truth is there, ready to be used.

But human beings don't operate that way. Minds don't automatically sort content and relate it to experiences. Content, taught as information, is filed away all right. *But without training, the student is unlikely to see its relationship to his life!*

If you doubt this, test yourself. Write down what you know about the present ministry of Christ in heaven. Now, jot down what this truth means to you personally. Write down how you *use* it. Difficult? Yet there's hardly a more relevant doctrine to Christian experience in the Word of God. But the chances are that unless you've been taught the doctrine *with a view to its meaning for life*, you can't apply it. And if you don't understand what it means for your life, you cannot possibly use it!

The idea that in patterning the mind with information individuals will develop ability to use that information has been thoroughly tested. And the tests show that this idea simply is not true.

What can we say then about the Bible teacher who covers only content and expects lives to change?

I have on my desk a senior high Sunday school lesson from a major curriculum publisher. It's a lesson on John the Baptist which talks of his character and way of life, and concludes by attempting *in a single sentence* to apply the lesson to teen lives: "Let's ask the Lord to help us be like John."

To close your lesson with a prayer or an exhortation to "use what we've studied today" is not to apply it—not so the truth is likely to affect the life.

GENERALIZATION

A better teacher, realizing that he must get beyond content, may move to generalization.

Take the John the Baptist lesson I mentioned above. The content is clearly organized. One section looks at John in the wilderness, pointing up his way of life, his clothing and diet. It stresses the idea that he did not find material comforts important. Another section looks at his sermons to the crowds. It points up his blunt honesty. He didn't pull his punches and tell people what they wanted to hear. He spoke God's message plainly, and no possible threat to his popularity could stay him. A third section looks at John after his disciples left him to follow Jesus. It points up his attitude: "He must increase, but I must decrease." John put Christ first.

The better teacher, unwilling to leave his class with only information, might ask, "What qualities of character set John apart from others—qualities that are important for Christians today?" And with this question he would lead his high schoolers to generalize. He would lead them from facts to principles.

This leading of students from facts to principles is important in effective application. *But it is not enough,* just as it wasn't enough for the teacher in chapter 7 to help his students discover the sources of Christian joy. To achieve response, the teacher must help his students see how to use the principle in their lives.

ILLUSTRATION

One way we can see a principle in operation is to give an illustration. But this has its problems.

Let's say that you've been teaching a class of seven-year-olds. In your lesson you've shown that being honest is one way to please the Lord. Your class expresses a desire to please the Lord, and is willing to be "honest" to do it. But you want to help them see that honesty means more than "don't steal." So, to bring this down on their own level, you use an illustration.

> Little Betsy found a jump rope on the playground! It had bright red handles and a colored rope, and she ran all the way home to show her mother! It was just like the one she had always wanted. But mother didn't seem too happy. "Betsy," mother asked, "is it really *yours?*" "Oh yes, Mother," Betsy said. "I found it." Mother still didn't look happy. She talked about the girl who had lost it and how she must feel. And she asked Betsy if it was really honest to have someone else's rope, even though she didn't steal it. Betsy went into her room and thought and thought. When she came out, she looked happy. "Mother," she said, "I'm going to take the rope back and give it to the teacher. If no one claims it, I can have it in two weeks. And," she smiled, "I really do want to be honest, to please the Lord Jesus."

The next day one of your class finds a doll on the playground, and takes it home. If it had been a jump rope, she'd have taken it to the teacher!

Think about that. Do you see why?

The illustration idea rests on the theory of "transfer by identical elements." You verbally create a "real" situation, as like an actual experience as possible. The hope is that when the learner finds himself in a similar situation, he'll remember and use the truth taught.

The difficulty is that elements of situations are seldom identical. To a literal-minded child, just the shift of one factor (a jump rope to a doll) may change the situation enough so that the relationship of the one to the other isn't noticed!

This happens with adults as well as children. A pastor cites as an illustration of failure to "provide things honest in the sight of all men" unwillingness to honor a commitment. But the illustration doesn't make you think of the vacation you're planning, even though you know it means late payment of some bills. And it doesn't make you think of the paper and pencils you bring home to your children from the office. The principle is the same, the illustration is a good one, *but it is not similar enough to your experiences to help you relate the truth to yourself.*

SO ALL FAIL

So none is really effective. None does a really good job in opening up your life to the illuminating ministry of the Holy Spirit.

Of the three, generalization *plus* illustration is best. The high schoolers studying John's life may see one of his qualities as "speaking up for God even when it's unpopular." The teacher may illustrate this, and tell of a teen who witnessed to teammates on a trip even though he knew they might laugh at him. This may hit one or more members of the class squarely, especially if the teacher knows his class well and chooses the illustration because he knows it is a problem area.

But this is unlikely to touch *all* the class. And it will not help *any* develop the ability to relate the principle to new life situations they'll face that week.

For truly effective application, we must look elsewhere.

GUIDED SELF-APPLICATION

In the introduction to this chapter we noted the relationship of individuality to application. Each student needs to see God's truth as it relates to his unique life. Each has different areas in which a lesson truth will apply, as well as some shared in common with his classmates.

The creative Bible teacher wants to expose a number of these areas, in order that the Holy Spirit might direct each student individually to the specific response(s) He wants him to make. Application, then, must be flexible enough to include all, yet individualized to touch the life of each.

PREREQUISITES OF EFFECTIVE APPLICATION

Truth must be related to "my" life. Some teachers try to hit all their class members with a shotgun burst of illustrations. This is better than using only one or two. But it still falls short. The reason goes back to the uniqueness of each individual life. Every person lives in his own peculiar situation, in a whole complex of relationships and personality that make his life uniquely *his*. Thus each individual has special opportunities to use a Bible truth, his own special areas of need.

It's true that we all share certain experiences. We have basic things in common. But because of our individuality we are tested in different points. I may see a neighbor child cut through my flower bed and, in a friendly way, ask him not to do it again. You may love your flowers so passionately that you struggle to resist hitting him! Or you may keep calm when someone disagrees with you, while I may become upset and angry, or even hurt. We each need God's strength, His calming grace. But we need it in different situations, at different points in our experience.

This clarifies the task of the creative Bible teacher. It's not to illustrate truth used in "life." It's to help each student discover how truth studied may be used in *his* life. And these situations, these personal points of need to which a word from God applies, *must be discovered by each of us for himself!*

Relevant areas must be explored. This seems to be the best way to help students to self-discovery. And such a course demands class participation. You can see why. The search for relationship of truth to life must be an active thing. Each of the learners must be involved. And participation stimulates thinking. It initiates the search.

There's another thing. When several people share their ideas, new ideas are born. Remember how in chapter 7 each suggestion of an application led to another? In talking about the gospel, the suggestion of one that others be invited to church made another think of VBS, and that made another think of transportation needs (C^{18}-C^{20}). The thought that sacrificial concern for other believers would lead some to serve in children's church led to suggestion of a number of other church-related services (C^{33}-C^{35}). And one member's report of someone who needed a demonstration of Christian concern stimulated awareness of others (C^{40}-C^{46}).

This is what happens when a whole class seeks together to put flesh on a Bible truth. New channels of thinking are opened for all. And as the group goes on to explore the areas exposed, the Lord gives each individual flashing insights into the meaning of the Word to his life and his needs.

In a process like this the teacher has to protect the class members. Each one, whether he realizes it or not, risks exposing his weaknesses and sins. The things he suggests reveal them.

The teacher in chapter 7 protected his students. He set up a situation in which ideas could be shared objectively. He didn't ask, "If you were living like Paul, how would your lives be different?" This is an invitation to open confession of sin, an invitation few are ready to accept! Instead, he talked about "the people in our church" (C^8). This is close enough to make the situation real, yet distant enough to permit objectivity. No one feels personally threatened.

Later the truth will become personal. The teacher suggests that each person plan to respond. But for open participation he sets up a situation in which each can express himself freely, without threat.

RESULTS OF GUIDED SELF-APPLICATION

The kind of application just described—a shared search for life-implications of a Bible truth, in which each pools his insights and experience—produces results. The primary result is that class members discover use for the truth in their lives. Only when use is known can a response be made. But there are other results too.

A sensitized life. A person who sees a variety of life-implications for a truth is likely to see more. After each class its members step back into life. None knows what new situations will arise that week, what new experiences wait. But if in the class a student has developed awareness of a wide range of situations to which a particular truth relates, he is likely to recognize new opportunities for response when they arise.

An independent ability to grow. An eleven-year-old once told me, "You're the teacher. You're supposed to talk. I'm just supposed to sit here." Already he had developed an approach to the Bible: "I listen. I'm not involved."

But for the Word of God to produce growth, we must be involved. We must be involved in actively searching for implications, in actively responding to every word from God. Students in a class using guided self-application are being trained to study the Word of God for growth. They are learning how to learn.

This should be one of the major goals of the Bible teacher: not to keep the learners dependent on him, but to equip them to study the Word independently, and to study it in such a way that they grow. When your teaching conforms to the pattern given in the Colossian cycle and you involve your class in the process, your students will develop the ability they need to grow.

THE PROCESS OF GUIDED SELF-APPLICATION

Last chapter we looked at the Hook, Book, Look and Took lesson structure. Application takes place in the last two steps, in which the student is guided to discover the relation of the truth studied to his life, and is encouraged to make a response. When we look at these steps in detail, the elements of the process become clear and take on a distinctive pattern.

The pattern described. Stated simply, the pattern is this:

GENERALIZATION→VARIED APPLICATION→EXAMI-
NATION OF SENSITIVE AREA→PERSONAL DECISION

This pattern is shown in figure 17.

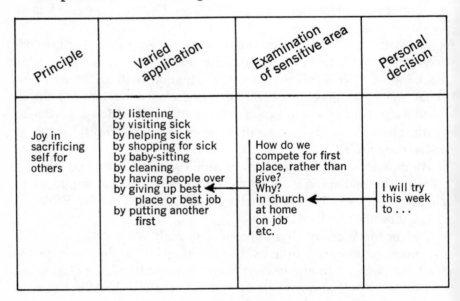

Principle	Varied application	Examination of sensitive area	Personal decision

Joy in sacrificing self for others	by listening
	by visiting sick
	by helping sick
	by shopping for sick
	by baby-sitting
	by cleaning
	by having people over
	by giving up best ◄
	   place or best job
	by putting another
	   first
		How do we compete for first place, rather than give?
		Why?
		in church ◄
		at home
		on job
		etc.
			I will try this week to . . .

Fig. 17

In *generalization*, discussed earlier in this chapter, a principle is discovered. Check for it in chapter 7. The class had discovered the major principles in each Philippians chapter. These were restated by the teacher (B[44]). Then he led his students to see contrasts between them and ways men seek happiness (C[1]-C[7]). When the principles and their nature were clearly defined, the teacher led the class beyond the generalizations to *varied application*. Rather than give illustrations, he forced his students to give illustrations themselves (C[13]-C[31]; C[32]-C[51]). Notice how the teacher guided his class to think of ways each principle might work out in their lives? Each question and suggestion was designed to stimulate or guide them to think concretely in a new area, or to think more deeply of one under consideration.

Gospel

Do you think this is the best way to get out the gospel? (C[13]).

What opportunities do we have to share Christ? Personal ones, I mean (C[15]).

You know, this neighbor business interests me. Why don't we have more impact as a church on our unsaved neighbors? We must have members living near dozens of unchurched families (C[21]).

What do you mean, too involved? Do you think church itself keeps us away from our neighbors? (C[33]).

Good point. How might a joy-side Christian show that kind of interest? (C[26]).

Serve others

How about areas besides church programming? What would we see that shows concern for other Christians? (C[36]).

Can you think of others who need our love and concern? (C[41]).

For instance? (C[45]).

Well, we've got a picture of some lonely Christians. What would a person who really cares do to help? (C[47]).

Under this friendly probing the class successfully described a variety of ways the principles could be worked out.

In the Philippians lesson the third element of the pattern (*closer examination of a sensitive area*) was not included. The teacher moved directly to encourage a decision to respond. But normally when a gentle exploration of varied applications uncovers an area in which most of the class is deeply concerned, it's good to go into it in depth.

The culmination of the process (the Took step in your lesson plan) is encouraging personal decision or in some other way helping students toward response.

In practice, decisions and responses will normally be made outside of class. During the week when situations arise, each individual will be faced anew with the opportunity to respond. But through the creative process in class you will have equipped your students with eyes opened to new meanings for God's truth, with new sensitivity to its relevance in their lives.

The process illustrated. Remember the John the Baptist lesson described at the beginning of this chapter? How might you teach it, using the guided self-application process? Let's see.

You've covered the content and begun generalizing. After some discussion, your teens suggest two qualities John had that they agree other Christians should share:

He pleased God, unconcerned about personal popularity.

He didn't place great importance on material things.

Now in various ways you lead your fellows and girls to see how these qualities would show up in life today. What pressures of popularity exist in the high school world? You think together of times when the desires of the crowd and of God pull different ways. And you get their ideas down on the chalkboard (see fig. 18). Moving on, you talk together of ways their friends put a premium on things. These too you record. This is varied application.

As your class suggests various applications, you notice that the idea of "outsiders" comes up several times. These are the kids who don't fit in, those who aren't in the "in" crowd. Often they are the kids without sharp clothes, a year behind the fashions; the ones without cars, without the looks or wealth that labels others "acceptable." So you now guide your class to think together about this group (*closer examination of sensitive area*). How would a person like John relate to these kids? What would his attitude be? His actions? What *does* count about a person, if not his money or clothes or appearance?

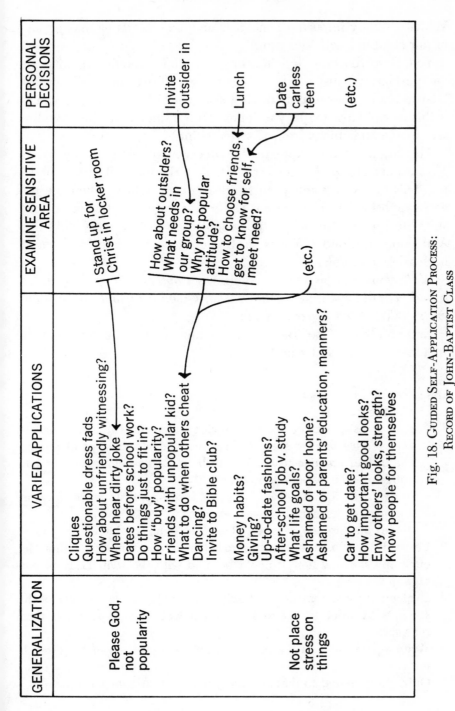

GENERALIZATION	VARIED APPLICATIONS	EXAMINE SENSITIVE AREA	PERSONAL DECISIONS
Please God, not popularity	Cliques Questionable dress fads How about unfriendly witnessing? When hear dirty joke Dates before school work? Do things just to fit in? How "buy" popularity? Friends with unpopular kid? What to do when others cheat Dancing? Invite to Bible club?	Stand up for Christ in locker room How about outsiders? What needs in our group? Why not popular attitude? How to choose friends, get to know for self, meet need?	Invite outsider in Lunch Date carless teen
Not place stress on things	Money habits? Giving? Up-to-date fashions? After-school job v. study What life goals? Ashamed of poor home? Ashamed of parents' education, manners? Car to get date? How important good looks? Envy others' looks, strength? Know people for themselves	(etc.)	(etc.)

FIG. 18. GUIDED SELF-APPLICATION PROCESS:
RECORD OF JOHN-BAPTIST CLASS

Which is really important: meeting another's needs or making sure of our standing with the gang?

You close the class by pointing out John's greatest quality, the one you haven't discussed. John put Jesus Christ first. And you ask, "If you really want to put Christ first in your life, how might you do it this week? How might you follow Him, rather than the crowd, or see people and things from His viewpoint?"

The results? Sally expresses her decision to try to bring a new girl into her group of special friends. Tom the football player, blushing, tells of his determination to speak up for Christ when the talk gets rough in the locker room. Little Gwen decides to ask an "outsider" to lunch with her in the school cafeteria the very next day. And popular, blond Jan says she'll even accept a date from one of her carless hopefuls!

Well, you think as you leave class, *serious or funny, they do respond. Tom in his quiet, serious way; Gwen, as usual, fluttery and enthusiastic; even superficial Jan.*

And you thank God. Because you realize that while you were the "teacher," it was God who taught.

Research and assignment
    for the student
1. Explain the significance of the following statements the author makes:
    The creative teacher seeks to lead his students to respond to God. The task of creative teaching is to help each student discover how truth studied may be used in *his* life.
    Students in a class using a guided self-application process are learning how to learn.
    While you were the "teacher," it was God who taught.
2. Be ready to illustrate each approach to application the author discusses by showing how it might be used with the John 11:17-44 passage.
3. Evaluate this statement: A teacher should visit the homes of his students in order to get to know them well enough to teach them relevantly.
4. Write a paragraph on the place of pupil *participation* in Bible teaching.
5. Quiz. Be prepared to diagram the guided self-application process.

6. Refine your lesson plan for the Look and Took of the John 11:17-44 lesson. Include questions (like those on p. 123) you might use to guide the process.

Exploration
    for the lay teacher
1. Recall the last lesson you taught, and try to diagram the application process (see fig. 18).
2. Restudy any areas in which completed exploration project number 1 showed weaknesses.
3. Plan next week's lesson on a Hook-Book-Look-Took chart, paying careful attention to the application process.
4. Read through the student research-and-assignment projects and jot down answers to numbers 1, 2 and 3.

11

MOTIVATING
THE LEARNER

Perhaps it looks too ideal, this picture of students eagerly and excitedly exploring the Bible together.

If you teach teens or adults, you may wonder how in the world to get them to speak, much less do the kind of thing described in the last chapter. If you teach children, you may wonder how to make them keep still! Or at least to keep on the subject. How could they be guided to explore Bible truths? They don't think deeply, and when they get started talking, there's no controlling them.

All these problems exist. No one ever suggested that creative Bible teaching is easy. But all can be solved. Even older adults, soberly stacked side by side on pews in the left front of the sanctuary in many churches, can be actively involved. And they can love it!

The solution lies partly in the area of teacher skills and training the class to take part in the creative process. But only partly. More basic is student motivation: that indispensable *desire* to take part, that *want* to learn.

Personal Factors in Motivation

It's an old evangelical cliché: "Visit your students, and spend time with them outside class. Then everything will go well in class." Like most clichés it's worn, and true—at least, true to some extent. But what it leaves out is more important than what it says. What's left out deals with the quality of the outside contacts, and with the fact that the *in class* teacher-student relationship is certainly as important as anything that takes place outside, if not more important! And that class group-life is involved in motivation too. That's a lot left out that ought to be in!

THE TEACHER-STUDENT RELATIONSHIP

Did you ever have a teacher who could say this? "My desire is to depart and be with Christ, which is far better. But to remain in the flesh is more necessary on your account. Convinced of this, I know that I shall remain and continue with you all, for your progress and joy in the faith." Or this? "I was gentle among you, like a nurse taking care of her children. So being affectionately desirous of you, we were ready to share with you not only the gospel of God, but also our own selves, because you had become very dear to us."

I don't mean, did you ever have a teacher actually say this. Paul said it, of course. It's written down in Philippians 1 and I Thessalonians 2. What I mean is, did you ever have a teacher who *could* say this and be believed?

Paul claimed to live for those he taught. And he did. When he rebuked them or counseled them or encouraged them, his students knew he spoke from love. His life with them breathed his love for them.

In living this kind of love, Paul was more like a lay Bible teacher than a pastor who, after all, is paid to love his flock. Paul worked "night and day so as not to be a burden to any" while he preached the gospel of God (I Thess. 2:9). Toiling over canvas in a tent shop, he earned his own living and gave his free time to his students.

Most lay Bible teachers have families, friends, neighbors. I'm not suggesting these be neglected. I'm simply pointing out that the depth of Paul's love for his students *could not be questioned*. In the context of unquestioned love, students can be motivated to learn.

Involvement in student lives. This is what love leads to. It can be expressed in different ways. When I served as director of Christian education, I saw it. In a preschool teacher who comes in Saturdays to prepare her room, who is always there Sunday to lovingly greet her earliest arriver. In the teacher of eight-year-old boys who ranks as such a favorite that fellows hope weeks before promotion time to be in his class. They know about the pancake breakfasts at his house some Sundays, and miniature golf expeditions. But it's not just these activities that make him popular. The boys know he cares, and they respond. I saw it too in the crusty teacher of teens, busy already with his teaching and on the church board, who cares enough to take on additional duty as a youth sponsor. And in the adult teacher whose concern leads him to meet with small groups for special study, and even to go weekly to meet with one man until a need is met.

There are many ways love can be expressed. But *real* love must be expressed. The prescription of a home visit or class activity is meaningless in itself. It may be done as a duty commanded by a restless conscience. As far as motivating learners is concerned, such empty activities are worthless. But involvement that flows from a selfless love is recognized. Such a teacher has won a hearing.

Attitude in class. Even a teacher who loves can destroy student motivation in class faster than he can create it outside class.

What do I mean? *Motivating students to learn is largely a function of teacher-student relationship in the class situation.* No matter how a teacher relates to his students out of class as a person, how he relates as a *teacher* is crucial.

Often people feel threatened when asked to teach. This shows up in little ways in the classroom situation: the extra demand that children pay attention, the irritation when a teen tries to express a different point of view, the sense of threat when someone asks a question that's hard to answer, the unwillingness to admit, "I don't know."

Each of these is an indicator that a person has taken on the job of teaching with a warped view of what a teacher is supposed to be. What is the warped view? That a teacher is an "authority."

It's dangerous to equate the words *teacher* and *authority.* An authority is by definition a person with power to settle issues, the right (even duty) to control, command and determine. And each of these activities is destructive of student motivation, a denial of the teacher's true role!

If the teacher is an authority, he must have the answers. He must give the answers. His students must look to him for answers, and, to be good students, accept his answers. This view subtly affects the relationship between the teacher and his students. He soon begins to treat his students as objects, not as people. He treats them as minds to be filled, as subjects to be ruled. As he tries to fill, to control, to rule, he ceases to teach.

People are not objects. They don't like to be treated as objects, and they will not want to learn if they are—especially when the teacher is no authority and has no authority. God is the authority, God speaking through the Word. The teacher is no mediator between God and man, no Protestant mini-Pope. The teacher is a *learner with* his students, one who comes to the Word of God as they do—eagerly, expectantly, humbly—looking to the Spirit of God to minister.

A teacher who sees himself this way has a different attitude toward his students. He doesn't have power to settle issues. God does. He's not in control or command of his class; he is to lead them in learning together. He shares with them in a great adventure, not determining the outcome, but structuring a situation in which God can determine as He chooses. In this situation he treats his students as people— people to whom and through whom God can speak as well as through him. He listens, he encourages questions. He's not afraid to admit, "I don't know," for he has no false status to maintain. He even expects God to speak to him through his students; he expects to learn from them in class!

A teacher who sees his role this way, and who sees his students as fully human, fully partners in the day's adventure in God's Word, treats them differently. There's a different attitude that shows up, in the things he says, in the way he says them, in the way he looks at a student who speaks. When the teacher by his attitude sets the tone of shared adventure in learning, his students will want to learn. His attitude in class is a key to motivating them.

THE LIFE OF THE GROUP

A teacher can set the tone for expectant learning. When the whole class shares his attitude, even deeper motivation develops. Students begin to see each other as persons, sharing a common life in Christ. Motivation that grows from such shared life spills over from Sundays into the weekday relationships and activities of each.

It's important to a class of older youth or adults to develop such a group-life. In the New Testament, this life is called fellowship. Fellowship *is* shared life, far more than the casual acquaintances that characterize relationships in so many churches and classes.

What in the learning situation leads to growth in fellowship? Basic is the attitude of the teacher, just described. He treats his students as fully human, fully partners. Also basic is the focus on *life*. When the study centers only on content, life is not shared; only information. Only when a class moves into the creative process of looking together at implications and responses is life introduced. Even then, growth into fellowship takes time. It may be six months, it may be a year. People hold back at first. They don't really talk about themselves, about their problems and their needs. There's a reason for this. It's dangerous to share your life with others. There are too many in our churches ready to gossip; too many ready to nod, clucking piously,"I knew there was *something* wrong with her."

It takes time to develop a climate for sharing of ourselves. Last time I saw it, it took about eight months. Then one day in a class exploring the biblical concept of "judging," a woman saw a fault of her own and almost involuntarily began, "Then I was wrong when I. . . ." As she talked, you could see it in the faces of the others. No one was sitting back, detached. All were fully involved, fully sympathetic, fully sharing the experience as participants in her failure and admitted need of grace. From this point the class became more and more open, more and more willing to share themselves honestly, to "bear one another's burdens, and thus fulfil the law of Christ" (Gal. 6:2). The class became a fellowship. And it took eight months to begin.

Group-life isn't only important as motivating. It's required for maximum spiritual growth. Paul points out in Ephesians that the body grows "by that which every joint supplies" (4:16). For growth, all must contribute. This isn't to say, of course, that contribution means talking up in class. It doesn't. It means sharing in the real lives of others, meeting in a variety of ways a wide range of needs. But *the context for contribution is developed through sharing, over a study of God's Word.* It's here, focusing together on the God of the

Word, that the Holy Spirit welds hearts and creates a unity that needs no organizational form, but must have a harmony of minds and hearts united in responsiveness to God's revealed will.

The personal factors, then, cannot be overlooked by the creative Bible teacher. Students must want to learn to learn. Such desire is most certainly kindled—or killed—by interpersonal relations.

Do your students know without question that you love them? Do you? All of us respond to a real (not selfish or forced) love. In class do you treat your students as people or objects? Are you an "authority"? Or are you a learner too, a learner who can lead others, but one who shares with them in a mutual quest for truth? Finally, if you teach teens or adults, is your class becoming a fellowship? If you teach as a colearner, and if you lead your students in a process that causes them to explore together their lives in light of the Word, this will come. God will bring it. Then, in the community of shared life and purpose, your students will truly want to learn.

STRUCTURAL FACTORS IN MOTIVATION

When Christian educators look at motivation, they usually see the personal factors. The Bible forces them to. In a Book that tells of a unique community, a unique oneness in Christ, of a life that develops through the shared contributions of all, you just can't overlook the personal dimensions. But often the structural factors *are* overlooked.

What are structural factors? Elements built into the structure of the lesson.

Educators have taken many different approaches to the study of learning. Some have tried to define learning, to discover how people learn. They haven't had much success. Others have looked at situations in which people seem to learn best, and tried to isolate conditions that facilitate learning. They've made more progress. Not that they've found buttons a teacher can push to turn on every student. But in situations where most people seem to learn, certain conditions do seem to exist. The Sunday school teacher and curriculum writer ought to be aware of these conditions, in order to build lessons that encourage the desire to learn.

We're going to look at four of these factors very briefly.

PEOPLE LEARN BEST WHEN THE LEARNING IS PATTERNED

What do we mean by *patterned*? Learning in which the student recognizes a goal and can see progress toward it. Remember the Hook? One of its functions was to set a goal that has meaning to the student. This is essential to patterning the class. It gives the learner a stake in the lesson, a reason to take part.

If you check through the Philippians lesson, you'll note that not only did the teacher state the purpose of the class; each activity from that point was clearly related to reaching that goal. When learning activities have no apparent relationship to the goal, students lose interest. So this, too, is part of patterning.

This doesn't rule out mystery or surprise. Sometimes parts of the lesson may have hidden purposes that show up after the learning activity is completed. But if a teacher regularly asks his class to take part in activities that have no apparent relationship to the class goals, students lose motivation.

This is one advantage of the structure suggested in chapter 9. When you build your lesson with a goal in mind, and in the initial minutes of class share that goal with the class in a way that makes the goal *theirs*, you're building motivation into its structure.

PEOPLE LEARN BEST WHEN THEY SEE RELEVANCE

This is a corollary of the first principle. Students need to see a relationship of what is being learned to their own lives and motives. When a goal is set that's important to the students, and when the class process involves a meaningful exploration of Bible truth in terms of life, students are motivated. This too is provided for in the chapter 9 lesson structure.

PEOPLE LEARN BEST WHEN THEY SENSE MASTERY

They learn best when they feel successful as learners, when they have evidence that they are mastering the material taught.

In a teacher-centered class, information passes one way—from teacher to learner. This doesn't give the students a chance to test their learning, to find out if they really understand the truths.

But when students have a chance to participate, they can express their ideas and in this way test their learning. They prove to themselves that they understand. In a Sunday school class this takes place in a climate of acceptance, where misunderstanding isn't held up to ridicule. Notice in chapter 7 how the teacher seldom *corrected* a learner? Instead he led each to clarify his thinking for himself. He led his learners to mastery.

In creative Bible teaching a sense of mastery in terms of *use* of biblical information is important. This comes in the sharing Look step of the lesson. The student's success in translating information into life, in seeing a new area of relevance, enhances his sense of mastery, and his motivation is increased.

PEOPLE LEARN BEST WHEN THEY SEE RESULTS IN THEIR LIVES

When a person responds to God he discovers that truths he has learned in class help him live successfully as a Christian. Such a person comes to class motivated, ready to learn. This too is encouraged by the lesson structure suggested in chapter 9. An effectively motivating class should encourage the student to respond.

Why not take a look at your class. Do students want to learn? Do your classes have a goal, one your students can see and one they feel is meaningful? Is there time for them to discuss the relationship of truth to life, to interact, and in talking to test their mastery of the truth studied? And do they see in culmination of the lesson just how they are to respond? Lessons structured to provide such opportunities do motivate. Your lessons can too.

Research and assignment
      for the student
1. Look through books written to aid lay teachers. What do they have to say on motivation? What do they omit?
2. Compare the personal and structural factors in motivation. Which do you feel are most important? Why?
3. Do you agree or disagree that "motivating students to learn is largely a function of teacher-student relationship in the class situation"?
4. How important is group-life? Look at Cecil G. Osborne, *The Art of Understanding Yourself* (Zondervan). What implications does this book suggest for Bible classes in the church?
5. Quiz: Explain what the author means by group-life and *why* it is important.

6. Study a junior lesson. What *structural* motivation is built in? How would you restructure the lesson to increase its motivation potential?
7. Visit and observe another class, looking especially for the use or failure to use personal and structural motivation. *Write out* a careful evaluation and a *thorough* description of how you could have improved the situation if you were teaching.

Exploration
    for the lay teacher
1. Evaluate your own teaching on the basis of personal motivating factors.
2. List specific things you can do to improve personal motivational factors in your class.
3. Rethink your lesson plan for your next class in terms of structural motivation. Can you see any ways to improve it?

CHOOSING AND USING CURRICULUM

I taught my first Sunday school class as a newly converted sailor, in a church where we "taught the Bible." Curriculum materials? We didn't use them.

I don't know whether my six primary boys suffered from the lack, but I surely did. It wasn't the easiest thing for a new Christian to select passages for eight-year-olds, to know how to plan a lesson that met their needs and captured their interest. Actually, it's never easy for a layman to teach without curriculum—and for a variety of reasons it's usually not *wise* either!

In this chapter we'll see why. We'll look at the values of using published lessons and at some of the things to look for when you try to find a good curriculum. (Not everything published that is conservative and evangelical is good, by any means!) Finally we'll suggest how a lay teacher can best use the resources a good curriculum provides.

CHOOSING CURRICULUM

IN THE VIEW of most conservatives, the Bible speaks for itself. We resent (rightly) the idea that some church authority must speak before we can know the true meaning of a passage, or before we can respond to God, who communicates Himself to us in His Word. In some churches, and to some individuals, this resentment carries over to Sunday school and other curricula. Writers and editors are viewed suspiciously as claimants of an authority not really theirs.

Certainly no writer or editor can stand as an authority. Even Paul, who actually had apostolic authority, commended the Berean believers for *not* taking his word for truth without checking. Each of us is personally responsible to search the Scriptures to see if the things taught are true. But users of curriculum materials normally aren't seeking an extrabiblical authority. They're users because they need help! They need the help of men trained in theology, just as a pastor needs the help of his commentaries and study resources. And laymen definitely need the help of those educationally expert.

It's help—not authority—that a good curriculum is designed to give.

VALUES OF A CURRICULUM

We see the values when we look at a few of the problems facing us in Christian education. Take, for example, the problem of progressive change. As children mature, they pass through stages marked by changing needs, interests and patterns of thinking and response. This is important, as the Hebrew text of Proverbs 22:6 points up. Children when old will not depart from the "way" they have been taught—*when taught the truths needed in the manner suitable at each stage of development.*

Most of us know that children pass through characteristic periods of change and development. But how many know the implications of these patterns well enough to be sure that a particular approach is geared to the way of thinking and feeling of their class? Few know the Word well enough to choose concepts and passages and stories that fit their students' changing pattern of needs. This is one advantage of using a curriculum. Curriculum writers can be (and usually are) experts on the characteristics of the age groups for which they write. Most laymen, possibly excepting public school teachers, need the expert help and guidance such people can give.

Another problem curricula help solve is sourced in the rapidly changing educational programming of the public schools. Each year new teaching techniques are developed. A lay Sunday school teacher isn't able to keep up. But an editor or writer can. Take, for instance, the primary department editor of one evangelical publisher. Go into her office, and you'll find master lists of vocabulary levels expected in various stages of first, second and third grades. You'll find current school texts, *My Weekly Reader*, etc. From these resources teaching methods are constantly checked, and new ways of learning introduced into Sunday school lessons. Such lessons are kept challenging and interesting, as new learning skills just mastered in the public schools are called for weekly.

Another closely related problem is found in the variety of resources now used in the public schools. A Christian publisher can match them and provide a variety of learning materials, including visuals, workbooks, take-home papers. When these are used, interest is increased, truths better grasped, and practical applications encouraged. No layman can produce the quantity and quality of supplementary teaching aids that publishing houses make available today.

Finally, there's the need for overall planning. Children develop in loose stages, usually of two or three years' duration. Most Sunday schools are graded to fit these stages, with nursery, beginner, primary, junior, etc., departments. When lessons are planned at a publishing house, the editor thinks in terms of the whole stage—the whole two or three years or more. The needs of the age group can be covered in a planned pattern of teaching that, left to themselves, few laymen would devise. For these and other reasons, good curriculum materials are an aid to creative Bible teaching. The creative teacher can draw on and adapt resources that few, if any, laymen can bring to their teaching without curriculum. The problem, then, isn't whether or not to use a curriculum; it's how to choose a good curriculum to use.

MARKS OF A GOOD CURRICULUM

It's a complicated task, evaluating curriculum. First the overall grading plan is studied. The theology of the materials is determined.

The pedagogy and relevance of the lessons at each age level are tested. Anyone interested in learning specifically how to test the Sunday school materials of various publishers and rank them can find out.* Our purpose at this point is simply to point out that, in the first and second sections of this book, a teacher or pastor can see crucial areas that *must* be right if a curriculum is to help laymen teach the Bible. What are they?

A correct view of Scripture and its function. Few conservatives choose curriculum materials that reflect the contemporary view of revelation (see chapters 2 and 3). Conservatives hold to a propositional concept of revelation: that God reveals true information in His Word. Materials which teach and reflect the view of the new orthodox simply are not acceptable, although some use them because of denominational pressures.

Many evangelical publishers, independent and denominational alike, provide materials that are based securely on the orthodox belief. But too few of these are as clear in their focus on the *function* of propositional revelation. They lose sight of the fact that revelation takes us beyond information to contact with God, and that it calls for appropriate response. Take the senior high lesson on John the Baptist we looked at earlier. It was designed to communicate information. It *did* communicate information, but the lesson was not structured to lead the student beyond the information, to confront God and His demands for a personal response. Because of this failure, the lesson is not acceptable theologically. The writer does not really understand the nature of the Word he teaches.

Another error, often found in children and youth materials, is to call for a conduct response, but *not the response demanded by the passage studied*. At times the lessons of most conservative publishers fall into this error. The writer wants the children to be kind and to share. So a passage, such as the feeding of the five thousand, is selected. The focus is on the little boy who shared his lunch. And from this passage, the commandment "You ought to share" is taught. But is this the meaning of the passage? Is "you ought to share" the teaching? Is sharing the appropriate response? Actually, little is said of the boy. He's not focal; Christ is. His act of sharing isn't held up

*For a guide to evaluating curriculum, including a carefully developed rating scale, see Lawrence O. Richards, *The Key to Sunday School Achievement*, chap. 4.

for others to imitate. Jesus Christ's power to meet every need is demonstrated for us to trust.

It's easy to set up our rules of conduct and then to find passages that seem to indicate some biblical support. But this isn't teaching the Bible. It's teaching a legalism that can become crushing. Such teaching obscures for teacher and learner alike the God who reveals Himself, and who demands not conformity to a code but response to a Person; a life lived not in cold conformity, but in spontaneous response to God the Spirit.

When a publisher's lessons characteristically fall into either pattern —information without response, or warped response—the lessons should be rejected.

A creative concept of Bible teaching. To discover these marks, just page through chapters 6 through 11. A good curriculum seeks to raise students' levels of Bible learning. Good curriculum follows (either in individual lessons or units of lessons) the pattern suggested in Colossians 1. Good curriculum reflects an awareness of the gaps that block response to God. Its lessons aim at response; they exhibit a structure which leads into the Word, explores the Word, and guides students to explore relevance and plan response. In a good curriculum, application is planned for flexibility, maximum student participation, and student self-discovery of the life implications of Bible truths. And good lessons reflect the writer's awareness of structural factors that help create the desire to learn.

What it really boils down to is this: good curriculum has a distinctive philosophy of Bible teaching, and this philosophy is carefully applied in developing each lesson series.

In point of fact, few publishers spell out their position on the theological and educational issues raised in this book. Even if they did, users would still have to check their practice against their claimed philosophy! And so the responsibility returns to the users, who expect and pay publishers for Bible teaching *help*. It's up to the men and women in our local churches to select lessons that are theologically and educationally sound.

USING CURRICULUM EFFECTIVELY

Published curricula are an aid, but not the answer. All lesson materials are limited in value. When used as a crutch even the best can stifle the freedom and spontaneity, so essential to creative Bible teaching, which the writer hopes to encourage.

A teacher then needs a healthy attitude toward his lesson materials. He'll look to them with appreciation for guidance in the choice of truths relevant to the age group he teaches. He'll expect ideas on the meaning of the passages taught, and a teaching plan that will lead to student response. He'll be glad for new methods and approaches lessons may suggest, and for visuals and other teaching materials. But he will not view his materials as setting a pattern he *must* follow in class.

A slavish reliance on printed plans, while helpful perhaps for an inexperienced teacher, cuts deeply into the potential for creativity. It's not hard to see why. Creative teaching is a process in which students are vitally involved. Often in this process, ideas are developed and needs revealed which no writer can plan for, nor teacher predict. The teacher has to feel free in such cases to respond to the lead of his class and spontaneously follow the guidance of the Holy Spirit. This may mean shortening some learning activities, adding unplanned ones, eliminating some that were planned. This kind of freedom just isn't possible to the teacher who relies slavishly on printed materials.

What then does the teacher need as he enters class? Not a detailed series of steps which he plans to take. He needs instead an overview of the process he hopes to stimulate. He needs a flexible view of the end toward which that process must move. And he needs a view so clear that he can feel free to adapt or change his plans in response to classroom developments, so clear that even with changes he still can lead his students to the climax of learning—response to the God who has spoken to them in His Word.

This need for spontaneity helps us see more clearly what a layman needs to become a creative Bible teacher. He needs first of all an understanding of the nature of the Bible he teaches, developed in chapters 1 through 5. Next he needs a clear understanding of how that Bible must be taught, a philosophy of teaching sketched in chapters 6 through 11. Finally he needs to develop skill in planning and using learning activities (methods) that will enable him to implement his philosophy!

It's to this last requirement that we now turn. The final section of this book, Guidelines to Creative Teaching, is designed to illustrate learning activities suitable to various age groups and purposes, and to help the teacher develop confidence in his ability to use them, to teach spontaneously and creatively.

Research and assignment
     for the student
1. Construct, to hand in, a curriculum evaluation guide.
2. List other values of using a curriculum in addition to those suggested by the author.
3. Evaluate three or more curricula using the evaluation guide provided in *The Key to Sunday School Achievement.*
4. Reconstruct the lesson plan of a lesson selected by your professor. Use a different learning activity (method) for each step in the lesson, but keep the *process* the same as that suggested in the original lesson plan.
5. Write to various publishers for a statement of their philosophy. Evaluate these carefully for position on each of the issues raised in this text.
6. Write two pages on the topic "The Nature and Need for Spontaneity in Bible Teaching."

Experimentation
     for the lay teacher
1. Check to see when your present Sunday school curriculum was last evaluated.
2. Evaluate your own lesson materials on the criteria suggested in this chapter.
3. Plan next Sunday's lesson as usual. Then review your plan. Can you use it spontaneously? Visualize the process apart from the specific methods you've selected. Try replacing each method with others.

PART III

GUIDELINES TO CREATIVE TEACHING

THE BIBLE
AND PRESCHOOLERS

When it comes to teaching preschoolers, we have problems. How do we teach *them* the Bible?

They certainly can't take part in guided self-application! And a Hook, Book, Look, Took hour structure won't work with tots whose attention wanders so easily.

There's an even greater problem. We've emphasized the idea that the Bible teacher teaches for response. Response to God is the big must when it comes to spiritual growth. But how about twos and threes and fours and fives? Spiritual *growth* presupposes spiritual birth!

And most of the children in the nursery and beginner departments aren't born again.

So our biggest task is to answer this question: What is the purpose of teaching preschoolers? It's not primarily to convert. It's not to produce spiritual growth in those who have no spiritual life. It's certainly not to help tots who aren't Christians act like Christians.

What then *is* our Bible teaching goal? When we know our goal, then perhaps we can see *how* to teach.

147

PAST AND PRESENT

ONLY DURING THE PAST twenty years has there been much concern in churches about preschoolers. Not until after psychologists and secular educators became convinced that the chances for healthy mental development are largely determined during the first six years of a child's life were Sunday school programs for preschoolers developed.

At first these Sunday school programs were patterned on secular nursery school ideas. Often Sunday school materials were written by women with experience in the secular schools. They naturally tended to think of teaching preschoolers in the familiar secular pattern. They built their programs, including goals and content, on the secular framework. Often there was hardly any difference between the church preschool class and the nursery school down the street! Preschoolers came to church, but they weren't really getting a Christian education.

WHY DID THEY GO?

The first Sunday school curriculum writers had no idea of "teaching the Bible." They never thought of teaching preschoolers in terms of content. Instead they carried over the goals that were common to secular nursery education. What were they trying to do?

> Nursery school educators have always felt a close kinship to psychiatry and psychology. Although such terms as "school" and "teacher" are borrowed from education and have an academic flavor, yet *the emphasis is on psychological concepts rather than teaching methods. The basic aim of most nursery schools for many years has been to help the child adjust* to the world away from home, to other children, new adults, and new surroundings. . . . It is generally accepted that *the teacher's duty is to help the child with his feelings* of jealousy, fear, anxiety, and aggression, to help him use his energies constructively, and *to feel secure* both in the family and with his peers.[1]

While helping young children find growing satisfaction in interpersonal relationships, helping the children adjust to and enjoy their surroundings, and helping them develop the full creative potentialities of their individual personalities is a worthwhile goal, it hardly can be the *distinctive* purpose of Christian training in the church.

Unfortunately, the basic assumption of the secular preschool movement—that good emotional adjustment is the sole function of nursery school—has led to strong criticism of *any* program that has "any connotation of stereotyped teacher-directed and dominated experiences." That is, you can't take objective truth as a starting point and force it on preschoolers. You have to deny "superimposed" experiences, and start with the immediate interest of the children as they develop.

Put this in Sunday school, and you have the idea that teaching a Bible story, leading tots to play out that story or review it with prepared handwork, is automatically ruled out. You teach to aid social and emotional development, not to communicate God's truth.

HOW ABOUT THEOLOGY?

At first church preschool programs were developed without too much thought about theology. It was more or less taken for granted that children didn't need to learn about God just yet, but they did need to develop emotionally. Mary Lloyd, for instance, in *Religious Nurture in Nursery Class and Home* suggests that even the words *God* and *Jesus* are "only words with practically no meaning for the 3." Thus "verbal interpretation is better left until children are a few years older."

Church preschool educators thought of the difference between secular preschool training and church training as residing in the *motivation of the teachers*, not in differences of program goal or method.

> We love him [the child] so that he will learn to love. We present ourselves to him as trustworthy and dependable so that he will learn to trust and grow in faith. We accept his angry feelings, understand his fears, forgive him his errors so that he can learn to handle his anger and his guilt. We deal with him in this way because God has so dealt with us. This is the way Christian people live together and treat one another. This is the life we want our children to live, because this is the gospel, the good news. The secular school has no such motivation.[2]

Perhaps you noticed in the preceding quote the idea, emphasized in neoorthodoxy, that Bible *truths* are communicated nonverbally. The same author goes on to say, "We are teaching them [Nursery children] the truths of the Bible by living these truths with them. They are learning love and kindness and forgiveness by experiencing them with a Christian teacher in a Christian church. This kind of relationship between the teacher and the child is at the core of the biblical faith."[3]

What the theory boils down to, then, is the idea that through guided "Christian" experiences, preschool children will develop Christian personalities and be "learning to live the Christian life as a three-year-old may live it."

IT JUST DOESN'T FIT

It doesn't fit the biblical pattern that we've seen in chapters 4 and 5. Not that exemplifying truths when we teach isn't important. It is— more important than most of us think. But Christian truth is communicated in *words*. Truths may be demonstrated and exemplified in life and by deed, but they must be understood conceptually. Ideas that can be communicated and understood stand at the heart of "the biblical faith"—not any relationship between teacher and child, no matter how fine.

And remember, too, that God reveals Himself *at the point of revelation*. It's in truth about God that we contact God. So, somehow, whatever approach we take to preschool Christian education, it cannot neglect the Word and words of God, made understandable to tots on the threshold of understanding.

Another thing this pattern of thinking doesn't fit is the biblical picture of a Christian. There is no scriptural justification for the idea that "Christian personalities" can be developed naturally through training in Christian moral principles. A Christian personality is produced *supernaturally*. Christian personality comes into being when a person exercises personal faith in Jesus Christ as Saviour, and a new, supernatural life is imparted by God. This supernatural life, lived out by the indwelling Spirit, is the only kind of life the Bible allows us to call "Christian."

So we can't take the position of suggesting that church preschool training is for the production of "Christian personalities," or even for helping tots live "the Christian life."

Actually, no conservative curriculum for preschoolers takes the extreme position of trying to teach Bible truths without any Bible. But nearly all do tend to be influenced by the "shaping Christian personality" school of thought—largely because no clear-cut alternative idea of the function of preschool teaching has been presented.

But we need such an alternative. We need to have clearly in mind our specific purpose in teaching the Bible to preschoolers. And that theory must fit both the Bible and its nature, and the child and his stage of development.

An Evangelical Alternative

A CLUE

Today secular preschool educators are rethinking their old ideas and are challenging the theory that preschoolers can develop emotionally, but must not be challenged to "learn." Their writings and their demand for a "bit of real, explicit teaching" help us understand the place of the Bible in our nursery and beginner Sunday school classrooms.

The most significant research has been performed by Dr. Kenneth D. Wann, professor of education, Teacher's College, Columbia University, New York. In a five-year study of concept development in preschool boys and girls, Dr. Wann and his associates observed that "the children employed all the processes involved in thinking and reasoning. . . . We were deeply impressed with the struggles of young children to *understand, to interpret, and to put together into a comprehensible pattern the pieces of the complex puzzle that is their world*" (italics added).

Dr. Wann's study and the changing climate of thought about preschool education (as illustrated in books such as Muriel Ward's *Young Minds Need Something to Grow On*) have made many more open to the idea that preschoolers should be taught, and can be taught, content. One sociologist, Omar K. Moore, reporting in *Today's Child* (February 1963), has even concluded that "the period from 2-4 years of age is a critical one for the development of a child's intellectual abilities. Then there is a period of maximum openness of the child's mind to learning complex subject matter."

Simply stated, the research indicates that *during the preschool years, children are involved in a process of building a world view—a way of looking at life.*

For instance, Dr. Wann's study tells of a four-year-old who watched thoughtfully as a giant machine scooped out the foundation for a New York skyscraper. After observing for a while, he turned to his teacher and asked, "What kind of machine made the world?"

This is what I mean by developing a world view. Preschoolers are using the information they have and, with that information, getting a picture of the way things are—an idea of what reality is. And this way of looking at things, formed so early in life, may persist through childhood and adolescence and into adulthood!

A ROLE

Until this crucial role played by the preschool years in concept development was recognized, we had no clear-cut alternative to the social-psychological theory of preschool education. If children really couldn't "learn" verbalized Bible truths, what was the use of teaching them?

But now we know that children can learn concepts. We know that children in their preschool years, in the words of Dr. Wann, "repeatedly sought more and more information about a given topic . . . and consciously tried to relate" it, while struggling to "organize and test one bit of information against another."

Relate this need of the growing preschooler for information about his world to the nature of Scripture as revealed truth about the nature of reality, and we come up with a distinctive purpose for Christian education of preschoolers. Simply stated, it's this: *The primary task of the nursery and beginner Sunday school teachers is to provide the basic concepts and information needed by their children to formulate a biblical view of the world.*

All this talk of a world view sounds obscure and difficult. But pull it down on the level of *what* is taught, and you can see what I mean. Children need to know who God is. It's vitally important that they look on the world as the creation of a loving God, that they develop the assurance that Jesus, God's Son, is a powerful Friend who loves them and cares for them. They need to know that God speaks to them in the Bible, His book; that He tells them there of His love, and how they can show love for Him. Children who grow in this knowledge, who have a place for God in their thoughts and a picture of the way things really are, will be ready to respond to the gospel message of God's love expressed in Christ's sacrifice when they've reached an age of understanding. Children who grow up without a biblical concept of God are those least likely to respond to the gospel message, for it will be completely foreign to their way of thinking about life and the world.

WHAT DOES IT MEAN IN PRACTICE?

The Bible must be taught. Nursery and beginner children need and must be taught biblical information. The information that's particularly relevant isn't moral in character—not telling them what God wants believers to do. The relevant truths are those that tell who God is—truths that give tots a biblical picture of the world, of themselves, of Christ. These ideas must be the core of the curriculum.

Response must be encouraged. Preschoolers can respond to Bible truths. A child who knows that "Jesus always sees me" can remember it and react when he's tempted to do something wrong out of mommy's sight, or when he's alone and afraid in the dark of his bedroom.

In asking for response, we're not expecting preschoolers without spiritual life to grow spiritually. We may encourage tots to share or to pray in response to a particular truth. But by this we're not suggesting that either activity pleases God. Before a child or adult can please God, he must be made acceptable to Him in Christ.

Why then the emphasis on response? *We're trying to establish early in life a pattern of response to truth.* We're trying to help children develop awareness that response is the normal and necessary companion of learning Bible truths. "I learn God's Word" and "I respond to God" *are* inseparable; and we dare not separate them, even when our teaching goal is primarily informational.

The Bible must be taught effectively. Biblical information must be taught on tot level. And it must be taught in ways that preschoolers can most easily grasp and learn it. We won't talk about omnipresence or omniscience to threes, but we can teach "Jesus always sees us."

Such Bible truths can be taught in a variety of ways. We can use a variety of methods that are fun for preschoolers. There's place in the nursery class, for instance, for interest-center play, for visualized stories, for fun-to-sing motion songs, for take-home items, finger plays, etc. But each such activity should be carefully planned to communicate one major and relevant Bible truth each Sunday. The major goal will still be to communicate Bible truth, Bible information.

With this goal clarified, then, our problem is to organize a learning situation in which preschoolers will most easily and meaningfully learn Bible truths. As noted earlier, the Hook, Book, Look, Took class structure just doesn't fit preschoolers' characteristics, needs, abilities and ways of learning. These patterns vary even between twos and threes and between fours and fives. And so we need to take a closer look at a program for each of these groups (nursery, 2-3; beginner, 4-5). We need to structure a program in which Bible truths can be effectively communicated.

Research and assignment
> for the student

1. Examine nursery curricula. Separate those which have a primary social adjustment purpose from those which seem to have a Bible teaching purpose.
2. Examine the social adjustment curricula. What reasons do they advance for their training? What view of verbalized teaching is stated? What theological justification is stated for their position?
3. Be prepared to criticize the social adjustment school in each of the above mentioned areas.
4. Look over the curriculum of lessons as well as the content of those which seem to teach the Bible. What stories and truths do they emphasize? List those lessons which effectively communicate truths you feel are important for developing a Christian world view.
5. Criticize (evaluate) in writing *one* of the above Bible-oriented curricula.
6. Plan a one-quarter curriculum for nursery-age children, stating the aim for each lesson, the Bible portion you would use, and the truth you seek to communicate.
7. Do the same as suggested in the first six assignments for beginner/ Kindergarten-age curricula.

Exploration
    for the lay teacher
1. If you teach preschoolers, evaluate your present materials by the criteria suggested in the chapter.
    —What is the apparent goal of the curriculum?
    —What Bible truths are being taught? What basic truths or moralisms?
2. Write out your personal goals in teaching your preschoolers.
3. Do you think that having a distinctive Bible teaching purpose in teaching necessarily reduces the love relationship so important between adults who work with preschoolers and their charges? If so, how?

14

TEACHING IN THE
NURSERY DEPARTMENT

Visit a Sunday school nursery department, and what you'll see probably won't look like teaching. Tots will be on the move, playing with blocks or dolls, or looking at colorful books. The room will be large and spacious—no cubicles for classes. And who can teach without classes!

But stay and listen awhile. Watch the pattern of the activities. Watch the teachers near each center of activity. Listen to the simple conversations they hold with boys and girls as they play.

Stay on through the hour and you'll observe a simple Bible story, told clearly and with a variety of visuals. Then more activities—motion songs, finger plays, playing of the story, working at simple paper projects—all of which reinforce the total learning impact.

A nursery department may not look like Sunday school; it may not seem that teaching takes place. Yet in a good department, tots *are* taught. What are keys to effective teaching of twos and threes? Let's see.

The Way Twos and Threes Learn

This is our starting point. Effective teaching teaches *pupils*. It's not simply "talking truths." Truth has to be communicated in such a way that pupils can learn.*

This is important to remember when we think about teaching twos and threes. Tots this age simply do not learn meaningfully (back to our learning levels!) when taught as older children are. Learning, for them, starts with activity, not with words.

It's true that TV has upped the vocabulary of young preschoolers. Recent research shows, for instance, that a child from a home with television starts school with a one-year vocabulary head start over a child from a home without it. But even so, the vocabulary of twos and young threes is severely limited. And what words do they know? Words that describe the important and familiar in their world. Words like *home, friend, mother, love, bad, food, play, sick, good, pretty*—a host of others that are related primarily to their experiences.

Of course new words constantly come. But when they come they're usually related to a tot's direct experiences. Meaning grows out of doing, feeling, seeing, testing, hearing. Words and ideas have meaning for preschoolers because they're real in the world of experience.

This is one reason why activity is important in a nursery department. Ideas take on meaning for preschoolers as they're associated with experiences. Thus the best way to communicate biblical ideas is to teach them in a context of activity and experience.

There's another reason why activity is important. Tots are naturally wiggly. It's not that they *can't* sit still, but they do have a built-in need to move. Twos and threes also come equipped with a wandering attention. When adults talk at them, things on the other side of the room just naturally draw small bodies off to a personal investigation. "Sitting still" is something preschoolers will learn—when they're old enough for public school! Even then it won't be easy for them. But in first grade they will finally be trained to sit still and be quiet,

*Some of the material in this chapter and the next is revised from the pamphlet *The Scripture Press Key to the Nursery Department*, prepared by the author for Scripture Press Publications, Wheaton, Illinois, and is used by their permission.

and they'll be taught new verbal ways of learning that do not demand direct experience. But until then, young preschoolers need activity and freedom to move.

Social characteristics, too, play a big part in guiding development of a teaching program for preschoolers. Young twos and threes normally aren't ready for *group* activities.

Turn a dozen threes loose in a well equipped nursery department and something interesting happens. They scatter. They'll move away from each other. Even when several go to the same area of the room, these won't be "together." They'll play beside each other, but they won't be playing *with* each other. Two will build with blocks—but each will build his own tower. Three may look at books, but each will look at his own book. Others may work simple wooden puzzles, but again each will work his own. Cooperative play—playing *with* others —comes later.

The fact is that at this stage of development, it's uncomfortable for children to be in larger groups. They like the presence of a friend or two, but eight or ten or more children—too close—are unsettling for tots whose days are spent in the relative solitude of home.

All this combines to highlight the fact that nursery tots are special, and must be taught in special ways. They're individualists who don't fit in groups, and who need to be taught and loved individually. They're wiggly and they need freedom to move. They're short on words and need to learn ideas in association with activities that will give the ideas meaning.

To communicate Bible truths meaningfully to children who are like this demands a uniquely structured teaching program.

A PLAN FOR TEACHING

A Sunday school nursery department is a teaching department. It's structured to communicate Bible truths. But in this department, teaching wears an unusual face. The hour is filled with activities, carried on with many shifts between active and quiet times. Yet the whole is carefully patterned. Overall the hour breaks down into three basic periods in which three *different approaches* to teaching should be followed.

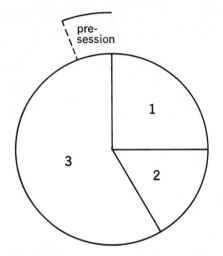

Fig. 19. SEGMENTS OF NURSERY HOUR

The first of these begins with presession and continues approximately fifteen to twenty minutes into the Sunday school hour itself. During this time, the children are free to take part in a variety of activities provided at centers in different parts of the room. In the second period, the Bible story is told. *Only during this short time* are tots together in a group. In the third teaching period, the boys and girls are again engaged in activities (singing, handwork, etc.). While they are all working on the same things at approximately the same time, they do them in different areas of the room (*not in a group*), with teachers guiding and helping the tots who gather in small clusters around them.

1: PRESESSION AND INTEREST-CENTER TIME

We previously noted that nursery-age children don't group together well. Instead they scatter and break up into smaller clusters. Larger groups distress twos and threes, and tots with little experience in groups are easily overstimulated when thrown into close contact with many others. This characteristic is one of the principle reasons for arranging the room as shown in figure 20. Notice that in each corner area an activity center is provided. These (called interest-centers) provide play materials that will capture and hold tot interest.

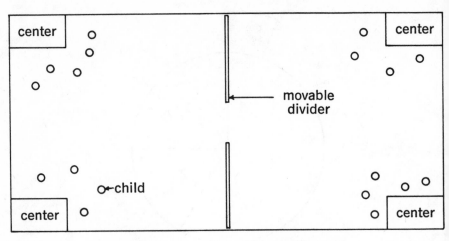

Fig. 20. NURSERY ROOM DURING PERIOD 1

But the nursery department is a *teaching* department, not just a play department. And so the materials which are provided are carefully selected to relate to the day's teaching aim and to provide experiences through which the day's Bible truth can be invested with meaning.

Four principles are important in making this "play time" a time of teaching:

1. *Have available only play materials which relate to the Bible teaching aim.* Aims for the nursery department are always simple and, as suggested in chapter 13, should relate to communication of a basic biblical concept. "Jesus always sees me" is one example of a theme on which to build an hour's teaching activities. Others about Jesus are appropriate. Develop the idea that He is God's Son, the children's Friend, who loves and cares for them. "Jesus gives us our food" might be one such idea, reflecting the truth that we can trace all blessings back to Him as Creator and Sustainer. For such a theme, blocks might become building units for farms, a housekeeping center a place to play at preparing and serving meals, magazine pictures of food a favorite meal to paste on paper plates. Each activity thus is related to the theme and provides an experience context in which the idea can be communicated meaningfully.

2. *Station a teacher or worker at each interest-center.* The play materials and the children's activities with them must be related to the day's theme. Tots won't fall into activity patterns that reinforce

the teaching by themselves. Yet twos and threes are highly suggest-
ible. They can easily be guided into play patterns that do fit.

For instance, listen in to the teacher at the housekeeping center:

> My, John, that looks like good food you're cooking. Are you
> going to put some on my plate? Thank you. It's good to say thank
> you, isn't it. Whom do we pray to and thank for our food when we
> sit down at the table? Yes, Jesus. Isn't Jesus good to give us our
> food. Let's thank Him now, shall we?

Occasionally a tot may object that *mommy* gives him *his* food.
Normally a simple explanation that Jesus makes the food grow, or
gives daddy strength to earn money to buy food, satisfies and helps
him see the relationship of Christ to the process.

Secular nursery school writers criticize this approach strongly as
"imposing" from outside "stereotyped ideas." They insist that the
child must be left free to develop his own pattern of play. This is
true—if you have the same goals in the Sunday school nursery department as the secular nursery school educator. But our goals are
very different. We're not trying primarily to encourage self-develop-
ment. We're trying to develop a biblically oriented picture of reality
and to help children develop patterns of response to truth.

3. *Allow the children freedom to move from one center to another.* Children do have wandering interests and wiggly bodies. So
during this period, freedom of movement is important. A child
should be allowed to go from center to center as he wishes.

The teaching focus of the hour isn't disturbed by this freedom of
movement, because no matter what center a child moves to, the
same simple truth is repeated.

If John tires of cooking and goes to play with the blocks, the
teacher there may say,

> Hello, John. I'm glad you've come. Tommy and Ann are playing
> farm. They're growing good food on their farm. Jesus sends the
> rain and the sunshine to make the food grow. Isn't Jesus good to
> give us food this way? Would you like to make a farm too? What
> will you ask Jesus to help you grow?

Thus through a variety of activities one simple idea is presented
and given meaning in terms of the child's own world and experience.

And the child develops further his picture of Jesus, who can do wonderful things, and who loves us.

4. *Separate the interest-centers visually.* While children are given freedom to move, rapid and repeated shifts from center to center aren't encouraged. Yet nursery tots are often distracted from activities by the sight of what others are doing. A movable room divider (made from plywood or purchased) can cut out distracting sights. Such dividers also give sensitive youngsters a sense of confidence by making them relatively unaware of the number of other children in the room. A divided room reduces contact of child with child and helps the whole program remain quieter and more stable.

Finally, note that this structure for the first period of the hour provides an individualized teaching situation. Teachers and workers are able to talk personally with each child as he joins the small cluster at their centers. And the constant repetition of the lesson's one main Bible truth sinks in.

2: BIBLE STORY TIME

In terms of communicating the day's Bible truth, the Bible story time is probably the least effective part of the hour.

Activities are a better media of communication than stories. The children will sit in a group for the Bible story—an unnatural situation for twos and threes. It will be hard to hold them together—to say nothing of holding interest and attention. Particularly difficult is the fact that the storyteller will be talking to the group, not to each child as an individual.

All of these factors limit the teaching value of the Bible story time. Why then have it? Primarily because each truth taught in the department should be associated with the Bible, God's Book. A Bible should be shown and opened by the teacher as if being read.

Actually, Bible stories can be made interesting and fun for tots. Visuals are important. Sand tables, flannelboard figures, murals, surprise aprons (with big pockets out of which can pop unexpected figures) all help arouse interest. If the story isn't too long, if the story is visualized, if the story is well told, a happy excitement about Bible time can grow. And developing an awareness of God's Book as interesting as well as a source of truth is an important goal of the nursery staff.

3: RELATED LEARNING ACTIVITIES

After the Bible story the group of children will break up. Tots can be free to circulate and join one of the small clusters that gather around each teacher.

A number of learning activities take place during the rest of the hour. One teacher may lead her cluster in a finger play that reviews the Bible story or restates the lesson truth. In another part of the room a teacher may lead a fun-to-do motion song with words that, again, are related to the day's lesson. Often activity in each cluster will parallel that in the others. All will be working on the handwork project at the same time, for instance. But still each teacher will work with only four or five tots, giving each individual attention and conversation.

Some of the learning activities commonly used in nursery programs are:

Songs. The teaching aim is central in all activities. It's central in songs too. Most courses for nursery-age children produced by evangelical publishers highlight songs that are especially written to impress Bible truths. Of course, some fun-to-do exercise songs are included for their own sake. But choruses that use symbolic words and phrases beyond the ability of young preschoolers to grasp are definitely ruled out.

A piano isn't needed for singing in the nursery department. Children this age find it much easier to match tones with a human voice than a musical instrument. But new songs must be hummed and sung often (as during the interest-center time) if tots are to learn their simple words and tunes.

Songs are especially good teaching tools, since a preschooler, after learning them, is likely to sing them over and over again at home, further impressing the biblical truth the words convey.

Handwork. Secular nursery school people insist that any handwork activity be entirely pupil-made. Preprinted, push-out or cut-out-and-color projects are ruled out. Again, this bias is based on their goals, which stress the development of the pupil and his growth in self-confidence and expressional abilities, etc. In the Sunday school the handwork project is designed to teach.

Handwork projects teach in one of two primary ways: (1) Some permit the child to replay the Bible story. Fold the paper so, and the sick girl sits up well! Thus the project taken home provides a built-in review of the lesson and a graphic play object that illustrates how wonderfully Jesus made the sick girl well. (2) Some projects demonstrate appropriate response to the Bible truth. Move Jeanie's arm (attached with a brass fastener to the picture) away from the cookies, and tell how she put back the cooky when she remembered that Jesus always sees her. She wanted to please Jesus, and she was glad Jesus could see her put it back. Projects like this encourage response to truth and demonstrate ways a preschooler can respond.

Handwork projects like these may often be completed by the teacher before class. In this case, handwork time isn't spent in *making* the item, but in learning how to use it. The teacher tells the story, and shows each child how to move or play with his item. While often some little thing is reserved for the child to do to "make" his project, the class emphasis still should be on helping him see how to *use* it. Handwork projects too are a teaching tool.

Each curriculum provides other ideas for pupil activities. Some have pupils' workbooks. Others suggest ways to play out the story. Others simple trips outdoors to find items associated with the day's lesson. Whatever methods are used, the basic function remains the same: to repeat, in a variety of situations and through a variety of activities, basic Bible truths which will structure the preschool child's thinking within a biblical framework.

And this happens in a relaxed, flexible, truly "fun" hour at church, highlighted by play activities the children enjoy and through which their adult friends *teach*.

Research and assignment
    for the student
1. Develop a complete listing of the basic Bible truths you feel a three-year-old should be taught.
2. Plan completely a teaching hour which you believe will communicate one of the truths you specified in answer to question 1. Be sure to plan for each part of the hour:
    Set up at least four different interest-center activities.
    Choose a Bible story demonstrating the lesson truth and show how it might be taught and visualized.
    Write at least one simple action song and sketch out a handwork project, plus one or two other activities for the after-story time.

3. View *Sunbeam in Your Hand*, a filmstrip which demonstrates the teaching ministry of the nursery department. Available from Scripture Press Publications (nonpromotional).
4. Visit and analyze the ministry in a nursery department in a church near you. Write up your observations and hand them in.
5. The optimum size of a nursery department is approximately fifteen children. From the material in the first part of the chapter, can you suggest reasons why this is so?

Exploration
    for the lay teacher
1. Obtain and view *Sunbeam in Your Hand*, a filmstrip which shows teaching taking place in the nursery department. It is available from Scripture Press Publications, 1825 College Avenue, Wheaton, Illinois 60187.
2. Develop a checklist from the second part of the chapter and compare the program in your nursery department to the pattern the chapter suggests.
3. List ways your nursery department ministry can be improved.

15

TEACHING IN THE BEGINNER/ KINDERGARTEN DEPARTMENT

How different they are! This may well be the first impression of a person who's used to twos and threes when he visits a beginner department.* Yes, fours and fives *are* different.

But there are important similarities too. Older preschoolers are still *pre*schoolers. They haven't yet been to grade school, and so aren't trained to sit still or to learn in ways schoolchildren are taught to learn. They can't read. While vocabularies are larger, these children still learn best when words are made meaningful by experience. They still need to wiggle and to move. Like younger nursery-age children, beginners are still building their pictures of the world.

They still need basic truths that will help them build a biblical picture of themselves and the world in which they live.

What about differences? These show up particularly in social areas. Beginners are interested in each other. They play together. They listen to each other. They cooperate. And—very important—a beginner can feel involved when part of a group. They don't require that talking-just-to-me approach used to hold the attention of a younger child.

All these—the differences and similarities—are important. And both point up an important fact: a teaching program must be tailored just for beginners, too.

*For brevity this department will be referred to as beginner.

THE WAY FOURS AND FIVES LEARN

"CAN YOU GROWL LIKE A HUNGRY LION?"

GRRR-rrr. GRRR-RRR!"

"Oh. Look, lions! Someone is opening the door of our den. Let's growl loud, to let him know how hungry we are."

"GRRR-RRR!"

A host of bright-eyed five-year-old "lions" in Mrs. Haleen's beginner department enthusiastically respond. "GRRR-rrr!"

"Look, lions! They're throwing something down to us! It's a 'people'! It's Daniel. Hurry, let's eat him right up. Come on—Oh, dear. Just a minute. What happens now?"

"God shuts the lions' mouths." "God wouldn't let the lions eat Daniel." "God took care of Daniel."

"Yes, He did. Can you all growl like hungry lions—with your mouths shut?"

"GR-MMMmmm."

*   *   *

Tommy plays Daniel. Then Sue wants a turn. Eagerly the children cluster around. "I'm next!" And so the Bible story is played and replayed, as each child *lives* the great event and experiences God's protection. God took care of Daniel. God wouldn't let the lions hurt Daniel.

The beginners in Mrs. Haleen's department are learning, in the way they learn best. They're playing. They're experiencing the biblical event, experiencing the joy of deliverance and finding confidence in God.

Later in the hour pictures of preschoolers in familiar situations may lead the fives to think of God's care for *them* while at play or riding in the car or on walks with mother. The children will have a chance to talk, to suggest places where God takes care of them. Jack may tell about the time he was in a boat, others may think of home, of playing in the yard, of being at church. Perhaps they'll draw pictures representing one of the experiences they talked about. Through it all—the imaginative play, the picture studies, the talking of personal experiences—the great fact of God's care for *them* will be impressed.

For fours and fives, this is the way to meaningful Bible learning.

What's involved in programming for this pattern of learning? "Fitting" to characteristics is especially important.

First, children become involved. This means *physically* involved in a variety of activities, as well as verbally involved in sharing and talking. Playing the story, motion set to music, acting out applications —all these require movement, activity. Such involvement demands a large and open room—a room with space in which to move and play.

Second, these activities are *group* activities. Beginners aren't broken up into little classes and forced to sit at "their" table and learn only through words. These children learn best through activities. They need to move, to be "lions," to be "Daniel" and jump down off a low chair into an imaginary den. Activities like these are noisy. They take space. Try them in each little class, and you'll disturb others who aren't at the same point in the lesson.

But the activities through which beginners learn are the kind of activities the whole group can do! And fours and fives are *able* to work together in a group. They can listen together to a single story-teller or follow a single song leader. They've come a long way from twos and threes.

Because of this social development, and because an activity-teaching program is needed for maximum beginner learning, keep them together in a group, except during handwork times.

What we need, then, is a teaching program patterned for the whole department group (usually a maximum of 25 is desirable). The pattern should provide for activities, yet also allow for quiet times of worship and listening as well. It's within a program so patterned that Bible truths can be most meaningfully communicated to fours and fives.

A Plan for Teaching

Sunday school is fun for beginners. But, as in the nursery department, the fun is purposive. Through each activity the children are to *learn.*

As in programs of the other departments, one main Bible truth is to be communicated during each Sunday's session, and response encouraged. The program, then, isn't "loose" (in the sense that children may choose any of a variety of activities and do as they please); it's "tight" (in that all activities are carefully planned to help children learn the day's Bible truth). Every activity must fit the lesson aim and give added dimension to the truth taught.

Yet, even with the "tight" structure, the hour itself is relaxed and flexible, and fun for children and teachers alike.

How is the beginner hour best broken down? Into clusters of activity that focus on the Bible story, worship and expression. And, of course, those minutes during which the children arrive before the hour begins.

Let's look at each segment in turn.

PRESESSION

Sunday school—and teaching—begins when the first child walks in the door of the department. This is a delightful time, when he can talk to one of the teachers, get adjusted to the room and the group, and get involved in activities that help him begin to think along the line of the day's theme.

In good curricula, presession activities that fit the theme are suggested for each lesson. "Free play" is discouraged. Presession activities may include choosing pictures and helping make a bulletin

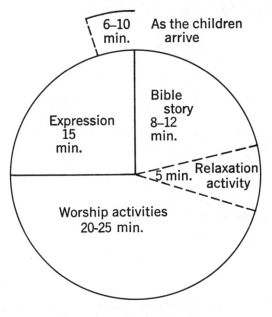

Fig. 21. THE BEGINNER HOUR

board, learning a new song, coloring or cutting out, a picture walk, acting out scenes, etc. But, again, these activities are related to the lesson aim. They may introduce new words and ideas the children need in order to understand the Bible story. They may simply help children recall experiences like those of people in the Bible story, or situations in which the Bible truth may be applied. In any case, the presession activities create a readiness for the lesson and the hour. And this is important.

Normally presession play doesn't extend deeply into the hour, as it does in the nursery. Yet presession activities may be extended occasionally, to involve all the children in the department.

Activities suggested may be carried on in small groups clustered around different teachers. At times the whole group will be together for presession fun. The procedure will depend on the kind of activity suggested for each hour.

THE BIBLE STORY

In most beginner programs the Bible story comes first. The rest of the hour is structured to lead to response of various sorts. The whole group is together for Bible story time. Thus there's no competition between noisy small classes. And, with the story told to all by one leader, the children all get to hear the department's best storyteller.

Picture studies and conversation are two activities normally clustered in the Bible story time. But relaxation activities are also needed. After ten or twelve minutes of sitting, beginners are ready to move. These activities should also be related to the lesson. A trip as thumping elephants going into Noah's ark, a chance to pretend to be the sick girl Jesus made well and to jump up at His imaginary touch, will meet the need of fours and fives for movement and change, and also contribute to the teaching impact of the hour.

For all of these—the listening, the conversation, the relaxation fun—the whole department group is together. And *one* teacher leads each learning experience.

WORSHIP ACTIVITIES

Following Bible story activities and the relaxation fun, beginners reassemble for activities that cluster around the idea of worship. In-

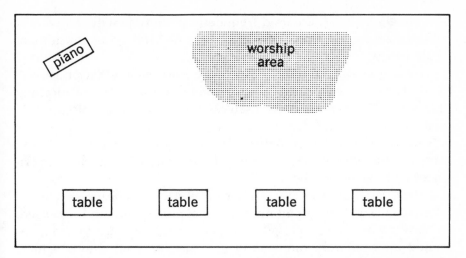

Fig. 22. A Good Beginner Room Has Space for Children to Move

Note that tables for handwork are at one end of the room. There is a large area for the fours and fives to act out the Bible story, to sing motion songs, to sit for worship activities.

Don't clutter up a beginner room with extra chairs. Let your fours and fives move the chairs if necessary. Remember, a good beginner room has space for children to move!

volved here are songs, prayer and conversation that help children relate the Bible truth to their lives and their experiences at home and play.

Songs. The message of beginner songs is of primary importance. Songs too should carry out the teaching aim and be of practical help to fours and fives. Words should contain concepts beginners can understand, speak of something they can experience, and be worth singing many times.

In good curricula, songs that meet these criteria are included. Songs should be used as suggested, and not replaced by choruses that the children sing noisily, yet without understanding.

Beginner songs should be explained as they're taught. This can be done by singing a song as a message before the children realize they're learning a new song, by using its words in conversation, by asking questions which the song answers and letting the children discover the answers, by illustrating the song with pictures as it's sung, etc.

As beginner songs are used frequently, each time within a context where meaning is emphasized, they become vital communicators of Bible truths.

Memory verses. Beginners can easily learn simple Scripture portions. Here, as with songs, the "learning" must focus on meaning rather than on the words themselves. Simply repeating Bible words isn't really learning God's Word.

During the worship activities, time will often be given to making words of the day's verse meaningful by relating them to class experiences or to weekday lives.

Conversation and prayer. Opportunities for simple prayers come spontaneously as songs and memory verses are taught and discussed, or as worship stories (provided in good curricula) are told. Prayer should be a natural expression of gratitude or need. Never a form through which children are forced to go. Prayer can be a natural and frequent experience in the beginner department as songs and conversation create a readiness.

EXPRESSIONAL ACTIVITIES

The general purpose of this cluster of activities is to guide beginners to actually *do* in Sunday school that which is stated as the response aim of the lesson.

Here fit such activities as playing the Bible story to make events more real, or playing out life situations in which a Bible truth is applied. Handwork should be designed to help beginners see how truth fits into their lives. It has a *teaching* purpose. While beginner handwork is more for use than to be made, fours and fives can do much to make their projects for themselves, and should be allowed to. Then the rest of the time can be spent showing the children how to use their project for play at church and later at home.

It's only (as a rule) during handwork time that the department group is broken down and seated around tables. During this time it's best to have one adult for every five or six children. As each worker assists her charges, her conversation can key their thinking to the meaning and use of the handwork.

The beginner program, then, with a variety of activities clustered around Bible story, worship and expression, fits the developmental characteristics of fours and fives and provides a framework for effective communication of Bible truths.

A CURRICULUM CORE FOR PRESCHOOLERS

In chapter 13 a distinctive purpose for Christian education of preschoolers was suggested. At this time, when research shows young children are developing their ways of looking at life, preschoolers must be given truths that are basic to a biblical understanding of life and their world.

This doesn't mean that teaching such Bible truths need be dull or academic. The pattern of teaching (described in chaps. 14-15) fits preschoolers, and instruction is carried on through activities that are fun and that will invest truths taught with meaning. Basic Bible truths must be taught in ways that preschoolers can understand and appreciate.

There's yet another dimension to teaching. The Bible truths taught in the nursery and beginner departments must be relevant to the lives and needs of preschoolers. Dr. Mary LeBar points out, "The only answer for the burdened individual—young or old—is found in relying on the wonderful Saviour who answers every need of the human heart. We are never too young, nor too old, for His ministration. At four and five, the need is not for heavy doctrine, but for the comfort of His presence, His love, His care."

Both these understandings guide in the selection of lesson topics for preschool curricula. No "heavy doctrine," yet basic truths must be taught. Stress must be on information, yet the needs of young children must be met, and Christ must be permitted to minister.*

What truths meet these criteria? Most conservative curricula have stressed these truths in the nursery department:

God: He knows and sees and can do all things.
       He takes care of us, hears us when we talk to Him.

*Curriculum writing is complicated even more by the need most conservative publishers feel to teach young children through Bible stories. There are few really suitable stories in Scripture. In practice the stories selected too often do not, in their context, actually demonstrate truths they are supposed to teach. It might be better if at times we could free ourselves from the compulsion to always teach with "stories."

He made all things, and gives us all things to enjoy: eyes to see, strong legs, parents, home, etc.

Jesus: He is God's Son, who loves us.

Jesus loves all children, and wants them to love Him.

Jesus can do all things, and will help us when we ask Him.

Jesus is alive, and watches over us all the time.

Bible: It is God's Word. He speaks to us in it.

It tells us about God and Jesus, and tells us how to please God.

In general, response activities suggested include praying (to thank God), giving (as an expression of love for God), helping, obeying and showing kindness to others.

In beginner departments the same truths are stressed, with additional ideas introduced. Among additional thoughts are:

World: God created it, and all good things in it.

Sin: Sin is disobeying God and displeasing Him.

God loves us even when we sin, though this makes Him unhappy.

Jesus can forgive our sin.

Jesus: He helps us to obey and to please God.

He died for our sin, and will forgive us.

He is alive today and is our best Friend.

The response patterns are approximately the same, although new information is also provided here. Giving is broadened to include missions, praying now involves intercession and petition as well as thanksgiving, etc.

The last word on preschool curricula surely isn't in yet. Nor on how much preschoolers can really understand and need to understand. It's not hard to teach Bible truths to young children. The real challenge is to understand the goal of preschool Christian education and to develop curricula that we're sure will help us reach it.

Research and assignment
    for the student
1. Visit and analyze the ministry in a beginner department in a church near you. Write up your observations and hand them in.

2. Develop a listing of truths you feel a five-year-old should be taught. How does this list go beyond the one that you developed for threes (R & A question 1, chap. 14)?
3. Interview a number of fours and fives who regularly attend an evangelical church Sunday school. Ask them to tell you what they know about God, Jesus, etc.
4. Select at least three Bible stories you feel could be taught to preschoolers and explain how you would use the stories and what truth you would teach through them.

Exploration
    for the lay teacher
1. Evaluate the ministry in your own beginner department on the basis of the elements described in this chapter.
2. Visit the beginner department in other churches in your area. Watch particularly for ideas you can use in strengthening your own ministry.
3. Carefully evaluate your present curriculum. Does it really teach Bible truths that children need and can apply? If not, obtain samples of other curriculum materials.

TEACHING CHILDREN

16

THE BIBLE
AND CHILDREN

"The Bible for children? Never!"

This idea appears over and over in Christian education magazines today. And with good reason. The Bible really is an adult book, written by adults and for adults. Major sections of the Bible, such as the prophets, most poetical books, and much of the closely reasoned teaching of the New Testament, *are* beyond a youngster's understanding. Who can imagine teaching seven-year-olds Zephaniah, verse by verse!

We Evangelicals, in a desperate search for something to teach to children, have often grasped at incidents in the Bible which aren't particularly relevant to childhood experiences. Or we've twisted a story to teach a "moral" which really wasn't there, such as teaching sharing from the feeding of the five thousand. Yes, a child *did* supply the loaves and fishes. But does the Bible really focus our attention on his unselfish act, as many curricula have it? Or is the biblical focus on the Lord Jesus Christ, who had compassion on the hungry crowd and the power to meet their need?

Even though much of the Bible is beyond children, God does have something to say in His Word to our six-year-olds, our sevens and eights, our nines and tens and elevens. And it's our task to communicate what He is actually saying *to them*.

WHAT DOES GOD HAVE TO SAY TO CHILDREN?

WHEN OUR SON PAUL was in the third grade he developed a very common and normal fear: a fear of the dark. Of course, he didn't come out and say, "I'm afraid of the dark." In fact, he denied the idea vigorously. But when bedtime came, it was amazing how many different excuses he could find for not going down the long dark hall to his room alone!

"Dad, will you get my pj's? I want to finish this picture." "Dad, I don't think my pj's are on my bed. Will you go look?" "Dad, come on down to my room with me. I want to show you something." The fear was there, unadmitted, denied, but there.

Then one evening I asked Paul into my study and suggested we write a book together. The book was to be one he could later read to his younger brother and sister to help them not to fear. I pointed out that as children grow, they often experience different kinds of fear. About three there's often a fear of loud noises. Sometimes there's a fear of other children—and fears in the Sunday school as mom or dad leaves. Our book was to help the little ones learn how to overcome their fears.

The first night we went through a concordance, looking for Bible portions where the words *fear* and *afraid* and *trust* occur. I read each part of a verse from the concordance and checked the ones Paul thought would be helpful for our book. The next night we looked up about half of those I'd checked. Paul found them in his Bible and read them off to me. I typed them on slips of paper. When this job was finished, we had about forty verses that spoke of fear and trust, and we were ready to start the book.

We bought a composition book and some construction paper and went to work. Paul first chose the verse for the title page: "Fear not, Abram," God had said, "for I am thy shield." Paul cut out a construction paper shield, and then a number of paper spears, which he showed striking the shield and breaking. The idea was his own, as was the insight: "This shows God protects us." That night he named the book and printed the title on the cover: *Paul's Not Being Afraid Book.*

We wrote several chapters. "What time I am afraid, I will trust" was one. We tried to think together of a Bible character who might have had reason to be afraid. Paul thought of Daniel, and drew several fearsome lions for illustrations. On the next page we listed times when children his age—the boys and girls he knew in school—might be afraid. His listing included fear of tornadoes, of kidnapping, and—of course—of the dark. Thinking in terms of others and understanding that fears were natural even for adults, Paul found it easier to face his own fears. And in the context of the Word it was easier for him to see that even when a believer is afraid, he is to trust in God.

We never did finish the book. But as we worked on it together over ten or so evenings, something happened in Paul. His terror of the dark gradually lessened. His calls on dad at bedtime, to go into the dark for him, diminished. And somehow his awareness that God went into the dark *with* him grew, until he was able to trust even in his fear.

CHILDREN HAVE NEEDS

It's not only adults who have needs that must be met by the Lord. Children do too. Trust in God, and personal experience with Him, do not suddenly come into style when a person reaches his teens. Childhood is a time for foundational experiences with God: finding Him able to help us in our fears, to comfort us in disappointment, to strengthen us for challenges we face. God does speak to children with the message of comfort or strength or encouragement that they need in their now, even as He speaks to us.

Children, then, need to meet God in the same way that adults need to meet Him. Children too need to hear His voice and learn the joy of responding.

Since God's point of communication with us all is the Word, it's clear that the Bible must be for children too. It's through the Bible that children come to know the person of God, to understand His love and steadfastness, to discern His character and care, and to know His will that they might be guided in their responses to Him in daily life. Through the Bible children too can become aware of the God who reveals Himself there.

As we noted in chapter 13, even preschoolers can apprehend basic truths about God, the world, Jesus and themselves. Children between six and eleven, initiated now into the school world with its wider variety of experiences and its new techniques for teaching concepts that are outside the direct experience of the children, can find much of what God says in the Bible meaningful.

One of the debates within evangelicalism relates to the meaningfulness of teaching salvation truths to younger children. Can children really understand the gospel and respond with trust in Christ? It's true that far too often we have concentrated on getting children to say "salvation words" rather than on guiding them to personal response to God based on an understanding of His work in Christ. For a seven-year-old to say, "I asked Jesus into my heart today" *may* be his expression of a real experience with the Lord. But it may just as well be his shy response of love to his teacher, who has urged her class to "do it!" Certainly, however, the facts of Christ's death and resurrection and their biblically defined meaning should be presented to children and response invited, if not urged.* God does speak to children. Our task is to communicate all that He has to say to them as meaningfully as we can.

CAN GOD SPEAK TO CHILDREN?

We have to say yes. The Bible is an "adult book," and many of its truths are beyond a child's comprehension. But much of the Word is not beyond them. And this we must teach.

There are several factors a children's Bible teacher must recognize when ministering to his or her class.

First, teaching should relate to a child's present needs and experiences. The goal in Bible teaching is not primarily to instill ideas which students will need to know "someday." The goal is to bring pupils into vital relationship with God *today!* Children, as suggested earlier in this chapter, do have experiences in which they need God. Children have fears that can be quieted by coming to trust God. Children do wrong and need to know God's forgiveness. Children are faced with choices and need to find strength to do what they know is right. God is eager to become real to each child, now, in his present life experiences. How foolish, then, and how tragic when children's

---

*For a discussion of children and salvation, see Marjorie Soderholm, *Explaining Salvation to Children*, Beacon Press, Minneapolis.

Bible teaching concentrates on things far removed from the child's now—as do such lessons as the quarterly temperance unit in some curricula.

Second, the teaching must be true to God's Word. Often children are taught "truths" they must *un*learn in later life. Like the idea that the Bible is a book of moral rules, of lists of dos and don'ts. The Christian life can't really be summed up as sharing or helping or being kind or obeying parents or being friendly. Yet sometimes this impression is given to children. The feeding of the five thousand is taught to promote sharing and the little boy exalted; Dorcas is held up as the shining example of a person who was kind to others; David and Jonathan are praised for their unusual friendship.

When this kind of thing becomes the central core of a curriculum where is God? A merit-centered works-righteousness replaces the biblical core of grace, and the biblical concept that human response is an expression of love to a God whose grace enables it is clouded and lost.

This isn't, of course, to suggest that the Bible doesn't reveal a distinctive moral expression of God's will for us all. It does. "Obey your parents" is a distinct command. "Love one another" is too. But these commands are given in the context of a response to God. Most of the stories through which children are taught do not teach morals at all! Both the feeding of the five thousand and the story of Dorcas focus on Christ and His power. The history of David and Jonathan *is* a wonderful story of human friendship, but the glory of it is that God should enable Jonathan to love David to the detriment of his own self-interest. The stories in context are not really there to be examples of morality principles.

The Bible is given to us that we might know and respond to God. How dare we tear incidents out of this context and use them to teach ideas they were never meant to communicate?

It's peculiar that in evangelicalism we seem to feel that all Bible teaching for children must be in "story" form. Certainly it's not wrong to use stories, when we retain the biblical emphasis. Stories of Christ's life and ministry recorded in the New Testament are a rich source of teaching material. How thrilling is the story of Christ's stilling of the storm, when the focus is placed on Christ and we (as did the disciples) learn the power of our Lord. How deeply meaningful the feeding of the five thousand can be when the focus is on

Christ's compassion and His willingness to act for those in need. So stories, taught in harmony with their purpose in the context, do have an important place in children's Bible teaching.

But so does the teaching of doctrine. Every child is aware of pressures inside him that lead him to do things he knows are wrong, things that make him feel guilty and unhappy. Children can understand this pressure as the Bible describes it, as sin. Understanding the biblical concept of sin, they can find sin's remedy in Christ and experience Christ's forgiveness on confession.

Not every biblical doctrine can be taught six- through eleven-year-olds. They have no current need to understand the doctrine of spiritual gifts, for example. But they do need to understand doctrines that tell them who God is and what He is like. They do need to understand doctrines (though perhaps their understanding will be rudimentary) that relate to their own Christian experience: doctrines such as those of Christ's indwelling and His personal presence providing power to obey Him.

Clear teaching of God's moral will also has a place. We *are* to love one another. And this has meaning to a child, who can express love in his own home and in school and play situations. Surely God's moral will must be known if children are to know how to respond to Him. But God's will should never be taught apart from *Him*; never as a set of rules, but always as the response of love.

All of this is involved in suggesting that our teaching of children be true to God's revelation. Surely the Bible contains objective truth, objective dos and don'ts. But the Bible is given primarily that we might meet and come to know God Himself. Only when behavior is presented as a response to God, whom we have met and come to love, is Bible teaching true to His revelation.

The weak moralizing of many lessons simply is not *Bible* teaching!

Third, the teaching must make the revelation relevant on the child's own level. It's one thing to say to a child who fears the dark, "Don't be afraid; God will take care of you." And it's quite another to structure a situation in which the child himself comes to recognize this truth and respond to God with trust.

Too often in teaching children, pat solutions to problems and easy formulas for meeting needs are offered. "Trust and obey, Jimmy." "Ask God to help you, Paul." "Sue, ask your friends to come to Sunday school." The pat solutions may well be the right ones. Trust and obedience *are* central in our life with God. But simply passing on truth as advice is not making God's revelation relevant to life—for child or adult!

What is involved in making revelation relevant? Our teaching must help the learner become aware of the crucial issues in his own life. It must lead him into contact with God, not rules. It must let him discover how God relates to his needs. It must help him discover his own opportunities to respond to God appropriately. While no child will have as deep an understanding of the Lord's relationship to the issues of his life as an adult may potentially have, the insights a child *does* have will be meaningful to him. And so our teaching must be structured to help children make their own discoveries and respond to God on their own level and in their own ways. When teaching children, the basic concepts outlined in earlier chapters must guide our expression.

How Can We Teach Children?

There are two primary requirements for Bible teaching that will best help children understand what God has to say to them. The first is being sure that what we teach is actually what God is saying. The second is creative structuring of the teaching-learning situation.

The process described and illustrated in chapters 6 through 10 should be used with children. The principles developed there apply to six- through eleven-year-olds as well as to older learners. But the teacher may find it more difficult to plan learning activities which will help the children discover relevant truth and motivate appropriate response.

The next four chapters of this book look at the lesson structure described in chapter 8 and give examples of a variety of learning activities that can be used to guide children through each step.

Methods, or learning activities as they are called in this book, are meaningful only when viewed in relation to the role they play in the structure of a lesson. These next chapters take two lessons and develop them, step by step, using a variety of learning activities. A teacher who learns to think first of the purpose to be accomplished at each step can then find any number of suitable learning activities. By illustrating this in these next chapters, I hope to enable you to visualize methods that will fit *your* teaching purposes.

Research and assignment
>   for the student

1. Look through contemporary religious education magazines for articles dealing with the Bible and children. What position is expressed? What are reasons for the position? Do you agree or disagree with each writer?
2. Choose any book of the New Testament and read through it, listing teachings which you believe are relevant to the needs of children.
3. How much of a child's understanding of the gospel is merely verbal? Ask children (in a nearby church) who profess Christ to answer the following questions:
   >   Do you ever do bad things?
   >   What does Jesus think when you do bad things?
   >   Does Jesus still like us when we do bad things?
   >   What is a cross?
   >   If children answer the above, then ask:
   >   Why did Jesus die on the cross?
   >   What is heaven?
   >   How does a person get to heaven?
   Compare notes and discuss the implications of your findings.
4. Study one quarter of curriculum materials on the primary level and evaluate the following:
   a. How does the teaching relate to children's present experiences?
   b. Is the teaching true to God's revelation?
   c. How is the teaching made relevant?

Exploration
>   for the lay teacher

1. Ask question 3 series to children in your own class. Do they have a more than verbal understanding of the gospel?
2. Look through the lessons you teach and evaluate them as suggested in question 4 above.

17

FOCUSING
ATTENTION

"All right, children. Let's review what we learned last week. David, what was our lesson about? Well, Karen, do *you* remember who we talked about last week?"

Hardly a fascinating beginning to a Sunday school class! Hardly the kind of activity that will grab the pupils' interest and focus it.

Hardly the kind of thing that will help them see and set a learning goal that will be meaningful to them.

Somehow, at the very beginning of your time together, interest has to be gained and focused, and a learning goal set. How? Let's see some ways.

STORY OR CONCEPT LESSON?

IN THE LAST CHAPTER I suggested that two kinds of studies may be particularly appropriate for children. The one builds on a story, on an event or incident recorded in the Bible. For such a study to be valid, the truth (or the lesson) must follow the writer's intent. This can be determined only by a careful study of the context, an examination of the theme and development of the book, an observation of the meaning the Scripture itself assigns.

One story in which these emphases are easily determined is that of Christ stilling the waves. It's recorded in Matthew 8:23-27, Mark 4:37-41 and Luke 8:22-25. In each book the section containing the record of this event is concerned with developing awareness of the person and power of Christ. And in each book the record contains a clear rebuke to the unbelief of the disciples, who had failed to trust a sleeping Saviour, and expresses the wonder of the disciples as the deity of Christ was vividly demonstrated to them. The event, a private miracle for the disciples, clearly served to nurture a growing faith in this Man to whom they had entrusted themselves.

This is a lesson we all need, adults and children. Christ stands to *us* as a Saviour who shares our lives, who is with us, although unseen and—sometimes, we fear—unseeing. Yet His power, as is His love, is unlimited. And we too can trust ourselves fully to Him.

In these next chapters we'll look at how this story might be developed if taught to younger children, say about seven years of age. The aim, growing out of the response which this recorded event clearly calls for, will be *to help primaries trust Jesus when they are afraid.*

As discussed in chapter 9, this aim presupposes that content will be taught and focuses on the response to God which the content calls forth.

The second kind of study I've suggested as appropriate for children is a doctrinal study, a lesson designed to make a basic teaching of Scripture meaningful to a child. This kind of lesson is more difficult, because historically we have developed methods of teaching children that revolve around a story, but have done little with teaching that revolves around a concept. Yet children, especially older children, are well able to grasp and to relate basic biblical *concepts* to their own experience.

One such concept, essential to our understanding of ourselves and of God's love for us, is the concept of sin. It's clear that the gospel becomes meaningful only when the nature and the effects of sin are understood. It is clear too that the biblical concept of sin is far too large to be communicated in a single lesson. Even a unit approach (a series of several lessons) can give only a superficial understanding.

To illustrate how a concept-oriented lesson might be taught, in these next chapters we'll also look at the development of one of a proposed unit of lessons on sin for juniors (nine- through eleven-year-olds). The unit as conceived contains the following lessons:

1. Sin:	2. Sin:	3. Sin:	4. Sin:	5. Sin:
what it is	what it does	what it does	Christ's power to free us	Christ's power to free us

The specific lesson chosen is the third in the series, in which the children are to be helped to evaluate their personal need for freedom from the power of sin in their lives. The lesson aim, which must be seen in the context of the whole unit, is *to motivate juniors to want freedom from sin's power in their lives.*

So let's turn our attention to the beginning of each of these lessons and discover what learning activities are available for use by the creative teacher who desires to (1) gain and focus attention, (2) lead into the Bible study, and (3) help the pupils set a learning goal which will be meaningful to them.

Philosophy of Approach

The concept of the Hook in lesson structure was discussed in chapter 9. But it's important here to restate some basic principles which underlie and control our method of approach.

Any learner whom we invite into our class has certain rights. One of these is the right to know *why* he should give us his time and his cooperation. He has a right to know that what we want him to learn will be important *to him.*

Also, it's important that his participation be called out because he senses that he has a definite stake in the lesson. As much as possible, we need to let our pupils, at the very beginning of the class session, set learning goals. We need to help them formulate as clearly as possible what they want out of the lesson.

The first kind of activity a teacher needs to structure, then, is one which will help pupils discover and define a learning goal which is meaningful to them. If the teacher and students are successful in this, they can then move on together in the learning experience.

In most Sunday school teaching, a teacher has chosen a portion of Scripture and a learning goal before class begins. The Scripture and the learning goal are set by the curriculum. In good curricula these will be relevant to the age group in general. It's the teacher's task to help each student become aware of personal need for the truth which will be taught. There must be a *personalization* of the general goal, a process by which each learner is enabled to see the relationship and the relevance of the general goal to *himself*, and thus be motivated to want to learn.

Jesus Stills the Storm

Teaching aim: to help primaries trust Jesus when they
are afraid

Approach 1

To encourage your primaries to think of situations in which they have experienced or do experience fear, play a "what's happening" game at the beginning of class. Tell your pupils that you'll describe how an eight-year-old friend of yours feels, and ask them to guess what he's doing or what's happening.

Begin by suggesting, "Jack is very excited." Let them tell you what they think might be happening. Then suggest, "Jack is sad," "Jack is happy." When the pupils are enthusiastically involved, tell them, "Jack is afraid."

Write down the possible "afraid" situations they suggest on the chalkboard. Encourage them to think of as many likely situations as possible. Normally they'll mention situations in which they themselves feel fear.

Then ask, "Is it fun to feel afraid? How do you think a person can keep from feeling so afraid?"

As your transition, after the class discusses this last question, state the learning goal which they are able to sense as important to them: "Today we'll see how Jesus helped His friends not to be afraid, and how Jesus can help us when we're afraid."

Approach 2

Give each child a sheet of paper and crayons. Show a picture you have previously drawn, using stick figures, illustrating a time in your life when you were afraid. Tell your pupils about the incident and then ask each one to draw a picture of one time when he has been afraid.

When all are finished, let each pupil tell about his picture. Encourage the class to talk about other times when children might be afraid. Ask, "How does it *feel* to be afraid? Do you enjoy it? Why not?" Then move into the lesson by stating the learning goal, which now you have helped personalize: "Today we'll see how Jesus helped His friends when they were afraid, and how Jesus can help us when we're afraid."

Approach 3

Tell your pupils this "open-ended" story. Explain that you're going to start a story about eight-year-old Jack, and ask each one to think of how he would finish it.

"It was terribly dark in the big, empty school. Jack pushed his back up against the corridor wall, afraid to move down the shadowy hall. How could he have been dumb enough to fall asleep in the gym behind that rolled-up wrestling pad? When he woke up it was dark. The school doors were locked, all the lights were out, and the trees outside made weird shadows that looked like giants creeping through the empty rooms.

"Suddenly Jack heard a loud thump against the outside doors, and someone or something began to shake them violently. They burst open with a loud crash, and a giant figure stood blackly in the entrance.

" 'Jack!' a voice cried. It was Dad! 'Dad!' Jack yelled and dashed down the corridor to throw himself against the warm strong arms.

"Later, at home, after a warm meal, Jack told Mom and Dad all about his experience. 'It was awful, Mom!' Jack said. 'I felt. . . .' "

Let each child tell what he thinks Jack told his mother. Write the words and phrases that describe the feelings on the chalkboard.

Then ask, "Can you think of other times when boys and girls might feel as Jack did?" Let your class think together for several minutes and list other occasions when they feel fear. Move to the transition, as suggested in the other approaches.

Approach 4

Divide your class into twos, and ask each pair to plan and act out (pantomime) one or two situations in which children their age might be afraid. Other teams will try to guess what is being represented.

Write each situation on the chalkboard as it is guessed. When each team has presented one or two pantomimes, discuss the situations they chose. Let the children talk about these questions: "Is it fun to be in situations like these? How do you think we could be helped when we're afraid?"

Move into the lesson by stating, "Today we'll see how Jesus helped His friends when they were afraid, and how Jesus can help us when we're afraid too."

Approach 5

List a number of common fears of children on the chalkboard (such as fear of dark, of big dogs, of bigger kids, of fire, of being alone, of thunderstorms, of monsters, of falling in the water, etc.). Ask your boys and girls which of these they think children would fear *most*. And add any other fears they suggest.

Encourage the children to talk about being afraid: "Is it fun to be afraid? How can we help being afraid?" Then state the learning goal as your transition into the next part of the lesson: "Today we'll see how Jesus can help His friends when we're afraid."

What Sin Does

Teaching aim: to motivate juniors to want freedom
from sin's power in their lives

Approach 1

Bring into class a large coin to which you've attached with cellophane tape two tiny slips of paper. On the heads side the slip should read "right"; on the tails side the slip should read "wrong."

Tell your juniors that they're to use the coin to make decisions about what to do in three situations: (1) their dad tells them to clean out the garage; (2) they're to decide whether to do their school homework or skip it and play with friends; (3) they find a friend's comic book outside his house and are tempted to take it home. Have your students flip the coin and say what they'd do in each situation when the coin indicates they're to do the "right" thing, and what they'd do when the coin indicates they're to do the "wrong" thing.

Suggest that no one really flips a coin when he has to decide between the right thing to do and the wrong thing to do. Ask, "What makes us decide to do the right thing or the wrong thing? Why might a fellow or girl choose the wrong thing in each of the three cases above?" List on the chalkboard the reasons your class suggests for each case.

Move into the lesson by pointing out that all of us do make wrong choices. Today they'll work together to find out why we make wrong choices, and what wrong choices do to us.

Approach 2

Give each junior a checklist on which to indicate by yes or no what he thinks boys and girls in his school would do in each situation.

Would fifth graders	If dad was watching	If no one was watching
Cheat	_____	_____
Lie	_____	_____
Fight	_____	_____
Take another person's comic book	_____	_____

Discuss the situations and the answers your students gave. If any indicated that fifth graders might cheat, lie or steal when no one was watching, ask *why* a child might choose to do something he knows is wrong. If no one gave a yes answer, ask your class *when* a child might choose to do the wrong thing. Encourage your pupils to share their ideas on why people do things they know are wrong. (Should one suggest too glibly that the reason is sin, ask why people choose to sin.) Force your juniors to think beneath the surface of the problem.

Then state your learning goal: "Today we'll find out more about why we make wrong choices, and also think about what wrong choices may mean for us."

Approach 3

Give each student a twelve- to eighteen-inch piece of soft, mallable wire. Show a straight piece of the same length and suggest that when the Bible describes God, it pictures Him as holy and just and good. There's no crookedness in Him.

Ask your students to take their pieces of wire and make a picture of what people are like inside. Are they straight, like God? Or aren't they perfectly holy and good as He is? Your pupils can do anything they wish with the wires, but the end result is to show what each thinks people are like inside.

Compare the pieces of wire. Encourage boys and girls who crumpled the wire completely, or who bent it just slightly, to tell why they shaped it as they did.

Then lay each piece of wire by the straight piece which represents God. Tell your class that today they will find out what it means to all of us to be sinners and twisted inside so that we sometimes or often do things which we know are wrong.

Approach 4

Read two case histories to your class, telling what Rick did in two different situations. Ask them to notice what's different about his decisions and *why* he might have made each decision.

Research and assignment
    for the student
1. Write up two additional learning activities which might be used to focus the attention of children on the learning goal of each of the two lessons suggested in this chapter.
2. Select one Bible story and one doctrine, then develop at least four different approaches for a lesson on each.
3. Survey one quarter of lesson materials for primaries and evaluate the effectiveness of the Hooks. Where necessary, rewrite to provide more meaningful approaches.
4. Survey one quarter of lesson materials for juniors and evaluate the effectiveness of the Hooks. Where necessary, rewrite to provide more meaningful approaches.

Exploration
    for the lay teacher
1. Evaluate the aim and the approach to your next Sunday's lesson. Try to develop at least two alternate learning activities you might use for focusing your pupils' attention on the learning goal.
2. Read through your quarterly and jot down the different kinds of learning activities the lesson writer suggests for the approach, or Hook step.
    If these fall into a pattern or routine, see if you can't develop other methods. (Note that in this chapter nine methods were used: a game, drawing a picture of an experience, an open-ended story, pantomime, ranking, an object [coin flip], a checklist, wire bending and case histories.) Can you think of at least three more learning activities that might have been suggested?

18

COMMUNICATING CONTENT

The Bible—that "adult" book—is central in evangelical teaching. So the Bible must be communicated to children.

Such communication encounters two main difficulties. First, what is communicated must be true to the Scriptures. The Word must be presented accurately, interpreted in full harmony with its literal, historical, grammatical meaning, with full attention given to the inspired writer's purpose. Second, what is communicated must be on the level of the children. The Word must be presented so that they can understand it—understand it as fully as possible not only within the framework of their mental level, but also within the framework of their current experience.

Teaching the Bible to children isn't easy. But it's necessary. And it can be done.

CHRIST STILLS THE STORM

Teaching aim: to help primaries trust Jesus
              when they are afraid

Background

In the biblical record this incident is sketched sharply and briefly.

> On that day, when evening had come, he said to them, "Let us go across to the other side." And leaving the crowd, they took him with them, just as he was, in the boat. And other boats were with him. And a great storm of wind arose, and the waves beat into the boat, so that the boat was already filling. But he was in the stern, asleep on the cushion; and they woke him and said to him, "Teacher, do you not care if we perish?" And he awoke and rebuked the wind, and said to the sea, "Peace! Be still!" And the wind ceased, and there was a great calm. He said to them, "Why are you afraid? Have you no faith?" And they were filled with awe, and said to one another, "Who then is this, that even wind and sea obey him?" (Mark 4:35-41, RSV).

The situation is clear: the raging storm, the terror of the disciples (many of whom were experienced fishermen) as they became convinced that they were about to die, the calm Christ, His quiet rebuke of the raging elements and their miraculous response, His gentle rebuke of the disciples for their fears, the awed response of those who had traveled with Him as once again they came face to face with His elemental power.

While the fear of the disciples was surely justified by the circumstances, the presence of Christ transformed the situation and should have enabled the disciples to trust even in their fear. The more you and I and our children are aware of the power and the presence of Christ in our experience, the more we too will be able to trust, even in our fears.

The "basic" approach taken in teaching younger children is *storytelling*. The elements of the biblical narrative are woven into a word picture which will interest and impress the children. It's built to appeal not only to the children's minds, but also to their emotions;

built with "tugs" to draw the listener and move him to think and feel and to experience and decide.

And storytelling, as we'll see, is also a method that provides for an almost infinite variety of learning experiences.

The basic story

Approach 1

When the first dark clouds began to pile up in the night sky, the men in the boat weren't worried. They were fishermen and had seen many storms. They weren't worried when the wind began to blow. They weren't worried when the waves began to pound against the side of their boat. They weren't even worried when the lightning started to flash and the thunder boomed out louder and louder.

But the wind blew harder and harder. And the waves got bigger and bigger. Now drops of cold water began to spray over the side of the boat. And the men began to shiver in the cold and wet. They shivered even more as the thunder crashed louder and louder, and the lightning cracked nearer and nearer.

But even then the men weren't worried. When they began to feel a little frightened, they looked toward the back of their little boat. And they saw Someone lying there, fast asleep. It was Jesus. *If Jesus can sleep,* the men must have thought, *the storm can't be too bad. If Jesus can sleep, we'll probably be all right.*

But the storm kept getting worse and worse! With a terrible ripping sound the wind tore the sail off the mast of the boat. With a crash, crash, crash, the pounding waves beat against the boat. The waves began to surge over the side of the boat, pouring gallons and gallons of water onto the men. All Jesus' friends grabbed buckets and basins and tried to throw water out of the boat. They dipped as fast and as hard as they could. But the waves poured more water in, faster and faster. The boat began to fill up! And now the men were really afraid. In the darkness and terrible noise of the great storm, they knew their boat was going to sink. And soon! They were lost!

But wait! What about Jesus. Where was Jesus? In the brightness of another lightning flash they saw Him. He was still asleep!

Terrified now, one of Jesus' friends shook Him and cried out, "Lord! Don't You care? We're sinking! We'll all be drowned!"

Then Jesus woke up. He looked around and saw the terrible storm. He saw the fear on the faces of His friends. And He stood up in the boat and told the wind, "Stop." And the wind stopped, just like that! And Jesus told the waves, "Be still." And they were still. Just like that. And suddenly, instead of being in a great storm, the boat was floating quietly on a flat, still sea. And the bright moonlight gave a calm peaceful light.

Then Jesus turned to look at His friends. Sadly He said to them, "Why were you afraid? Don't you trust Me?"

And Jesus' friends were amazed. Who else could have made the storm stop and the seas be calm? No one, no one but Jesus. "Who can this Jesus really be?" Jesus' friends wondered. And deep down inside they must have thought, *We really could have trusted Jesus all the time. We didn't have to be afraid, because Jesus was with us. We'll never forget to trust Jesus when we're afraid again.*

And you know, boys and girls, we can trust Jesus when we're afraid, too. Jesus loves us, and He has promised, "I will never leave you" [Heb. 13:5]. We don't have to be afraid, because Jesus is with *us!*

Variations on the story

Approach 2

In the foregoing basic story the teacher drew out and stated the *generalization* (see pp.   ). By cutting the last two paragraphs off the story and using a question/answer technique, the storyteller can guide his young pupils to discover and state the generalization themselves.

A question series such as the following might be used to lead children to such discovery and statement:

question	*expected response pattern*
Why were Jesus' friends afraid?	restatement of storm situation
Why wasn't Jesus afraid?	Jesus knew He could stop the storm, had more power, was God, etc.

How did Jesus show His power to help?	Jesus stopped the storm.
Now, stop and think a minute. If Jesus was in the boat, did His friends have to be afraid? Why? Why not?	No, because Jesus was with them, He could and would take care of them.
Do you think Jesus takes care of us today?	Normally children who have been brought up in church or in Christian homes will respond with yes. Either yes or no responses call for a verse like Hebrews 13:5 which may serve as a memory verse or key verse.

Approach 3

Large colorful pictures of most Bible stories are available from many Christian publishers. A picture study, calling for the children to observe and to relate significant events, can also be used following the basic story. Again questions can be used to guide the thinking of the children.

"Look at the faces of the men. How do you think they feel?" "Why are they afraid?" "But look, who is this standing up in the boat?" (Jesus.) "Does He seem to be afraid?" "Why isn't He afraid?" "Can you think of any reasons why Jesus' friends didn't have to be afraid either?" "The Bible tells us that Jesus will never leave us nor forsake us. What does that mean for us when we start to be afraid?"

Approach 4

Flannelgraph is another method of visualizing often used in evangelical churches. After telling the basic story, let the children use the flannelgraph figures to retell it. As each child tells and shows his part, ask questions in a pattern like those suggested above, to help the children move toward interpretation and understanding of the story's meaning.

Approach 5

Another variation is to let the children act out the story after it's been heard. Where space (and soundproofing!) permit, this kind of experience uniquely lets the children enter into and participate in the total experience, to thus sense vicariously the comforting presence of Christ.

Approach 6

A variation which can be very effective is to encourage the children to pretend they were actually in the boat, and "interview" them. A tape recorder for the "reporter" makes the experience especially exciting.

In using this technique with older children, divide the class into two groups, one of which is to be reporters and the others disciples who were in the boat. The reporters can decide what questions they would like to ask, and the disciples discuss the experience, before the interview takes place.

What Sin Does

Teaching aim: to motivate juniors to want freedom
from sin's power in their lives

Background

The biblical concept of sin is extremely complex, and yet comprehensively developed in Scripture. The usage of the word ranges from the designation of an action itself as sin, to a conceptualization of sin as a condition or characteristic quality of man, on to its portrait as a power which deceives and directs men who are its slaves. Sin, that warping of man's mind and heart and will out of harmony with God, is both the producer of guilt feelings and the ground on which men are held to be in fact guilty. Thus sin twists our actions and spoils our lives and brings us under the wrath of God. Existentially sin is both appealing and defiling, both desirable and repellent. And all of us are aware that there is some principle within, some fact of our existence, that spoils our lives and keeps us from doing and being all that we should do and be.

In the lessons for juniors which preceded this third session of our unit on sin, something of the nature of sin and its wrath-producing results has been developed and understood. In this lesson the focus is on the existential effects of sin: the personal awareness we all have of its presence and the difficulty we have in resisting its power.

The content section of this particular lesson needs to focus on (1) the fact of sin's presence and (2) the believer's reaction to sin's pull.

Each of these ideas needs to be developed in sequence. The basic section to be taught, one selected here just because of its doctrinal complexity, is Romans 7:14-19, 24:

> For we know that the Law is spiritual; but I am of flesh, sold into bondage to sin. For that which I am doing, I do not understand; for I am not practicing what I would like to do, but I am doing the very thing I hate. But if I do the very thing I do not wish to do, I agree with the Law, confessing that it is good. So now, no longer am I the one doing it, but sin which indwells me. For I know that nothing good dwells in me, that is, in my flesh; for the wishing is present in me, but the doing of the good is not. For the good that I wish, I do not do; but I practice the very evil that I do not wish. Wretched man that I am! Who will set me free from the body of this death?

In approaching any such section as this, ground rules must be laid by lecture. For this lesson we'll suggest that the teacher begin by either discussing or listing definitions on the chalkboard, to clarify such vital terms as *spiritual* and *flesh* in this passage. The teacher will also need to point out that sin shows up in our lives in at least two ways. Sin makes us *want* to do something wrong or it makes us do something wrong that we don't really want to do. (At this point the juniors might be asked to think of cases of each type.)

Beyond this point, a variety of learning activities can be introduced to help the learner interact with the passage and the concepts under consideration.

Stage One

"What does the passage say?"

Approach 1

Give a chalk talk to illustrate biblical concepts. "Mr. Everyman" can be sketched as a person who stands with his feet pointed in opposite directions. Like the apostle Paul, we all know certain things are right and others are wrong. We really *believe* that these are right or wrong. But while part of us recognizes and wants to do the right, part of us wants to do the wrong. Paul says that the cause of this pull toward the wrong is sin which lives within us. That sin often wins out in our lives and we do the wrong.

Another way of visualizing this concept is with a wagon (representing us), pulled in opposite directions by two horses, one of which pulls us toward the right, the other toward the wrong.

right ←——   ——→ wrong
Mr. Everyman

Approach 2

To help the juniors understand the passage even more graphically, give each a sheet of paper and ask him to do an "incident paraphrase." That is, ask your students to substitute some specific wrong for the general idea of doing wrong or sinning. Thus the verse might read "I do not really want to cheat, but I do cheat even though I hate it," etc.

Approach 3

After the introduction give your juniors a series of questions. Let them work together by twos to answer each. A question series for this passage might be:

1. What does Paul *want* to do?
2. What does Paul end up doing?
3. Why does Paul do what he does?
4. How does Paul feel about what he does?

Stage two

"How are we to feel about sin?"

Approach 4

Ask the juniors to look for "feeling words," for phrases or words that show how Paul feels about the sin within him. List these on the chalkboard as they are discovered. Then encourage the children to share how *they* feel about doing wrong. Do they ever feel unhappy about doing wrong, as Paul did? Can they think of any reasons why Paul might have been unhappy about doing wrong?

In this approach it's important to accept both the answers and the feelings of the juniors, then help them deepen their sense of concern about sin. Answers to the question of *why* Paul might care about sin (which may range from "Because he wanted to please Jesus" to "Because he was afraid he'd be punished" to "He just didn't feel right inside") will give clues as to where the children are in their personal feelings about themselves and about sin.

Approach 5

Ask your juniors to recall Bible stories about sin or about people who sinned. They may be familiar with stories of individuals (such as Saul or Achan or Judas).

Talk with them about what happened to the individuals who sinned. Were they happy? How did their sin affect other people? Did it help or harm other people? How did God feel about the sin? What did God do about the sin?

How big a problem does Paul have then (and we also) if he finds he's doing the wrong things he doesn't even want to do?

Approach 6

Point out that others who have loved God have done wrong and felt bad about it. Let your juniors read Psalm 32:3-4 and discuss how David felt after he had sinned. Did he feel as Paul felt? Why were David and Paul so unhappy about having sinned? Do your juniors ever feel like either of these men when they do something they know is wrong?

When your juniors have grasped the basic teaching of the Romans passage that "sin" is inside us and causes us to do things that we know are wrong, and when your juniors have sensed something of the unhappiness sin's power has caused, you're ready to move on to the next step in your lesson, guiding to insight.

Research and assignment
    for the student
1. From the ideas on storytelling suggested in this chapter, develop a set of criteria to guide you in telling a Bible story to children.
2. Read a good book on storytelling and compare the criteria you developed in response to question 1 with the criteria suggested in the book.
3. Select three incidents recorded in the Bible and develop them for telling to seven- or eight-year-olds. Be sure to write out each story as you would tell it, then check your story against the criteria you have established.
4. Try to think of at least two learning activities other than those suggested in this chapter that might grow out of storytelling.
5. Make a list of methods you believe best suited to communicating doctrinal content to older children. Write up at least two and show how you might use them to teach Romans 7:14 f.
6. Survey one quarter of materials for primaries and one quarter of materials for juniors and list all the methods the writers suggest for communicating content. What conclusions can you draw from this study?
7. Develop at least four ways to communicate the content segment of the story and the doctrine you selected to fulfill assignment 2 at the end of the last chapter.

Exploration
    for the lay teacher
1. Buy and read one good book on storytelling (such as Ethel Barrett's *Storytelling—It's Easy!*).
2. Do at least one of the seven assignments suggested above.

19

GUIDING TO INSIGHT

We come now to the very heart of teaching, to the process that distinguishes teaching from preaching; the process that is at once the most difficult and the most challenging aspect of creative Bible teaching.

Any of us can know what the Word says without a significant awareness of what the Word says—and means—*to us*. Guiding learners from the place where they understand content to the place where they clearly sense its meaning for them challenges the best of teachers.

It's particularly difficult for teachers of children. With older students and adults a discussion technique alone can help learners confront the personal implications of truth. But younger children don't operate facilely on a merely verbal level. They don't think well or deeply in words alone. Guiding children to insight—to self-discovery of how truth taught fits into *their* experience—requires far firmer handles than words. Far firmer and more graphic handles—like those described in this chapter.

LEARNER PARTICIPATION

BASIC CONCEPTS which determine our approach to this part of the lesson (the Look) are described in some detail on pages 110 and 119-27. Central among them is this: the learners need to participate freely. Insights into how the Word applies should come, to a great extent, from the learner. The teacher's task, then, is to structure learning activities with solid enough handles for children to grasp; learning activities that help children work with concrete situations and ideas rather than with concepts and abstractions.

It's important also to recall that the response which is appropriate to a given truth about or from God *may* be an action, but it may as well be a change in attitude or motivation. These later responses are not immediately perceptible to the teacher nor even to the learner! The learning activity chosen, then, must help children focus for themselves on what the appropriate response to the truth studied actually is, and must facilitate that response.

Christ Stills the Storm

Teaching aim: to help primaries trust Jesus
when they are afraid

The Look step in this lesson might helpfully focus on developing the children's awareness of uncomfortable situations in which they can trust themselves to an ever present Christ. Or it might focus on encouraging the children to think through *how* they might turn to Him when afraid. The learning activities suggested here focus on one or the other. In the class you may want to use two activities, which would permit you to help the children in both these ways.

Approach 1

Discuss each time "when we're afraid" is listed during a Hook activity (chap. 17), and ask the children to decide for each item whether or not Jesus is with them in this situation.

Approach 2

Ask the children to draw pictures of times when they feel it is especially important for them to know that Jesus is with *them*. Then compare these pictures with the listings or the pictures drawn during the Hook activity. If the children have drawn the same situations as they discussed earlier, ask them how remembering Jesus is with them helps. Ask also how a child in the situation pictured might feel *before* he remembers Jesus is with him. How might he feel *after* he remembers?

Approach 3

Cut from a catalog pictures of a man, a woman, and two or three children. Back the pictures with cardboard. Introduce the paper doll "family" to your class and tell a story about one primary-age child who became lost. Move the figures appropriately as you tell the story. Tell how worried mother and dad were, and how frightened the child was when he (or she) realized he was lost. Then tell how each remembered that the Lord was with the lost child, for He has promised never to leave or forsake us. Tell how each prayed and asked the Lord for help (as the disciples in the boat had) and how they then were comforted as they trusted Him till the child was found.

Then let each child who wants to use the doll family tell his or her own story about trusting. Remind the class of the various situations they discussed at the beginning of the period. Thus primed, the children will have plenty of ideas for their own stories.

This same approach may be used with finger puppets, paper bag puppets, etc.

Approach 4

Prepare for each child four picture panels that show a situation in which a child or adult feels fear. One of the panels ought to show the child in the situation. A second should be a close-up of his face showing his fear or unhappiness. A third might show him praying or thinking of the Lord. And the fourth should show him trusting the Lord with fears lessened.

Ask the children to make up a story about the child in the four

pictures, telling in some detail what is happening. You may wish to write the story down as the children dictate.

Another variation on this approach is to leave one of the four picture squares blank (preferably either frame 3 or frame 4) and ask each child to draw in the picture that he feels will help complete the story.

Approach 5

A hymn study, in which the children learn a hymn or review one they know well, provides another good stimulus to thought. Such a hymn can help carry the impact of the class over into the week, as the children hum or sing to themselves during the week (as my children do).

A gospel song which would fit quite well for primaries with this lesson is "Anywhere with Jesus":

> Anywhere with Jesus I can safely go,
> Anywhere with Jesus in this world below,
> Anywhere without Him dearest joys would fade;
> Anywhere with Jesus I am not afraid.
>
> Anywhere, anywhere, fear I cannot know
> Anywhere with Jesus I can safely go.

Discuss each phrase as it is sung, and relate the ideas to specific situations in which the children might feel fear or in which they have already said they do tend to fear.

What Sin Does

Teaching aim: to motivate juniors to want freedom
from sin's power in their lives

In this lesson (which, again, is only one of a unit of five lessons on sin), the goal lies in the realm of affecting attitude and motivation rather than in the realm of affecting an overt action-type response. The purpose of this lesson in the unit is to *prepare* for personal response to Christ by deepening the juniors' awareness of sin and its meaning in their own experience.

Specifically, then, the Look step in this lesson is designed to help juniors become more sensitive to the pull of sin in their own lives and to deepen their awareness of the guilt and sense of guilt which sin brings.

Approach 1

Give your juniors copies of the following story. Ask them to read the whole story, then to go over it again and underline on their own copies wherever they think the story is wrong or that what is written isn't really what would have happened.

> "Tad," Mom called, "please do your homework before you play this afternoon. It should only take you about twenty minutes."
>
> "OK, Mom," Tad said. *Homework! Phooey! Aw, why bother?* Tad thought. *I'll just go play anyway.*
>
> Tad felt real happy about his decision and dashed out the door after stopping to tell Mom that he wasn't going to do the homework.
>
> Outside Tad played with his friends for a while, then dropped in to Bill's to play with his matchbox cars. When Bill wasn't looking, Tad slipped Bill's favorite car into his pocket.
>
> Later, at home, Tad's dad asked him how his day had been. "Great!" Tad said. "I got out of doing my homework and I swiped a real keen car from Bill—one I've wanted for a long time."

That night when he went to bed, Tad prayed, "Thank you, God, for giving me such a happy day. Amen."

At each criticized point encourage discussion. Ask, "How do you think he *would* feel?" "What do you think he *would* do?" "Why do you think he'd do [or feel] that?" etc.

Encourage them to talk about how they feel when they do something they know is wrong. Happy? Can they tell dad about their wrong choices? Or God? Why or why not?

Approach 2

Show a filmstrip on a Bible character, such as Saul, who made wrong choices. Let your juniors then think about the filmstrip and discuss key points.

What did Saul do that was wrong? How do you think Saul felt when he sinned? How can you tell? What happened to Saul and to his people because of his wrong choices? How do sin and our wrong choices harm us? How do they harm others?

Would Saul have been happier if he had not sinned and had made right choices? Would *we* be happier? Why then do we choose wrong so often?

Approach 3

Give your juniors elements of a basic situation. For instance, in the story of Tad, key elements might be Mom's telling Tad to do his homework and Tad's later temptation to take Bill's matchbox car. Divide your juniors into two teams. Each is to write a skit about Tad. One skit is to show him making wrong choices, showing how he feels after making them. One is to show him making right choices, showing how he feels after making *them*. Each group is to put on its skit for the class.

Then let the class discuss the two skits. Why were Tad's reactions shown as they were? How does doing wrong make us feel? Why then do we ever do wrong?

Approach 4

Ask your juniors to write out a story telling of the incident Jim is thinking of:

Say, Jim thought as the class talked about the way the apostle Paul and King David had felt when they sinned. *I know just how they must have felt. I remember the last time that I* . . .

When the juniors have finished their stories, read each aloud to the whole class. Discuss the incidents described. Ask if there are other times when they are particularly aware of guilt feelings. Do they ever do the things they feel guilty about again? Why? How important do they think it would be if they could always do the right thing, not the things that make them feel guilty and wrong?

SUMMARY

The relationship of the preceding learning activities to the biblical content should be carefully noted. In each of the two lessons developed here, the learning activities suggested in this chapter presuppose the biblical content. They are based on the Scripture study. *They would not be valid apart from preceding Bible study.*

This is not because they *could* not be effectively used apart from Bible study. In one sense, they could be so used. However, the basic concept on which this book is based is that Bible teaching must be structured to lead students to a response *to God*. This concept rests on the conviction that God confronts us personally in His Word. *Response which is not response to God as met in the Word deteriorates to legalism.* Any behavior which might be motivated by such techniques apart from Scripture would fall short of being spiritually meaningful.

Paul states strongly in I Corinthians 13 that *any* behavior—even the most commendable—if not motivated by love, if not flowing as a heart response to God, is of no profit. This defines the position we must take. Action must flow as a heart response to God as He is met, and His will discerned, in the Word.

Thus the Look activities suggested in the chapter are intrinsically related to the biblical study preceding it. Here the students have confronted God in His revelation. Now, the Look activities are to guide the students to a response which is appropriate.

In the first lesson, Look learning activities are designed to encourage a trusting response in time of fear, helping the children vicariously work through an appropriate response with puppets or pictures. Thus they are helped to see when and how they can themselves turn trustingly to Christ.

In the second lesson, the learning activities are designed, not to encourage immediate response, but to lay a groundwork for future response. They are to help the juniors to the same awareness of sin's power and to the same sense of unhappiness about sin that is portrayed in Scripture as an appropriate response to God's verdict that we *are* sinners and that we stand in terrible need of Christ and His help.

The learning activities suggested here, then, *must* be understood in the context of the total lesson structure and must be understood as attempts to deepen the understanding and impact of the Word studied on the learner.

Research and assignment
        for the student
1. Write out at least two more learning activities appropriate to each of the lessons described in this chapter.
2. Make a study of the use of questions as demonstrated in the learning activities suggested in this chapter and in chapters 18–19. Write out a two-page article for Sunday school teachers on the subject "Using Questions in Your Teaching."
3. Study curriculum materials for either primary or junior age. Prepare a *written evaluation* of one publisher's philosophy and practice of transfer of learning (see chap. 10), as demonstrated by the effectiveness or ineffectiveness of Look activities.
4. Complete through the Look step the development of the lesson begun as part of chapter 17's assignment 2.

Exploration
        for the lay teacher
1. Evaluate the Look activities in the Sunday school materials you teach. Are good learning activities provided?
2. Plan two or three different learning activities which you could use with your lesson this coming Sunday. Use one or two of them with your class.

3. Note that the learning activities suggested in this chapter require a large block of time to allow for student involvement and discussion. Estimate the amount of time you should spend on each segment this week. After teaching, reevaluate your time estimates. How much time did you use? Are you satisfied that the time was used to best advantage? What changes might you have made to gain better use of the time?

20

ENCOURAGING RESPONSE

Response to God is always an intimately personal thing. Only God knows the heart; only He can sovereignly move to touch our motives and our wills, and to create the love which makes an action a true response to Him.

Yet from the point of view of our perception, response is our choice, our decision. And from the point of view of the teacher's responsibility, our students must and can be encouraged to respond, to decide, to choose to do God's will.

When we think of guiding children to response, it is necessary to think beyond the class situation. It's true that there are learning activities which the teacher can plan which will bring children to the brink of decision. In this chapter we'll look at some of them. But it is also true that children need out-of-class *guidance* in actualizing response. They need the kind of loving supervision of daily life that no Sunday school or Bible class teacher can provide, the kind of informal instruction and guidance that only a parent can provide. And this too will be considered here.

OBTAINING LEARNER RESPONSE

THE TEACHER in the class has the task of leading the learner to the brink of decision.

That is, the teacher needs to help the young learner face the necessity to respond, giving whatever help is appropriate to the age group without coercing a response.

Children often need an external stimulus to help them respond, but not the stimulus of a prize or an award, which stimulates response to the reward rather than to God. Children need the kind of stimulus that will help them respond appropriately in the life situation outside of class. They need the kind of support that will help them be alert for response opportunities.

What kind of learning activities might serve this function? Let's look at some, as we conclude the two lessons begun in chapter 17.

Christ Stills the Storm

Teaching aim: to help primaries trust Jesus
when they are afraid

The Took step in this lesson is designed to help the children be aware of opportunities to respond to Christ with trust and to remind them of the constant presence of Christ with them.

Approach 1

Give each child a postcard, addressed to you (the teacher). On the postcard place a picture seal of Christ and print this incomplete statement: "Today I remembered to trust the Lord when. . . ." Encourage the children to complete the card during the week whenever they've found the Lord has helped them, then to mail the card to you.

Next Sunday bring the cards you received to class and post them. Also let the children share with the rest of the class how the Lord comforted and helped them.

Approach 2

Make of several four- by six-inch slips of paper, stapled together, a "Chapter-a-Day" book on trusting. Have each child print his name on the cover of his book, and also the day's key verse ("I will never leave you"), or some such phrase as "I can trust Jesus."

Encourage the children to keep the daily diary on trusting by drawing in, each day, a picture of some situation in which they were conscious that Jesus was with them and taking care of them.

The books can be discussed in presession the next Sunday.

Approach 3

Provide each child with a small take-home picture of Jesus stilling the storm. Suggest that the picture be placed near his bed, and that as he goes to sleep he look at the picture and remember that Jesus is with him, too, and that he can trust the Lord.

You might also give each child several stars with gummed backs. Tell him that if he has remembered to trust the Lord at any time during the day, he can place a star for that day on the picture.

Give the children an opportunity to share their experiences the next Sunday morning.

Approach 4

Phone the children during the week and talk with them about the lesson. Let them share any times they have trusted the Lord in a special way since class.

Or mail each a personal note.

Approach 5

Duplicate for each child a copy of the song that was learned or reviewed as part of the Look activity. Encourage each to ask his mom and dad to learn the song and to sing it during the week at devotions. If the family has no devotional time, they could sing it together at bedtime.

What Sin Does

Teaching aim: to motivate juniors to want freedom
from sin's power in their lives

In the previous lesson, the focus of the Took was on providing spurs to specific response to Christ in life situations.

This lesson on sin, as part of a unit, does not culminate in any such definite action-response. Yet, at the same time, the Took step must help the junior who has explored the meaning of sin in others' lives to move on to exploration of the meaning of sin in his own life. The learning activities must help him face the fact of his own sin, and thus his own need for freedom in Christ which will be presented in subsequent studies.

The learning activities appropriate in this lesson, then, are activities which will help the juniors sense for themselves the ideas and feelings they have discussed, and will deepen their awareness of their own nature and need.

Approach 1

Follow up the wire-bending Hook activity (chap. 17). Give each junior a second piece of wire. Ask him now to bend the wire to show how he feels *he* is inside.

When each has completed this exercise, which encourages an honest self-evaluation, point out that Paul says in Romans 7:25 that he can thank God, for through Jesus Christ he can be freed from the power of sin which is inside him.

Close in prayer that each who feels an honest need for Christ's help to free him from sin's power might trust the Lord for help this week. And promise your juniors that next week you'll all find out more about how Christ can and will help them.

Approach 2

Develop a self-evaluation guide that each junior can use to evaluate the hold sin has on him.

A continuum scale (see fig. 23) is probably the best rating device. Items on the scale should be chosen from the problem areas your juniors themselves have mentioned during the class. Thus if they've said that they have trouble with cheating or with obeying their parents, those items would appear on the evaluation guide.

When each junior has completed his self-evaluation, take time to discuss how much each wants to be free from sin's power.

Close as suggested for approach 1.

PART ONE: SIN'S PULL

no temptation	strong temptation

to lie _____

to cheat _____

to disobey _____

(etc.) _____

PART TWO: SIN'S POWER

never give in	usually give in

to lie _____

to cheat _____

to disobey _____

(etc.) _____

Fig. 23. SELF-EVALUATION CHART

Mark on the line the place where you believe *you* belong for each item listed.

Approach 3

Ask each student to write a brief paragraph or story about how *he* feels about sin. Encourage each to use as many *feeling* words as he can.

Then list feeling words each junior has used on the chalkboard, and close as suggested in approach 1.

Approach 4

Ask each junior to think of one situation in which he feels sin's pull, and in which he really wants to do right but finds it difficult.

With this specific situation in mind, ask your juniors to write a paragraph on "What I would like most then."

When the paragraphs are written, close as suggested in approach 1. Or first collect and read each anonymous statement to the group.

THE LARGER CONTEXT OF LIFE

As suggested earlier, response to God is normally made in the context of life. And life is lived outside the church and outside the classroom.

It has been the thesis of this book that ultimately Christianity is not intellectual. That is, Christian education and Christian training cannot concern themselves only with intellectual exercises, only with the transferring of concepts from mind to mind. Christianity cannot be mere mental mastery and manipulation of revealed truths.

As we have seen, the Christian does have a body of revealed, propositional truth. This truth is presented in the Word of God. And these truths must be known. But the biblical focus is not on the intellectual mastery of such truths; it is on our personal *response* to truth.

But response is necessarily tied to life. Response has to be made in the context of our total experience. Bible truths, to be real to us and to seem real to us, must be lived and seen in the context of daily life.

Our faith is to be *lived*.

Thus the Christian teacher and the Christian parent need to be clear on one basic point: the formal instruction in the classroom cannot in itself develop strong Christians or nurture children and youth in the Christian faith.

To be in harmony with the nature of our faith, Christian education must be integrated with daily living. Students *should* study the Bible in class, certainly. But they *must also be guided to experience the truths studied in the context of daily life.*

Who is in a position to fulfill this responsibility? Certainly not the Sunday school teacher. Only the parent. Note that this is in harmony with the pattern of teaching the Word given in the Old Testament:

And these words, which I command thee this day, shall be in thine heart: and thou shalt teach them diligently unto thy children, and shalt talk of them when thou sittest in thine house, and when thou walkest by the way, and when thou liest down, and when thou risest up (Deut. 6:6-7).

The words of God are basic. *But they are to be communicated informally in the context of life.* They are communicated as life is being lived, as we talk in the home, walk along the road, in the morning and in the evening. For maximum impact on children, teaching in the agencies of the church must be integrated with a ministry of informal guidance in the home. While such integration is seldom accomplished, it *can* be. What does it take? Here are a few simple suggestions.

1. Acquaint parents with their responsibility. Church leaders should make sure neither parents nor teachers trust in church-centered training to accomplish nurture goals.

2. Keep parents aware of what teachers are teaching. Plan PTA meetings. Publishers often provide take-home materials which can be used in family devotions and which acquaint parents with weekly lesson themes. Teachers can and should visit homes to explain the use of take-home materials.

3. Superintendents of teaching departments and teachers should be made more sensitive to the need for working *with* the home. Parents need help to relate daily experience to Bible truths. For instance, each Sunday school department might prepare an information sheet to be sent home at the beginning of each unit of lessons. The sheet can contain copies of new songs, memory verses the children will learn, etc. Most important, the sheets can summarize the Bible content taught each Sunday and suggest to parents the general trend of application suggested in class. Often lessons for older children and youth contain suggestions for carry-over projects. These too can be reproduced and passed on to parents.

While this book deals primarily with the classroom situation, the reader ought to recognize the limitations inherent in even the best classroom teaching. He should seriously consider, when teaching children, how the teaching ministry can be integrated with a guidance ministry of the home.

Research and assignment
> for the student

1. Develop two Took activities to complete the two lessons you have been developing.
2. Develop two different learning activities which would accomplish the Took goals for the lessons discussed in this chapter.
3. Go back through chapters 17–20 and list *all* methods (learning activities) illustrated, plus any you have developed as part of your assignments.

   Begin a file of methods to expand the number of learning activities you have at your command.
4. Evaluate the author's contention that Christianity is not intellectual and that it must thus be lived. Think through the implications of this suggestion for Christian education.
5. Survey parents of children in a primary or junior department to see if they are *in any way* working cooperatively with the church teaching agencies. What do the survey results indicate? What do you project as the *causes* of the situation you discovered?
6. Take one quarter of primary materials and develop, as a class project, a full "home support" program—writing additional materials you feel parents would need, planning meetings between teachers and parents, etc.
7. Write to several evangelical publishers and ask them how the materials they publish for the church are correlated with the ministry of the home. Then check out their answers by seeing how local churches using their curricula implement their suggestions.

Exploration
> for the lay teacher

1. Plan Took learning activities for this week's class. Be sure you also think through the total lesson structure as suggested in the earlier chapters.
2. Check out the parents of children in *your* class. Are they working with you to fulfill your teaching ministry? If not, why not? Which of the suggestions in this chapter do you feel you and your department most need to follow?

TEACHING YOUTH AND ADULTS

21

FOCUSING ATTENTION

The Bible, youth and adults: it's here that the principles suggested in this book find their fullest application.

Adults, in ways children simply cannot, are able to understand and to respond to God's call to them in the Word. With adolescents and adults the teacher's goal of stimulating a deeply personal, shared interaction with the Word can be fully realized. And maturing students can be taken as full partners into the learning experience. And such students can gain the fullest insight into the meaning of the Word *for them* and make the fullest response to the God who says, "Keep My words."

It's the teacher's task to build toward such a responsive, responsible fellowship.

TRUTH IN LIFE CONTEXT

WHEN I WAS CONVERTED, while in the Navy, I began to attempt to share my faith in Christ with those on my base. It was hard. I had been brought up in a Christian home, but there was so much I didn't know. So an army sergeant friend and I spent hours studying the Bible together, discovering truths that are so familiar to most of you who read, and trying to understand their meanings. I was motivated to learn, for life had thrown me into contact with many who did not believe and thus challenged my faith. And so I struggled to understand what God had done and was doing for me.

Ideally, motivation for learning should grow out of experience, and will exist as a tension which the learner feels a need to resolve.

Much later I taught a Sunday school class of young marrieds. In our discussion it became clear that many of us were concerned about unresolved tensions in our homes. What were the role and the responsibilities of the husband, of the wife? What was the best way to discipline children? How could we guide the total development of our children—and be sure to promote a balanced spiritual growth? As this tension, growing out of our experience, was focused, the class and I worked together to structure a series of studies that would help us discover and examine biblical guidelines for family living. Again, motivation was strong. A tension was sensed by us all, and our investigations were directly related to resolving them.

It should be clear that the *best* structure for an adolescent or adult class is one in which the curriculum is developed spontaneously as an outgrowth of the tensions already existing in the lives of those in the group. When these tensions are focused, and we direct our attention to the Word, seeking God's solutions and His direction for life, the greatest possible opportunity for relevant Bible study and response exists. No class of older learners should ever be so tied to "the lesson" that freedom to turn to sensed needs does not exist. And, in a very real sense, the ultimate in a Bible learning situation may well exist when a group of believers meets together with no curriculum, but with a determination to share their needs and tensions, and to search the Scriptures to find—and to do—God's will.

In most Sunday school or "class" learning situations the core of the curriculum is not the ongoing experiences of the group, but rather blocks of biblical content. This is certainly not "bad." But it does create certain difficulties which the creative teacher must recognize and plan to resolve.

For one thing, it is easy to approach and cover the biblical content block simply on the idea level. We find out what the Bible says. We relate it to other passages of Scripture and to our total understanding of God's revealed plan and purposes. While this is basic, for maximum spiritual growth it is *necessary* to go on—not only to understand the truth in the biblical context, but to understand truth in the context of life now, to discover what God is saying to *me*, and how in this passage of His Word He calls me to respond to His words. The block of Bible content must, then, be taught with the focus on the existential, on the response God calls me to make.

A second problem is this. While all Scripture has response implications, and thus is practical and relevant for me now, I *may not sense a need for the truth taught*. In the experience core curriculum, this sense of need is the starting point, thus providing motivation both for learning and for response. In the Bible core curriculum, *the sense of need must often be created*.

By this I don't mean that a *false* sense of need must be developed in the learner. I mean that a real need does exist, always, for response to the Word God speaks to us. But we may not be aware that a need exists! The teacher must help the learner become aware of a need that is really there, but not yet felt.

Awakening a sense of need often takes place in the Look step of the learning process, where the Word, now understood, is related to our daily life. But for maximum motivation some steps toward the awakening of a sense of need must be taken at the beginning of the lesson. The Bible portion to be studied must be shown to have relevance. It must be seen by the learner as able to resolve a tension which, when pointed out, the learner will realize does exist. *The learner must see that he has a stake in the learning*. Thus we see again, and particularly so with the maturing student, the need for a Hook in the learning process.

The Scriptures

In this unit on teaching older students, as in the last unit on teaching children, I propose to illustrate a variety of learning activities which the creative teacher can adapt to accomplish the goals of each part of the learning process. A number of learning activities can be used to focus attention (which involves creating a sense of need and setting a learning goal), others for communicating content, still others for guiding to insight and for encouraging response.

I've chosen two passages of Scripture to develop in these chapters: John 14:22-24 and the book of Malachi. The first will be developed as a single lesson, the second as a unit of lessons in which each part of the teaching-learning process may take one or more sessions.

JOHN 14:22-24

This short segment records Jesus' answer to a question one of His disciples raised as He was about to be crucified. Christ had told of His departure and had promised that although He would not be physically present and thus could not be "seen" by the world, He would manifest Himself to these friends. The question raised is an extremely significant one:

> Lord, what then has happened that You are going to disclose Yourself to us, and not to the world? Jesus answered and said to him, If anyone loves Me, he will keep My word; and My Father will love him, and We will come to him, and make Our abode with him. He who does not love Me does not keep My words; and the word which you hear is not Mine, but the Father's who sent Me.

And the answer is *most* significant, for it reveals the secret of the believer's direct, personal experience of Christ, the One who makes His home with and within us.

The teaching aim, framed again in terms of the response desired, is

> to help each learner experience Jesus Christ
> as a Person who is real and present with him

MALACHI

This short four-chapter book concludes the Old Testament canon. It pictures God's people settled down again in indifference to Him, even though just a short half century has passed since the rebuilding of the walls of Jerusalem under the leadership of Nehemiah, marking an end to some of the major effects of the Babylonian captivity—a captivity ordained as a judgment for just the kind of sin and indifference we see reflected in this book!

The book pictures an indifferent society, a company of saints who slipped from coldness toward God into positive rebellion to His ways, while all the time justifying themselves and their behavior.

The book portrays a total pattern of unresponsiveness toward God which is too often characteristic of the life of the church today. And it clearly reveals God, in His character, His motives, His actions, and in His desire toward men who reject Him.

The teaching aim, necessarily a general one because of the complex of possible applications of the book to individuals and congregations today, is

> to become more responsive to God by evaluating
> our sensitivity to His will, using criteria revealed
> in Malachi

Experiencing Christ
(John 14:22-24)

Teaching aim: to help each learner experience Jesus Christ
as a Person who is real and present with him

The Hook activities for this lesson should be geared to awaken the learner's sense of need for personal experience with Christ—for a faith that exists as a vital relationship, not merely as a mental assent to biblical doctrines.

Approach 1

Display the following statement and ask for your students' reactions: "If I couldn't experience Christ's presence every day, I'd doubt the truth of Christianity."

If the class is unused to participation, you might attempt circular conversation (asking each to give his reaction in a sentence or two and moving from left to right around the circle) or neighbor nudging (pairs of students sharing their thinking with each other before throwing their ideas out to the whole group).

As reactions come, there will probably be both agreement and disagreement with the statement. Help bring the issue into focus by questions: How important is it that the Christian actually experience Christ? What is the role of a daily personal relationship with Christ in the believer's life? Are we satisfied that our Christian experience is real and vital and meaningful? Why or why not? What makes Christian experience "vital and meaningful"? Is a rather mystic awareness of the presence of Christ important for believers? etc.

The questions used will vary with the way discussion of the starter statement develops. But the teacher must attempt to help the class focus on and explore their experience of, or need for, actual *experience* of Christ.

Approach 2

Open the session by singing a hymn (such as "O Jesus, I Have Promised" or "I Need Thee Every Hour").

Then read through the words:

> O Jesus, I have promised to serve Thee to the end;
> Be Thou forever near me, my Master and my Friend:
> I shall not fear the battle if Thou art by my side,
> Nor wander from the pathway if Thou wilt be my guide.
>
> O let me feel Thee near me; the world is ever near;
> I see the sights that dazzle, the tempting sounds I hear:
> My foes are ever near me, around me and within;
> But, Jesus, draw Thou nearer, and shield my soul from sin.

Discuss these phrases, asking your class whether they are merely nice sentiments to sing or if the songwriter pictures hard reality. Can we "feel Thee ever near"? Can we sense Jesus at our side or know His guidance? Is this the common experience of Christians? Why or why not? Are Christians missing out on God's best if they don't *experience* Christ as "here" as well as believe that He is real "out there"?

Approach 3

Ask two members of your class to prepare to debate the following:

Resolved: No one can really know that Jesus Christ is alive today.
The person taking the affirmative should emphasize the "scientific
method" sense of knowing, stressing that there is no possible way to
empirically verify Christ's present existence or state. The one taking
the negative should stress not only biblical teachings but particularly
the claims of believers (in Scripture, throughout history, and in
modern days) to have experienced a daily relationship with Him.

After the debate has focused the issue, let class members discuss
the positions represented and share their ideas. Encourage them to
explore their own personal experience with Christ. Are they satisfied? Do they think there may be more of a depth relationship available to them? How important is it for the Christian to experience
Christ?

Approach 4

As class members come in, give each a poll slip, asking him to
respond anonymously and then return it. On the slip have the following:

> How would you be *most likely* to respond if a friend said, "I don't
> see how anyone today can believe that Jesus was anything more
> than a good man."
>
> _____ (a)   Turn to Bible prophecy to prove Christ is God.
> _____ (b)   Point to Christ's own claim of deity as recorded in
>   the gospels.
> _____ (c)   Tell of your personal daily experience with Christ.
> _____ (d)   Other (explain) _____

Tabulate the results and discuss the reasons for each response
given. When you discuss (*c*), encourage the students who did *not*
check it to explain why. Encourage those who did to explain also.

Lead the group to a discussion of the role of direct daily experience of Christ in the Christian life. Use question patterns like those
suggested in earlier approaches.

Approach 5

Give each student a blank sheet of paper and ask him to write a brief description of one time this past week when he was aware of the presence of Christ: when he might say that Christ "showed" Himself to him. Anyone who is uncertain can either leave the sheet blank or briefly share uncertainties he has about the task.

Collect the papers and read one or two. Then invite discussion of the task assigned. Should we be able to describe such a time? Can we expect Christ to be real in our daily experience? How? Or why not? What is the role of personal relationship with Christ in Christian experience? etc.

In each case a simple statement of the goal of the day's learning—that we might each actually experience Jesus Christ as a Person who is real and really with us—can serve as a transition into the study of the biblical content.

Routine and Reality?

(Malachi)

Teaching aim: to become more responsive to God by evaluating
our sensitivity to His will, using criteria
revealed in Malachi

The study of Malachi demands an extended, or unit, approach. The unit developed in these chapters is in eight basic sessions, any of which can be expanded to two or more sessions as the class may desire. The whole unit, visualized below, expands the Hook, Book, Look and Took processes and gives one or more whole sessions to each segment of the total learning experience.

Thus in Hook activity options developed in this chapter, far greater creative possibilities exist. And there is room within the structure for the use of several activities, which together focus the learner's awareness of need for this study. All, however, need to help the learner sense a personal need for evaluation—of himself and of the fellowship of which he is a part.

MALACHI

HOOK	BOOK			LOOK			TOOK
1. Launching	2. Malachi 1:1—2:9	3. Malachi 2:10—3:5	4. Malachi 3:6—4:6	5. Team	6. Study	7. Reports	8. Response

Fig. 24. STRUCTURE OF THE LEARNING UNIT

Preparation

In preparation for launching, prepare and display posters of biblical injunctions for self-judgment. Such verses as these may be used: "We shall all stand before the judgment-seat of God" (Rom. 14:10); "For it is time for judgment to begin with the household of God" (I Peter 4:17); "Let him who thinks he stands take heed lest he fall" (I Cor. 10:12); etc.

The teacher will also need to prepare materials to be used (see suggestions in various approaches, below).

Approach 1

Prepare a slide/tape presentation designed to challenge the group's acceptance of common personal and church practices. The presentation is not designed to *condemn* individuals or the church, but rather to forcefully present the need for critical self-evaluation.

Tape-record a dynamic and impressive reading of Isaiah 1:1-17. Take pictures of a variety of situations in your church and community which will correlate with the passages read. For instance, verses 11-13 (RSV):

"What to me is the multitude of your
        sacrifices? says the Lord;
I have had enough of burnt offerings
        of rams

and of the fat of fed beasts;
I do not delight in the blood of bulls,
    or of lambs, or of he-goats.

"When you come to appear before me,
    who requires of you
    this trampling of my courts?
Bring no more empty offerings."

When this passage is read, show scenes of your own members at worship, giving their offerings, standing outside the church in "Sunday best," teaching, etc.
    Or Isaiah 1:15-17:

"When you spread forth your hands,
    I will hide my eyes from you;
even though you make many prayers,
    I will not listen;
    your hands are full of blood.
Wash yourselves; make yourselves
    clean;
    remove the evil of your doings
    from before my eyes;
cease to do evil,
    learn to do good;
seek justice,
    correct oppression;
defend the fatherless,
    plead for the widow."

With such a passage you might show pictures of the sex magazines at the corner drugstore, composite headlines on youth crime in your community, substandard housing, an orphanage, etc.
    Your group may strongly react to the implication that we and our churches are like the nation Judah which God condemned. Let everyone express himself and argue all he wishes for or against the implied judgment. Then raise the issue of criteria. How do we tell if our worship is an empty show? If our religious habits are just that

—habits—how do we know if we're fulfilling our responsibilities as Christ's representatives to those in need? How do we know if our church is?

Conclude the discussion and the session with a brief introduction to the book of Malachi—it's historical setting, and the fact that in it God provides clear guidelines by which we can measure our sensitivity and responsiveness to Him. State the goal for the series—that we all might become more responsive to God by evaluating our present sensitivity to His will, using criteria revealed in Malachi.

Approach 2

Tape-record the following statements for your group to evaluate:

I think I must be the worst Christian that ever lived. I try to do better but—well, to be honest, too many times I don't even try. I don't know why I don't care more about what God wants. It seems that whenever there's a choice to make, I do what appeals to me, without thinking about what He'd like me to do. Maybe it's partly the church's fault. Everyone goes to church and goes through the motions. They sing loud, and bow their heads when the pastor prays, and look at him when he preaches, but as soon as they're outside they talk about everything but the Lord. I get the feeling that sometimes they just can't wait to get outside.

But I guess I shouldn't blame them for my failings. I know it's not their fault if I feel so helpless and so useless all the time. It's my fault. I know I can't live up to anything God wants. They just don't come any more worthless than me.

* * *

If there's anything that we've got to be proud of in this church, it's the way we go all out for the Lord. Why, look at our missions budget. It's up $2,300 over last year! And we were the highest in our state association then. And we're always out to church for the meetings. The church is full Sunday mornings, Sunday evenings, and even for Wednesday prayer meeting.

Personally, I'm thrilled to have a place in this church. An important one, too. I'm chairman of the finance committee, on the board, and one they always call on when it comes to helping with any problem. My wife teaches Sunday school, and my son is the president of the youth fellowship. And last year my youngest daughter won a week at camp by memorizing Bible verses.

Now, I'm not proud or anything. I know that the Lord has blessed, and I want to give Him all the credit. But it sure is great to be so blessed, and to know that you're really going all out for God. They just don't come any more dedicated than we are here.

Play both tapes, asking each member of your group to jot down his thoughts after each is played. Give your group a few minutes to compare, in twos, their evaluations of the two monologues. Move then into a general discussion. What seems to be the basic attitude of each individual about himself? About his church? About his relationship with the Lord? On what is this thinking based? How can we tell whether or not such evaluations are accurate? Throughout the discussion of the above questions, keep a chalkboard list of class ideas, comparisons and contrasts.

As the group becomes more involved, the class can be divided into smaller buzz groups of four to six individuals to discuss issues like the following: If we were to evaluate our own church, which of the two would we say is *more like* ours? If we were to evaluate ourselves, which person would we be more like? Why? On what criteria did we decide?

One member of each group should keep a listing of the *criteria* by which the members felt individuals and a church might be evaluated. These can be reported to the whole class when the buzz sessions are over. Near the end of the class, the leader should summarize, and introduce the study of Malachi as suggested in approach 1.

Approach 3

In preparation for this unit, select three class members to attempt an evaluation of the general sensitivity of the church and of class members to God's will. Each of the three might be given a separate area of research, roughly paralleling the three areas covered in Malachi: personal relationship with God; commitment to God's standards of concern and righteousness in interpersonal and community relations; demonstrated values and priorities. Each of the three should be free to develop his own ideas. On the launching day, the three can serve on a panel and each report his research and thinking. The panel might then briefly discuss "The Status Quo."

Then involve the whole class in interaction with the panel. Encourage all to express agreement with the panel or to challenge it. After a time of free discussion, lead the group to think of criteria by which such areas might be evaluated. Why is evaluation important? How *do* we know whether we're really sensitive to God's leading or if we've just fallen into a routine and a rut? Near the end of the period, introduce Malachi and the unit.

Approach 4

Give an evaluation form (see fig. 25) to each member of the group. Encourage each to place both *himself* and your *church* on continuum scale. When all have finished evaluating, draw the form on the board and ask for reports on where the group placed your church in each item.

Watch for areas in which there are discrepancies in evaluation. In such cases ask those who disagree with each other to explain the criteria on which they made their determination. Encourage class discussion through the process of working out a composite evaluation.

When the composite evaluation is completed, ask your group to say how they *know* the evaluation is accurate? Are the criteria on which they evaluated God's criteria? How does God judge a congregation or an individual? What does He expect?

Near the end of class, introduce Malachi as previously suggested. Be sure to record the class composite evaluation for later use. And encourage each individual to keep his own self-evaluation.

How Do We Rate?

Place the appropriate sign on each continuous line below, to indicate your evaluation of our church (o) and yourself (x) in each area.

not honoring God _____	honoring God fully
in-different to God _____	totally committed to bring Him praise
morally stained _____	living in full holiness
indifferent to injustice around _____	deeply concerned with justice for all
withholding money, time and self _____	fully committing finances, time, self to God
concerned primarily about own well-being _____	concerned primarily about God's will

Fig. 25. CHART FOR APPROACH 4

Research and assignment
    for the student

1. Examine several publishers' adult curricula and evaluate (a) the overall philosophy of the lessons, (b) the effectiveness and function of the Hook activities.
2. For each of the two passages being developed in these chapters write up, to hand in, two more Hook learning activities.
3. Select a passage of no more than twenty verses in the New Testament to develop as a one-session adult lesson. Write out your aim and three different Hook learning activities.
4. Be prepared to relate what the author says in chapter 11 concerning motivating the learner to the learning activities suggested for the Malachi lesson. Show carefully which structural and relationship factors are present, and how they are being worked out. If you feel any approaches can be improved, show specifically how motivational factors can be injected.
5. *Before reading on,* study the book of Malachi and jot down how you might plan to cover the content in each of the three segments suggested in figure 24.

Exploration
    for the lay teacher
1. Look through all the lessons in your curriculum materials for this
   quarter and evaluate the Hook learning activities. Do they actually
   give the learner a stake in the lesson? A reason to learn?
2. Plan at least two Hook activities for your next lesson and try one of
   them. Evaluate the results.

22

COMMUNICATING CONTENT

Teaching, for Evangelicals, is *Bible* teaching. And so the communication of content takes a central and often dominating role in the class session.

It is, of course, right that the communication of content be considered basic. Content *is* basic. We meet God in His Word. He communicates truth and Himself to us there. And thus it is essential that the Word be taught and that the

words of Scripture be rightly interpreted and understood.

But it is not necessary that communication of content—particularly a teacher-given monologue or sermon—dominate classtime. It's possible to communicate content creatively. It's possible to encourage each class member to take responsibility for personal study. It's possible to make the study of the Book an interactive process.

ACTIVE STUDENT PARTICIPATION

ONE MAJOR PURPOSE of teaching in our churches should be to encourage and help older students learn how to study the Bible for themselves. The kind of class that is built around the biblical knowledge and skills of an "expert" (be he a lay teacher or the pastor) does not normally encourage the average member to personal involvement with Scripture. In practice today we too often *discourage* such involvement and promote the idea that only a specially gifted individual can handle and understand the Word of God right.

Not that we believe this. We believe that God speaks to each believer who searches His Word. We believe that the Holy Spirit is our Teacher. But in practice we tend to make passive listeners, not active participants, of older learners.

The learning activities suggested in this chapter highlight approaches which encourage the active involvement of all class members in direct Bible study.

This is not to say that lecture is not a valid or important method in Bible teaching. Lecture is important—and has many advantages. When, for economy of time, much material needs to be covered and covered clearly, lecture is probably the best method. But lecture cannot become the *only* method of communicating content, not if high schoolers and adults really should be encouraged to get into the Word for themselves.

In this segment of the lesson, then, we are concerned with discovering what God is actually saying in the passage studied, and with helping the learners to a clear understanding of His message.

Experiencing Christ
(John 14:22-24)

Teaching aim: to help each learner experience Jesus Christ
                  as a Person who is real and present with him

Approach 1

Content can be easily and quickly covered by taking a lecture approach. For this passage the teacher should first sketch the situation (the context) in which the question is first raised, and which forms the background for Christ's answer.

The key points in these verses hinge on the meaning of *to manifest* and the role given here to the Word. These can be covered by explaining that the word *manifest* means, in the original, "to make visible," "to make known, clear." Thus the disciple is asking how Christ can be an experienced reality to the believer, while He is not so known by the world.

The Word, which, Christ stresses, is the Father's, is to be kept (obeyed) by the believer. Only when the life of the believer is lived in obedience to the words of Christ will the Father and Son be present in his life in such a way that this presence is experienced.

What is the relationship between the Word and experiencing Christ's presence? It might be visualized as in figure 26. The Bible consistently presents the Word as in full harmony with ultimate reality. Scripture is God's Word. Because God is the Creator and Sustainer, He is the One who defines what is truly *real*; real in relationship with Him, in interpersonal relationships, in all things. Thus Christ's words not only command us, but guide us into the kind of life which is in full and complete harmony with redeemed human nature and God's will. The one who loves Christ keeps His words, and thus his *experience* begins to match up with what is real! And it is at this place where God is known experientially, where Christ is "made visible."

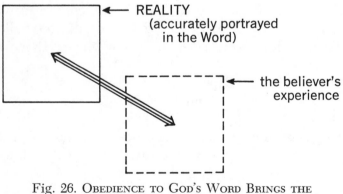

Fig. 26. OBEDIENCE TO GOD'S WORD BRINGS THE BELIEVER'S EXPERIENCE INTO HARMONY WITH REALITY

There are many competing philosophies of life, many seemingly wise ways, but all are mirages. Only God's way, as revealed in words in Scripture, leads us past the mirages of life to find and to experience reality.

Approach 2

Rather than cover the material yourself, ask two students to research the two key areas and prepare reports for the class. One should be assigned the word *manifest*, and asked to learn what the original word means and how it is used in Scripture. Anyone with a concordance which distinguishes the words used in the original (such as *Young's Analytical Concordance to the Bible*) can discover which Greek word was used and what it means. Further research might be done in a commentary or in one of the excellent Greek-English helps available.

A second student should be asked to research the interplay in the passage of *word* and *words*. Why is the last phrase of verse 24 significant?

After the reports are given, summarize and integrate the information they provide, using the chart suggested with approach 1.

Approach 3

Rather than lecturing, divide your class into twos, giving each pair a list of key questions they are to attempt to answer from a study of the passage. Encourage your class members to use different translations when undertaking such a study.

Questions which might be used with this passage are

1. What led up to the disciple's question (cf. 14:18-21)?
2. What does *manifest* seem to mean in this context?
3. What condition(s) does Christ set down that must be met if He is to be manifested to the believer?
4. What promises are associated with the conditions?
5. What reason is suggested or implied for the importance of keeping Christ's Word? Why does the Word play such a vital role?

When the questions have been discussed by the twosomes, their answers can be shared with the group; then a summary by you can point up the ideas expressed in approach 1.

Approach 4

Divide the class into buzz groups of four to six individuals for a study of related passages which may clarify the meaning and impact of this passage.

Sketch the background of the question and point up the nature of the question Christ's disciple was asking. Have prepared slips of paper on which assignments for the buzz groups are written.

Give each group two or more of the questions suggested above. Or choose other parallel passages of Scripture (such as I Cor. 2:9– 3:13; James 1:19-25; I John 3:19-24) which may give your students insights into the passage being studied.

Approach 5

The week before you cover this passage in class, ask each class member to read the larger context at home and to look up John 14:22-24 in at least one commentary.

If you wish, you may also give out a guide question list (such as is included in approach 3).

Classtime can then be used by the students to share their discoveries and broaden the understanding of Christ's answer to His disciple's question.

Additional methods

There are many methods available for encouraging preparation by the students for the class hour. Approach 5 illustrates just one. Here is a partial listing of other approaches which might be taken, depending on their suitability to the particular passage to be covered.

Readings

1. Read different interpretations of the passage to be studied.
2. Read from a preselected bibliography.
3. Read parallel accounts in Scripture.
4. Read various versions.
5. Read as specific preparation for discussion.
6. Read to prepare an oral or written report.

7. Read looking for relationships (why, where, when, which, how).
8. Read to survey, evaluate, defend, compare, solve.
9. Read to outline or summarize.
10. Read repeatedly.
11. Read to memorize.
12. Read to answer prepared questions.

Projects

1. Construct charts and graphs.
2. Diagram a passage of Scripture.
3. Prepare a quiz or test on the subject being studied.
4. Develop outline of subject.
5. Prepare oral report.
6. Prepare a research paper on topic.
7. Prepare for a drama in class.
8. Prepare for a panel, forum or discussion.
9. Prepare with others for a debate.
10. Prepare audio-visuals to present topic.
11. Write subject up as a story or newspaper article.
12. Define terms without any outside aid.
13. Conduct a personal-opinion poll on topic.
14. Develop time-line for history.
15. Create a poster, display or exhibit for the hour.
16. Share with class a poem or story in own words.

Interviews and Surveys

1. Interview resource individuals on subject.
2. Interview "man on the street" for his opinion.
3. Prepare and distribute a questionnaire.
4. Collate and analyze responses to survey.
5. Make list of problems people have with this subject.

Questions

1. Give questions to be answered in class.
2. Give questions to be answered by selected readings.
3. Give questions to be answered in writing.
4. Give questions to be answered by experience.

5. Give questions based on previous classes as foundation for next session.
6. Have students prepare a list of personal questions they have regarding the subject.
7. Give thought-provoking questions.
8. Have students prepare a set of questions they would ask on an examination of the subject.

Problem Solving

1. Give a real-life problem to be solved.
2. Give opposite view as a problem to be solved.
3. Use case studies as problem for solving.
4. Make up a hypothetical problem related to subject.
5. Set up problem in class, then dismiss and allow class to work on it.
6. State problem and various solutions, asking class to pick the best.
7. Allow students to create or relate their own problems and then solve them.
8. Have students list all possible solutions to a problem.
9. Have students develop a method for solving problems.
10. Give erroneous facts or materials on some problem.

Written Assignments
1. List implications of truth on this subject.
2. Write a commentary, report, paper, etc.
3. Write out answers to questions and solution to problem.
4. Write a defense for your position.
5. Write out a list of personal definitions on topic.
6. Write letters, tracts, poems, drama, testimony, etc.
7. Outline a reading or Scripture passage.
8. Paraphrase a Scripture portion.
9. Write a paper on "What _____ Means to Me."

Group Work
1. Discussion with others in small informal groups before class session.
2. Discussion between opponents on topic.
3. Meet in group to plan and prepare to teach the class.
4. Group work on projects to present in class.

5. Meet to prepare a debate, panel, drama, etc., for class.
6. Assign different groups to work on separate aspects of the subject and report to class.
7. Meet after individual readings and preparation to discuss topic.

Routine or Reality?

(Malachi)

Teaching aim: to become more responsive to God by evaluating our sensitivity to His will, using criteria revealed in Malachi

In the basic plan of approach to Malachi (see fig. 24) three separate class sessions are devoted to a study of biblical content. The whole book might be outlined, and the content presentation surveyed, as follows:

Segment	Session	Source
I. Historical setting	Launching (1)	Collateral readings
II. Relationship with God	(2)	Malachi 1:1–2:9
III. Relationship with men	(3)	Malachi 2:10–3:5
IV. Relationship with self	(4)	Malachi 3:6-15
V. Warning and hope	(4)	Malachi 3:16–4:6

In summary, Malachi shows that the people of God, even after the judgment of God on their fathers, were now unresponsive and indifferent to Him (II), were uncaring and heedless of others' needs and rights (III), and were completely self-centered in all they did and thought and valued (IV). While the society was thus abandoned by God to judgment, individuals who feared the Lord came together to speak of Him and encourage each other in obedience (V). These were remembered and honored by the God whom they honored; the rest were warned of judgment to come.

The task now is to discover why God judges these people. What are the criteria on which He rejects them? Let's see a number of ways in which our students can become involved (in class or before class) in studying the message of the passage. For brevity's sake, we'll look at the approaches tailored to segment II, Malachi 1:1–2:9.

Approach 1

Give each student a chart (fig. 27), which organizes the passage around the three cynical questions asked God by His people. Have each student study the passage and complete the chart by filling in the blank columns.

Question	God seen as	The appropriate response to God	Their response to God
How have You loved us? (1:2)	loving		
How have we despised Your name? (1:6)	a Father a Master		
How have we polluted Your altar?	Lord of hosts the great King		

Fig. 27. MALACHI CHART

Then discuss in some depth the response God's character called for, and the response these people made. Or this may be done by the entire class during your session.

Approach 2

Ask each student to write a two-paragraph summary of the heart of the message of Malachi 1:1–2:9. Compare the summaries and discuss differences. This will drive your students back into the passage to explain their impressions, and it will involve the whole group in a joint effort to locate and clarify the major issues.

Approach 3

Ask each student to read through the passage and place the following symbols beside each verse which

a. raises a question in his mind (?)
b. tells something about the person of God ( )
c. pictures the thinking or actions of God's people ( )
d. seems to have parallels in modern life ( )

Each should compare those verses beside which symbols *b* and *c* have been placed, to get a clearer picture of what the passage teaches in each area.

Most students, by the way, will question such phrases as "Jacob have I loved, but Esau have I hated" (1:2-3). The teacher will need to explain that this is a common Near Eastern formula used by a father in his will. The word *loved* indicates the one whom the father has chosen to inherit; *hated* indicates a decisive legal rejection of any rival claim. The formula does not necessarily imply animosity or anger, as *hated* does in our culture.

Approach 4

Ask each student to write out a character sketch of (*a*) God's people as portrayed in Malachi 1:1–2:9 and of (*b*) God as portrayed in the same passage.

Read several sketches and then discuss the biblical evidence on which these are developed. In what ways was the character of the people evidenced? How is such character manifested today?

Approach 5

Have each student make an analytical outline of the passage. Outlining should point up the major thrust of the passage clearly, and need not be completely accurate to be of great value.

For instance here is one adult's outline:

I. God's Love for Israel (1:1-5)
   A. God expresses love for Israel (1:2)
   B. Israel questions God's love (1:2)
   C. God demonstrates His love (1:2-5)
      1. God chose Jacob over Esau
      2. God has wasted Esau's country
      3. God will keep on tearing down his country
         (Note: it is for their "wickedness," 1:5)
      4. God will keep His people's borders

II. Israel's Dishonoring God (1:6-9)
   A. God says He gets no honor from Israel (1:6)
   B. Israel questions this (1:6)
   C. God proves His point
      1. Offer of polluted food on the altar
      2. Sacrifice of worthless animals
         (something they wouldn't dare give to a human governor!)
   D. God refuses to accept their offerings
      1. He is great over all the world
      2. They give of their worst
      3. They are bored with His worship
   E. God warns the priests
      1. He will curse them if they do not give Him glory
      2. They don't really worship or fear God
      3. They don't live uprightly
      4. They have led others astray, away from God

Approach 6

Note that in each of the approaches suggested above a necessary next step is to relate the failings of God's Old Testament people, together with the criteria God used to judge them, to us today.

While it is true that in the unit approach most of the Look process, of seeking insight into the meaning of the biblical message for twentieth century life, will take place later in other sessions, some definite attempt to begin that relating process must take place in the Book sessions.

Each of the methods suggested above are easily taken this step further. Two new columns can be added to the chart (fig. 27) in approach 1: "What should *our* response be?" and "What *is* our response?" In other approaches a shift to modern life is equally as easy. In the last approach, for instance, the question can be raised, "If God were writing about us today, what would be His possible evidence under I:C and II:C?

At the same time, some approaches to content demand both a careful study of the text and a thoughtful attempt to spell out its implications.

One of these is the "modern paraphrase." Select one or two significant segments of the passage and ask the students to rewrite them as though they were being spoken to us in America today. For this passage you might select Malachi 1:6-9, 1:11-13, and perhaps 2:6-9.

Approach 7

Divide your class into three teams, each of which is to present one of the three major sections of Malachi. Ask the team assigned the first section to develop and present a two-part drama, which will portray in the lives of twentieth century people the characteristics which God condemned in the people of Malachi's day.

One of the team members should lead a general discussion of the drama afterward, showing the parallels between Malachi and modern life that exist and that were dramatically developed.

The challenge to justify or to invalidate the conclusions thus presented will drive the whole group into the text for further study and discussion.

Research and assignment
    for the student
1. Use the guidelines given in this chapter to develop, in detail, three alternate approaches for covering the content of the next two sessions on Malachi (2:10—3:5; 3:6—4:6).
2. Study the presentation of content suggested in one adult curriculum. What methods are suggested? What conclusions can you draw from your study?
3. Evaluate the differences between content coverage possibilities in a unit approach to Bible teaching v. a "single class" approach.
4. Evaluate the methods suggested and those illustrated in this chapter.

Which are most adapted to an "in class" study of content, and which to a "before class" study by the students?

5. Write out: What are the implications for creative Bible teaching of preparation by older students before class?

6. Continue to work on the New Testament passage for which you began to construct a lesson plan (chap. 21, R & A 4). Develop at least five approaches to covering its content.

7. The author suggests that one goal of teaching is to help learners get into the Bible for themselves. Evaluate each of the learning activities illustrated in this chapter as to its effectiveness for this purpose. How important do *you* feel this goal is in Bible teaching?

Exploration
    for the lay teacher

1. Evaluate the approach to content communication taken in your present curriculum. Is it satisfactory? Why or why not?

2. Plan at least three ways of gaining student involvement in the content segment of your next Sunday's lesson. Use one of them. Then write out an evaluation of what happened and why.

23

GUIDING
TO INSIGHT

"Open up your life, and let the Word shine in."

No, that's not what the old familiar chorus really says. But that's what has to happen when youth and adults come together to study the Bible.

God's Word has to shine into every relationship, every activity. We have to discover what it means for us, individually, to keep His words, and Christ has to be invited in to control. We have to be "doers of the word, and not hearers only."

For the Word to so permeate our experience, we have to open up our life. We have to open it up to ourselves and consciously explore the harmony or disharmony of our experience with God's will. We have to open it up to God and be honest with Him and ourselves. And, strikingly, we have to open ourselves to one another, to be willing to share not only our experiences with Christ, but also our needs and failures.

This isn't easy for any of us. But this is what has to happen if we're truly going to guide our learners to insight.

EXERCISE OF SPIRITUAL GIFTS

IN EARLIER CHAPTERS (8, 10, 11) we've discussed the importance of encouraging and guiding our learners to make their own application of Scripture, to discover for themselves where and how a passage studied relates to their experience, to define for themselves just what response God is calling them to make.

As we think of guiding youth and adults in this process, it's important to note another dimension of the process which we want to develop. And that dimension relates to the exercise of spiritual gifts.

We've all read in the Bible of "spiritual gifts"—special abilities, or special ways the Holy Spirit chooses to work through individuals. There are representative lists of such gifts, or special ministries, in Romans 12, in I Corinthians 12, and in Ephesians 4.

What is significant for us is that (1) the Bible says *every* believer has a spiritual gift—a special ministry to perform—and (2) the Bible ties spiritual growth of the church to the exercise of these gifts! The Bible says the whole body grows "by that which every joint supplies, according to the proper working of each individual part" (Eph. 4:16). Spiritual growth for the group and for individuals is dependent on each believer's ministering to others, and being himself ministered to.

This is a dimension we have lost in much contemporary church life. Too often "ministry" has been seen as the work of the pastor or appointed teacher, and the layman in the class and church service has been a passive listener. One of the most exciting developments in our day is the growing movement to return to the practice of *mutual ministry*—of believers sharing with believers in groups which together study the Word of God.

The Look step in the process we've described in this book demands just this kind of open sharing—sharing which is clearly centered on the Word of God and which encourages expression of each person's experience with Christ. *It is this context that gives maximum opportunity for exercise of spiritual gifts.* And it is this context of openness which Look learning activities must encourage and develop.

Openness and meaningful sharing do not come quickly or easily. But they do come. They come when the teacher understands what the Look process is to be. They come when the teacher resists taking an authoritarian role and instead stimulates his students to take full responsibility for discovering and discussing the implications of the Word studied. They come when the teacher encourages a free and spontaneously developing discussion.

Let's see some learning activities that can be used to help reach this goal.

Experiencing Christ
(John 14:22-24)

Teaching aim: to help each learner experience Jesus Christ
as a Person who is real and present with him

The stress in this passage, as developed in the last chapter, is on the relationship of keeping Christ's words to reality in Christian experience. The generalization might be stated this way: Christ is experienced as a real, present Person when the believer is responsive and obedient to His Word.

The Look activities should help the group explore the implications of this truth for them, help them define in what areas of life each needs to become more responsive and obedient, and help them see how this might be done.

Approach 1

Give each class member an area checklist (see fig. 28). Ask all individually, in pairs, or in groups of three or four, to check those areas in which they feel most of us today find it difficult to remain in full harmony with Scripture's teaching. Ask them then to indicate in one of the two columns to the right the most likely reason for this difficulty.

When the class has finished, compare and discuss their evaluations. As discussion develops, encourage the group to share ideas as to what they need to do to become more responsive.

Approach 2

Ask your class to analyze one or more of the following case histories and apply the teaching of John 14:22-24 as it seems relevant.

Areas of Life	Difficulty level	Reason for Difficulty	
		Don't <u>know</u> biblical principles	Unwilling to apply biblical principles
Home			

Relationships
  husband/wife
  children
  other			

Responsibilities
  material
  social
  spiritual
  (etc.)			

Job			

Relationships
  boss
  co-workers
  subordinates			

Responsibilities
  to company
  to customers
  to fellow employees
  witness
  (etc.)			

Church			

Relationships
  pastor
  friends
  members			

Responsibilities
  financial involvement
  (etc.)			

Neighbors (etc.)			
Community (etc.)			

Fig. 28. LIFE-RESPONSE AREA CHECKLIST
Rank level of difficulty (1-high to 3-low)

The cases are designed to bring into focus different points at which an individual's ability or willingness to respond to God might break down. Encourage the class to identify these points as they discuss the cases, then to develop constructive suggestions on how to help each person.

Case one

Jack is a new believer who expected that becoming a Christian would solve all his problems. After his conversion, life at first seemed very exciting—sort of a daily adventure. But then things began to go wrong. Jack discovered he still had many of his old habits and desires, and that their pull was as strong as ever. He had a setback at work, and discovered that being a Christian didn't guarantee a comfortable life either. About now Jack is wondering if what he felt in those first weeks as a Christian wasn't all self-delusion.

Case two

Carol Ann has been going to church and Sunday school from early childhood. To her, Christianity has always been a part of life—but not the most significant part. The new pastor has been talking much of "dedication" and "reality," and this has disturbed Carol Ann. "What," she wonders, "does he mean? I've been a good Christian and a good person. But all this talk of 'reality' sounds so strange and foreign."

Case three

Frank is one of the leaders of the church, a person who knows his Bible well. He can quote down a lot of ministers when it comes to arguments on Scripture (and has done it!). But no one in the church really likes or trusts Frank. He has the reputation of being a politician and a manipulator. He's been known to cut down other Christians behind their backs. And in the business community he's regarded as too sharp to be trusted.

Approach 3

Ask two of your class to role-play a situation in which a person with a problem comes to a friend for counseling.

Give the one taking the part of the counselee enough information to form a picture of the feelings and character of the individual he's asked to play. Such information as is included in the case histories above (approach 2) is needed. Other than this basic picture of the person to be played, and a brief statement of the occasion on which they meet, no script is needed. Each speaks as he thinks the person he plays would speak.

Let the role play develop freely. When its direction and the approach of the counselor is defined, stop the action. Explore the feelings and ideas of each participant about the situation, then involve the group in evaluation. Did the counselor recognize the problem? How do *you* see the problem? Was the counselor able to help? How? What would help a person who is in this particular situation? Is there any way in which we are in situations similar to that shown in the role play? How? What are our problems? How does the passage we studied speak to us? What are we to do?

Approach 4

Write on the chalkboard several statements for the class to evaluate in view of John 14:22-24.

One or more statements, like

Most Christians today are only interested in God's second best for their lives.

Members of this class daily experience the reality which relationship with Christ makes possible.

We can help each other, as families and as friends, to experience Christ in the way He promised in this passage.

There is only one possible cause for our failure to go on as Christians and to develop a vital daily relationship with Christ.

Experiencing Christ sounds great, but there are a lot of good reasons why it's not for me.

I'd be willing to "do Christ's words" if I wasn't afraid of all the changes I'd have to make.

I don't really know anyone who honestly makes it his goal to do daily just what Christ wants him to do—in everything.

Is there a "first class" and "second class" for Christians, or do we all have to be in such terrible subjection?

If obedience to Christ is the measurement of our love for God, I guess we rate. . . .

One or more of these statements, or statements like them, should help to stimulate discussion and to guide your class toward exploring the implications of the truth studied in this passage.

Note that not all the statements are "true." Some even express a warped view. But each demands evaluation, not a yes or no reaction. And each is related to the truth revealed in the Bible passage studied.

Routine or Reality?
(Malachi)

Teaching aim: to become more responsive to God by evaluating our sensitivity to His will, using criteria revealed in Malachi

In structuring the unit on Malachi, several options as to arrangement of sessions and learning activities exist.

For instance, it would be possible to organize the unit with a Look session following each content unit, like this:

Launch	Malachi 1:1—2:9	Look	Malachi 2:10—3:5	Look	Malachi 3:6—4:6	Look	Took

Or the unit could be organized to permit a series of Look sessions following a series of content coverage sessions, like this:

Launch	Malachi 1:1—2:9	Malachi 2:10—3:5	Malachi 3:6—4:6	Look			Took
				─────────────────────────►			

This second option opens up at least two possible approaches. (1) The implications of the message of Malachi as a whole can be discussed in the three sessions set apart for guiding to insight. (2) One of the three sessions can be related to each of the three content sessions. It is this second approach that is suggested here. Why? Because application of the message of Malachi to today demands a careful investigation of our contemporary church and personal practices. Adequate application to twentieth century America of Malachi's revelation of God's expectations for His people demands that we get beneath the surface of what is so commonly accepted, and thus so seldom honestly examined.

I noted in the last chapter that we should begin to explore the implications of Malachi as a part of our study of the biblical text. Thus the methods suggested for communicating content contained questions and activities which encouraged the students to seek parallels in modern life (see pp. 249 f.). For a series such as this to be most meaningful to the students, and for it to utilize the factors discussed in chapter 11, some relationship of Malachi to our lives, *now*, should be established in the content segments—although they need not necessarily be *developed* there.

The approach taken in this unit, then, requires that some awareness of the relevance of Malachi be established in the content study itself. And it expects that students who are particularly interested in an aspect of the study will take responsibility for further research.

The relationship of the Book and Look sessions in this unit might be visualized as follows:

Thus the Look process, begun in session 2, will be continued and completed in session 5, *with the delay designed to enable a team of class members to examine in some depth practices of our own which Malachi's message may call into question.*

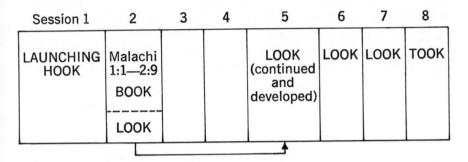

Session 1	2	3	4	5	6	7	8
LAUNCHING HOOK	Malachi 1:1—2:9 BOOK ------- LOOK			LOOK (continued and developed)	LOOK	LOOK	TOOK

LOOK ACTIVITIES IN THE CONTENT SESSION

When thinking, then, of the Look process, we need to remember that learning activities should be structured for sessions 2, 3 and 4, which will help the group *begin* to explore contemporary questions the Malachi message may raise. What might such activities be?

Approach 1

Add two columns to the chart suggested for approach 1 in chapter 22 (fig. 27). One column should be captioned "What should our response be?" and the other "What *is* our response?"

As these columns are completed by the class, ask how we can be sure that our practices are not as routinized and unrelated to God's desire for us as were the practices of Malachi's day.

Approach 2

Tape-record comments of several college youth on Sunday school and church. Young people today tend to be critical of the institutional church. Many feel that we *are* expressing a deadened ritualization like that of the Old Testament.

To stimulate their comments, read Isaiah 1:11-12 and ask a young person whether or not he feels this might be God's attitude toward the contemporary church. And ask why he feels as he does.

Play the reactions in class. Then ask your students to evaluate. Why do youth feel as they do? Is it possible that we *are*, in some ways at least, like the men of Malachi's day? How?

Approach 3

Ask the class what, if God were writing to us today, He might present to us as evidence of indifference and unresponsiveness to Him (see chap. 22, approach 5, p. 244).

Approach 4

Incorporate *application* as an integral part of the content covering technique. Note suggestions in chapter 22, approaches 6 and 7, on creative paraphrase and drama.

LOOK ACTIVITIES BEYOND THE CONTENT SESSION

In none of the approaches suggested above can any firm determination be made, nor can the actual situation be accurately sketched.

In this study, and *in many other Bible studies*, assessment of the implications of the Word for our day and our lives demands in-depth, continuing exploration. In this particular study let's suppose that several of the class members are concerned about our religious practices, as God was about the approaches of the Israelites (Mal. 1:6—2:9). Ask for five or six interested volunteers to look into the area and report back to the class in three weeks. At this point your role is to help the research team plan how to gather information for the report to the class in the later session. The learning activities they now undertake are *out of class* activities, which upon report to the class will stimulate more intelligent discussion in the follow-up session.

How then can the team explore the meaningfulness of our church life and practices?

Approach 1

Provide books and materials on the contemporary church. While much available today is simply critical, some writers attempt to evaluate and give constructive suggestions.

Materials which might be particularly helpful to such a team would include Keith Miller, *Taste of New Wine*; Walden Howard,

Nine Roads to Renewal; Wallace E. Fisher, *From Tradition to Mission*; Larry Richards, NAE study booklet, *Tomorrow's Church*, and others. Have each team member read at least one book or booklet and attempt to relate what is said to the Malachi passage. They should meet together to share their discoveries after one week.

The readings may open up several ways of reporting to the entire class, planned for session 5 of this study. Team members may serve as a panel, to summarize the thrust and ideas of contemporary writers; or quotes from the readings may be reproduced and mailed before class to each class member. The class members can then make comparison criticisms with Malachi 1:6–2:9 as preparation for class discussion.

Approach 2

After reading, the study team may decide that further research is needed. Areas of contemporary church life which are being questioned today may be isolated, and research may be done within their own congregation.

For instance, how effective is the church in reaching others in the community with the gospel? A survey of membership additions (checked whether by conversion or letter) or of recorded results of various agency ministries might be made. Or a spot check of the witnessing by lay members might be taken. Or a questionnaire asking church members to evaluate the contribution of the church to their lives (and giving specific criteria for the evaluation) might be developed and passed out.

Or a study of the youth in the church might be undertaken. How many drop out of church when they reach high school? Why do they leave? What is the attitude of those who stay on? Do they stay because they *want* to or because they have to? How do the youth evaluate the relevancy of the church ministries and activities to their lives?

Information thus gathered may be reported to the class, through charts, verbally, etc. Thus information needed to correctly assess the implications of Scripture to this particular fellowship can be provided.

Approach 3

The group might attempt to find believers in other churches who are experiencing what Keith Miller calls "the taste of new wine." Or a member of a church that is trying in various ways to make its services and ministries more relevant might be invited to share with the class what has been happening in his church.

Note that all of these approaches are designed to gather information to stimulate (1) further discussion and (2) evaluation of the impact of the Scripture studied. Each presumes that the hour set aside for further discussion will be a *discussion* session, a session in which the study team introduces enough information to make discussion meaningful, to give the group a basis for evaluation of the ideas under consideration.

The easy "Oh, we're all right" and the too quick "Everything today is horribly wrong" are both put to rest when facts replace unreasoned opinion in discussion, when that discussion is an open sharing between group members who are determined to understand and to do God's will as revealed in Scripture and applied under the Spirit's direction to the real situation in which they live.

In this process—this time of examining together the *meaning* of Scripture for us—the basic and ultimate method is discussion.

A quick check over the learning activities suggested in this chapter will demonstrate a significant fact: each is designed to stimulate discussion of the implications of God's Word for *us*, now!

In such discussion we exercise our spiritual gifts, and we minister to each other, *when we say what we really think and believe and feel in full commitment to each other and to the authority of the Word in our lives.* In this context of fellowship (Greek, *koinonia*, "sharing") the Holy Spirit works through each of us to minister to the others, and He leads each of us to a knowledge of His will for our lives. We discover together new unexpected ways in which God's Word calls us to response to Him.

TRANSFORMATION OF THE CLASS

I suggested in the introduction to this chapter that it isn't easy for us to enter into true fellowship with each other. To open up—to ourselves, to others, or even to God.

How does a traditional Sunday school class move from its traditional form—with a "teacher" telling truth and its "learners" passive listeners—to a group in which each ministers and each takes full responsibility for studying and applying the Word of God?

Part of the solution, I am convinced, is in understanding the process of interaction with Scripture presented in this book. As we come to the Word, not merely to learn information, but to open our lives to God's scrutiny and to seek out ways we can respond to Him, we will begin to grow spiritually.

Thus the learning activities a teacher plans must bring into clear focus the processes designed to guide the learners through the Colossian cycle (Hook, Book, Look, Took).

As we learn to share our thoughts and our experiences with each other, we come to know, to love, and to trust each other in Christ. It is then that we become a *fellowship*. Thus the learning activities a teacher plans must encourage interaction between the class members. They cannot be merely different ways for the teacher to perform.

Class members must become involved, involved with the Word and with each other.

Normally transformation from the "traditional" to the "fellowship" learning group will follow a pattern like this:

Phase 1. The teacher is the dominant figure in the group. He studies and prepares the lesson. In class he presents what he has learned from Scripture. In the majority of cases he also suggests several possible applications of the passage, which he presents with illustrations designed to help the students relate the truth taught to their lives. In this approach the teacher is the only truly active person and the only real learner! The students are passive, and are expected only to listen.

Phase 2. The teacher is still firmly in control of the class, but now has a clearer concept of planning the class session. He has begun to introduce participative methods, though he still tends to cover the biblical content in a lecture approach (to save time for the other parts of the lesson). All parts of the lesson are capsuled within the one hour available for class. And the major emphasis on class participation is found in the Look learning activities.

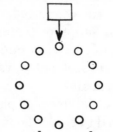

In initiating this phase, the teacher introduces participative methods slowly. He uses only one or two each session at first, still lecturing enough to help those feel secure for whom change is threatening. During a period of several months, more and more methods are introduced, until one or more learning activities are used for each process in the lesson structure.

After several months, the class will begin to *think* in the Colossians pattern. At that time the class members will begin to complain about the use of so many methods!

Why? Because the methods that at the beginning were needed to *stimulate* discussion will now be seen by the class as *inhibiting* it! The class will not *need* a structured learning activity to lead them to think together about practical implications of the Word studied. They will have learned how to learn together! They will be ready and eager to share and to discuss.

At this point, with the exception of retaining a good Hook and preparing several questions to help focus the discussion, the teacher will drop the use of methods and permit the class to explore the passage's meaning freely and *without direction from him*. The teacher will be ready to take his place as a learner with other learners, and will expect the Holy Spirit to guide in the class as each believer shares what the Word means to him.

Phase 3. The students are now willing to take responsibility for before-class study of the Scripture to be discussed. The teacher helps to design materials which will guide each in a personal study of the chosen passage. The group then comes together and the whole class period becomes, in effect, a Look discussion. The Book step has

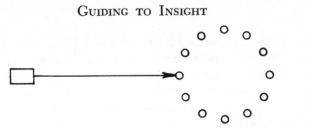

already been taken before class! Except for clarification of misunderstandings (which will come out in the discussion), the members understand that they are gathered for the purpose of discussing the implications of the Word for their lives, and to support one another in shared commitment to Jesus Christ.

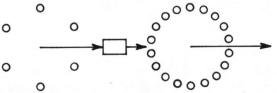

Phase 4. The teacher now is simply another member of the group, and the group takes full responsibility for all processes associated with the learning experience. The content to be covered is chosen by the group as the sharing members express needs they have in common. A resource library and the Bible knowledge of group members serve to locate portions of the Word which can be studied to discover God's answers in each area of need. And the group begins to have a life of its own, a life of spontaneous sharing of Christ's life, and one of mutual submission to His will.

Research and Assignment
    for the student
1. Evaluate the author's emphasis on "openness" and "meaningful sharing." Relate these ideas to (a) the transfer of learning process described in chapter 11, (b) the doctrine of spiritual gifts, and (c) the growth of the early church as recorded in Acts. What Acts passages imply the kind of situation the author describes? What other learning situations does Acts imply? How are these related?
2. Study the relationship of learning activity suggested in this chapter to *discussion.*
3. Read one secular and one religious education book on discussion. How does each view the importance of the role of discussion in learning? What guidelines for effective discussion are given? What are possible difficulties? How might these be overcome?

4. Develop from your own study of Malachi 2:10—3:5 and 3:6—4:6 three different "in class" and three "beyond class" Look learning activities which would be appropriate to the passages.
5. Continue to work on your New Testament passage lesson plan. Develop at least four learning activities which would help lead your students to insight.
6. Write a thoughtful evaluation of the approach the author takes to the study of Malachi. What are its advantages? Its disadvantages?
7. Be prepared for class discussion on the "transformation of the class" section of this chapter. Do you think this is needed in today's church? Why? Is it possible to remain at Phase 2, yet provide maximum guidance for lay learners? Why or why not?

Exploration
    for the lay teacher
1. Evaluate your present curriculum for Look activities. Does the lesson writer seem concerned with motivating class members to discuss the meaning of the Word, or is he satisfied to give you a "canned" application?
2. Plan three different Look activities for your lesson for next Sunday. Use at least one of them.
3. Where do you feel your class is in relationship to the phases of class development defined by the author? If you feel you need to move on to another phase, jot down the list of things you can do to help the class develop change.

24

ENCOURAGING
RESPONSE

"How should *I* respond to God?" This is ultimately and intensely a personal question. Each of us must respond as God the Holy Spirit leads—and He may lead each of us differently. The single command to witness, given to us all, may be used by God to point me to a neighbor, to direct him to establish a home Bible class, and to send you to the mission field.

Each life is different from each other—with its own opportunities, its own contacts, its own experiences. And only Jesus Christ, who is Lord of our lives and head of the church, has a right to direct us, by His words, into His perfect will for each individual.

Certainly God's Word is one. But our opportunities for response are infinite.

How then do we in teaching help each learner face the necessity of a **personal** response to God? How do we encourage each to seek God's leading for his own "doing" of the Word?

This we must do, for such is our task.

RESPONSE THROUGH FELLOWSHIP

SOMETIMES WE TEND to treat each other like mass-produced products. We teach a lesson on witnessing—and for an application ask everyone to pass out ten tracts during the next week. We teach a lesson on family living—and ask every dad to spend two hours alone with his oldest son during the next three days. We teach a lesson on Christian concern for others—and for application ask everyone to give one afternoon for visiting a shut-in. We teach a lesson—and plan a response *for everyone*, as if believers were rows of identical computers, waiting to be fed punched cards and then to whir into synchronized action.

But people aren't duplicates of each other. We're not mass-produced products. We're all handcrafted. We're all shaped by God's own hand, and each of us is unique, each fitted to just the tasks He has planned especially for us. And only God Himself can show a believer what *his* task is and how he is to perform it.

Thus the creative Bible teacher resists the temptation to make mass applications. Instead he plans ways to encourage learners to face the necessity of response and to seek God's leading for just the specific response each is to make.

This is one more reason why the Bible encourages us to develop a fellowship relationship with other Christians. It's one more reason why, when believers are ministering to each other, the church grows spiritually and numerically (Eph. 4:16). And this is another reason why the kind of Bible teaching presented in this book is vital. We must be involved in the Word of God, involved in the lives of one another, if we are to become all we can be in Christ. In many cases, learning activities designed to encourage response are actually ineffective apart from a fellowship context. Fellowship is basic to spiritual growth.

But what kind of learning activities can a teacher structure which, while the class is growing together, will help each realize his own need for response? What kind of learning activities will move the learner toward a personal decision to respond?

Experiencing Christ
(John 14:22-24)

Teaching aim: to help each learner experience Jesus Christ
as a Person who is real and present with him

The Look activities for this lesson have helped the group explore
some reasons for unresponsiveness and some ways a believer might
become more responsive. Some Look activities helped the class explore specific areas of life in which responsiveness to God was particularly needed. Took activities should correlate with the emphasis
in this class discussion.

Some possible Took activities are:

Approach 1

Ask each individual to circle or otherwise indicate the one area on
his chart (fig. 28) in which he feels a need to become more responsive to God. Conclude class by asking several class members to pray.
Ask the Lord to help each member experience Christ's presence as
he seeks to know and do God's will in the area circled.

Approach 2

At the conclusion of the case history analyses or the role play
situations suggested in the last chapter, ask each student to decide
which of the individuals discussed he is *more like*. What steps does
he need to take to become more responsive to God? Give time for a
short written self-analysis, then close in conversational prayer.

Approach 3

Ask the group to pray together about each one's responsiveness to
God this coming week. Tell the group that you'll give time next week
for sharing what God has done in their lives.

Approach 4

Give or send each married couple a follow-up question to discuss
during the week. "How can we guide our children to be more responsive to God?" or "How does our conversation at home show our
children that Christ is real to us?"

Approach 5

If the class has become a fellowship, in which each can trust the other, take time at the end of the discussion to share prayer requests. Encourage individuals to ask for support of the group as they sense personal problems and needs.

Routine or Reality?
(Malachi)

Teaching aim: to become more responsive to God by evaluating
our sensitivity to His will, using criteria
revealed in Malachi

Like the Look process, the Took in a unit study may begin in any of the sessions. Individuals may hear God's call to them as the Word is studied. Others may see more clearly what He desires as the implications of the Word are explored in the session set aside for that purpose. But a unit study normally demands at least one session of hard, conscious consideration by the group of the question "What must *we* do?"

A variety of approaches can be designed to help the group ask and answer that question. Here are some:

Approach 1

Repeat the slide/tape presentation with which the unit was launched (p. 233). Ask, "How did you react when you first saw this presentation? How do you feel about it now?"

As the learnings of the unit are summarized, challenge the group to define what, in light of the Word of God and the meanings they've discovered it has for them, they must do. What response does God demand of them?

Approach 2

Ask each study team, on the basis of the class discussion of their report, to draw up a series of proposals, attempting to define the action that they feel individuals and the class as a whole ought to take in response to God's Word.

Have each team present its proposals for discussion by the class, for any action the group may decide to take.

Approach 3

Place on the chalkboard the composite evaluation chart (fig. 25) which the class constructed during the unit launching. Ask the group how, after the study, they would now evaluate their congregation. As changes are logged, ask the group to suggest *how* they might move to achieve the goals. What must be done? How might it be done? What role can/should the class play? What is the role of the individual?

In suggesting the above activities I have apparently presupposed that the Took process is always to be a part of the class session. This, actually, is not necessarily true. It is important to plan Took activities as a class is introduced to a structure patterned on the Colossians cycle. Youth and adults need to "learn how to learn" when it comes to studying the Bible.

But when the group becomes response-oriented—when the class moves spontaneously into an open discussion of the meaning of the Word for their lives—then special Took activities become less and less necessary. For the group is learning to think response when they come to the Word, and their hearts and minds are opened up to the ministry of the Holy Spirit. At this point each class member tends to take personal responsibility for doing the Word.

In an open, sharing discussion this sense of personal responsibility *to do* the Word of God, to which the whole group is committed, becomes the primary and only necessary means of creating motivation.

CREATING MOTIVATION

Throughout the book I've used the term *creative* often. And now I've written *creating motivation*. Before the last page is turned it's important to state one more vital truth about creative teaching.

Teaching the Bible is essentially a creative ministry—but the task of creating is not ours. Only one Person can create—whether it be the creation of a universe, the creation of motivation, or the creation, in a heart of a human being, of response to God's Word.

That task is the Holy Spirit's. He and He alone is *the* Teacher.

I'm particularly conscious that what I've written in this book focuses on the activity of the master Teacher's human partner in the teaching ministry. I may be understood, because of this, to imply that teaching the Bible is merely a matter of skill, of fitting a pattern or of pushing a button. Bible teaching is not this, and never can be. For the Word of God is unique among all subject matter, and the task of teaching it unique in the whole realm of teaching. *For no one can communicate God's truth in such a way that it calls forth response except the sovereign God whose truth it is.* "Success" in Bible teaching depends on God alone.

What is taught in this book—and what you do in teaching the Word of God—is valid only to the extent that it conforms to and reflects the way God has chosen to work through His Word and through His church. Yet even teaching that harmonizes in its methods with the divine purpose of God for the Word will not change lives apart from the creative work of the Holy Spirit.

So teach. Be a creative teacher. Learn all you can of how to handle the Word of God, conscious of whose word the Scripture is. Learn all you can of how God works through the Word, and develop skills that will help you lead learners to response. And when you have done all, bow your head and commit all your efforts to God, in complete dependence on His Spirit, who alone can truly teach the Word.

Research and assignment
     for the student

1. Examine each of the learning activities suggested in this chapter and show how the author kept *flexibility* a basic feature.
2. Develop two more Took activities for each of the lessons concluded in this chapter.
3. Complete your lesson plans for the other two segments of Malachi.
4. Complete your lesson plan for the New Testament passage you have been developing.
5. Write up a *complete* evaluation of youth or adult materials from one Sunday school publisher, using criteria developed through this study.

6. Visit an adult or youth Sunday school class and write an evaluation of the session. Include specific suggestions on how you would modify the approach taken, if you would.
7. As a class project, develop a teacher-training course for use with teachers of youth or adults in the local church. If possible, teach it in a church.
8. Read *The Holy Spirit and Your Teaching* by Roy Zuck and relate the ministries of the Holy Spirit to each part of the teaching-learning process as developed in this book.
9. Teach in a local church (a) the New Testament lesson you have developed and (b) the unit of lessons on Malachi.

Exploration
   for the lay teacher
1. Teach the John 14:22-24 lesson to your Sunday school class, selecting learning activities which you feel would fit your group.
2. Teach the Malachi unit, after developing your own sessions on the portions of the book not covered in these chapters.
3. Set definite goals for your class and your own teaching. Write them down. Review chapters of this text until you are able to see *how* you can reach the goals. Then commit your class and teaching to God's Spirit, and be a creative Bible teacher.

APPENDIX 1

Using "Creative Bible Teaching" as a Textbook

THIS BOOK is designed to serve a double purpose. It is written to help the layman who teaches to understand his ministry and to perform it more effectively. It is also written to serve as a framework around which academic courses, such as a philosophy of Christian education or a pedagogy class, can be built. As a text, it does not offer an exhaustive treatment of the areas on which it touches. My purpose rather has been to crystallize issues and to present a theologically and educationally sound approach to Bible teaching. This book is designed as a starting point for deeper studies.

You'll note that each chapter concludes with a research-and-assignment section. These suggest a variety of learning activities for the Bible school, college, or seminary student, correlated with the chapter content. They are given with the idea that the instructor will select and assign those which fit his class and his approach to the subject, and omit the rest.

Because the approach to the topics covered in this book is not exhaustive, many teachers will want to go more deeply into some of the issues raised. This Appendix is to help them do so. In it I suggest additional readings to go with each chapter, and possible avenues of approach in teaching.

Let's turn, then, to an overview of the book, and move on to supplementary resources to use with each chapter.

THE BOOK AS A WHOLE

The overall plan is simple. Section one, The Bible We Teach, looks at the theology of Bible teaching. It first sketches the dominant contemporary view, then presents in more detail an evangelical position. A grasp of the theological issues involved is essential for anyone in the professional Christian education ministry.

Section two, Teaching the Bible Creatively, develops an approach to Bible teaching that is consistent with the nature and purpose of the Bible, as understood by evangelical Christians. The *how* as well as the *why* is developed to help the student understand teaching that leads to spiritual growth.

Section three, Guidelines to Creative Teaching, goes into the application of the philosophy earlier developed to teaching on different age levels. It seeks to help the reader become flexible and confident of his ability to guide learners in a variety of learning-experiences, within the framework of a process that will lead the learner to spiritual growth.

CHAPTER BY CHAPTER DEVELOPMENT

UNIT I

Chapter 1 raises the question of the nature of the Bible and asks, "How can we teach the Bible effectively if we do not fully understand how God uses it to transform?" The illustrations are designed to show that holding an orthodox view of Scripture is, in itself, no guarantee that we will teach it effectively.

The chapter suggests two alternative views of the Bible and indicates that one of the alternatives dominates contemporary Christendom. Because of this domination, and because orthodox doctrine doesn't guarantee effective teaching, the chapter suggests that the Bible teacher *must* come to understand the Word he teaches.

If your purpose is to motivate your class for this course, one class session on the chapter should be enough. If your purpose is to help your students to a fuller understanding of the contemporary scene, you'll probably want to spend several class hours. For your own reading, Kendig Cully, *The Search for a Christian Education—Since 1940* is essential. Your students might sample Elliott, *Can Religious Education Be Christian?* And you can then point up in class the dominant theological and educational ideas of that time. For a second session your students might study more carefully H. S. Smith's critique, *Faith and Nurture.* In class the criticisms and the theological presuppositions of neoorthodoxy can be clarified. In a final session, Zuck's "commendable emphases" might be explored in detail, with students expected to give their views on why each emphasis is commendable in Bible teaching.

With this general background laid, you can lead your class into a closer examination of present-day Christian educational thought.

Chapter 2 attempts to simplify the basic elements of contemporary thinking on revelation and the Bible. These concepts are completely foreign to most conservatives, and in my simplification some important aspects of contemporary theory are left out and others merely mentioned. For anyone studying for a professional Christian education ministry, this area ought to be developed. No one can avoid meeting this pattern of thinking in future professional reading.

There are four areas which I try to develop in my own classes, guiding students to representative reading in each area:

1. *The nature of revelation and the Bible.* Sara Little, *The Bible in Christian Education* is a basic text for this area. Also instructive are chapter 3 of Shinn, *Educational Mission of the Church*; chapter 4 of Sherrill, *Gift of Power*; chapter 4 of Miller, *Education for Christian Living*; and Iris Cully, *Imparting the Word*. Chapters 1, 3, 6 and 7 of this last book show how evangelical the contemporary position can sound.

For your own background, Hyatt's new *How Encounter Yields Revelation* is must reading, particularly for its critique of encounter theology.

Normally two class sessions are needed to help students grasp the idea of a completely noninformational revelation. Usually the full impact of the outside readings is not achieved until after some in-class introduction to the area.

2. *The focus of encounter teaching.* I next try to help my students think through to the goal, for teaching such an idea of revelation makes for contemporary Christian education. Contrasts are drawn between an informational learning focus and an encounter focus. This helps students understand contemporary curriculum theory and challenges them to see the weakness of Bible teaching which is *simply* informational. Helpful readings in this area are L. Harold DeWolf, *Teaching Our Faith in God*; pp. 108 f chapters 7, 9 and 10 of Schreyer, *Christian Education in Theological Focus*; and chapter 3 of David R. Hunter, *Christian Education as Engagement*. This is in addition to helpful books mentioned in the previous section.

3. *Methods in teaching.* Many of the contemporary writers go into

interesting detail on methods designed to promote encounter. I usually ask students to read in several, to get an idea of the methods they suggest, and to *contrast* them with methods they might use in teaching. The methods actually are similar—the purpose differs.

Good readings are chapter 5 of Kendig Cully, *The Teaching Church*; chapters 6 and 7 of Iris Cully, *The Dynamics of Christian Education*; and chapter 10 of Schreyer. Key reading for you, which develops the ideas hinted at in the second chapter of this text, are Iris Cully, *Imparting the Word*; pp. 117 f, and Dendry, pp. 88 and 89.

4. *Place of relationships.* This area, neglected in chapter 2, is so important in contemporary thinking that it should be carefully explored in two or more class sessions. Basic ideas can be discovered in Miller, in chapter 2 of Shinn, on pages 237-38 of Butler, in chapter 3 of Sherrill, in chapter 12 of Schreyer, and in chapter 3 of DeWolf.

Chapter 3 suggests two approaches to evaluating the contemporary concept of revelation. The first is by examination of its fruit. What has it produced? Quotes included in the chapter enable students to get the picture! The second is by pointing up a philosophical and practical problem: How does one who will not take Scripture literally know how to interpret it? If one deserts literal interpretation, he has to find some key to understanding the message of the Bible, and he can *never be sure his key is the right one!*

These ideas can be covered thoroughly in a single class session. It is important, though, if Christian education students are not introduced to hermeneutical principles in any other course, to see that they understand what is meant by "literal interpretation." Here Ramm's book (see R & A assignment 5) is a standard text in many seminaries.

For a simple survey of current theological ferment on revelation, see Carl F. H. Henry, *Frontiers in Modern Theology.*

Chapter 4 develops from the Bible a meaning of revelation that is distinctively different from the contemporary view. Revelation is defined lexically, and its component elements charted from relevant passages of Scripture. A brief survey indicates that the Bible writers were convinced that they had received and were communicating true information from God.

The fact of nonverbal revelation is discussed, but the vital point—that the interpretation of nonverbal revelation is itself communicated in words—is made. This should be emphasized in class.

Revelation is related to inspiration in the chapter, and the point is made that while the whole Bible is inspired, it is not all revelation in the lexical sense. Yet the value of Scripture—and its character as the Word of God—extends to the entire Old and New Testaments.

The length of time you'll spend on this area should again depend on the background and other training available to your students, as well as their own questionings in this area. Each Christian education student *should* be confident of his Bible and should understand the doctrines on which this confidence rests.

Good books with which to supplement study of revelation and inspiration are Walvoord (ed.), *Inspiration and Interpretation* and Henry (ed.), *Revelation and the Bible.*

Chapter 5 presents the thesis that God makes Himself known through information about Himself. Information is the point of contact we have with God, and in information about Himself, God Himself confronts us. Man's *response* to God, as He shows Himself in His Word, determines the outcome of any initial contact. Only an appropriate response, as determined by the nature of the truth we come to know, can lead to a deeper personal experience with God.

The crucial issue in Christian education thus is not communicating information as information. It is guiding learners to respond appropriately to God as He shows Himself in the particular information taught. Bible teaching must communicate truth, but with an emphasis on personal response. (This idea is further developed in chap. 8.)

Several issues raised in this chapter deserve closer study. One relates to the nature of response. Response to God cannot be the product of unaided human effort. Response is intrinsically related to the New Testament concept of faith. Biblical faith always has a dimension of response; without that it becomes the "dead" faith James speaks of (2:14-26). A study of obedience as response to God (not as works) should also prove_helpful, if time permits. Several research-and-assignment questions focus on this kind of study.

While faith is by nature responsive, the teacher needs to remember that he is to teach in harmony with the workings and the purposes of Scripture and to be a tool of the Holy Spirit. To work in such harmony, teaching *must* have a response goal. The research-and-assignment section provides a stimulating exercise along this line which will introduce the students to the next section of the book.

UNIT II

In this study of *teaching the Bible creatively*, creative teaching is defined as that which "consciously and effectively focuses on activities which raise the student's level of learning." Chapter 6 suggests different ways in which we may be said to learn. The teaching process by which learning levels can be raised to response and application is demonstrated in chapter 7; theological foundations of the process are explained in chapter 8; more detailed examination of crucial steps in the teaching process is undertaken in chapters 9 and 10. Chapter 11 looks at motivation in relation to learning, and 12 gives suggestions for choosing and using curricula.

Chapter 6 stretches students to rethink their concept of learning. If you want to go deeply into this, it's best to approach the area from the standpoint of educational philosophy. A number of standard texts (Lodge, Phoenix, Weber, etc.) discuss the classic educational approaches and their various concepts of the nature and goal of learning. While much study is currently being done in learning theory, little of value seems to have surfaced as yet.

Extra study in this area is valuable, but may be off the track at this point. Enough classtime must be spent (perhaps using several R & A assignments) to lead a class to rethink their presuppositions about learning, and to grapple with some of the basic issues.

Chapter 7 should be read and discussed, perhaps in light of ideas expressed in the adult teacher training filmstrip *Out on a Limb* (Scripture Press). The film might be shown before the chapter is read, as background to make the class more sensitive to the place of participation. This chapter will be referred to often in later sections of the book as a model for demonstration purposes.

Chapter 8 picks up the theme of response from chapter 5 and shows how Colossians 1:9-11 systematizes (in terms of process, not of steps) movement from information to response. As well as systematizing the process, Paul's prayer recorded here focuses attention on crucial areas of potential breakdown in teaching and in personal life.

Research-and-assignment questions suggest a variety of supplementary activities you may find of value. However, the basic concepts expressed so clearly in Paul's prayer *must be understood*. This is the foundation (rather than educational psychology or philosophy) of the process of creative teaching as developed in this book.

Chapter 9 explores two implications that arise from the Colossians study: the nature of the teaching aim is defined, and the structure of the teaching-learning process is revealed.

My position is slightly different from that of others who have written on aims. Note the reason: in this text the stress is on teaching the Bible for growth—and this demands a response aim. Classtime should definitely be taken to guide the class in evaluating aims and in gaining skill in writing teaching aims.

The second part of the chapter breaks down into four steps the structure of the lesson designed to call out response. The text presents specific tasks for each step. These tasks and the steps themselves (title mnemonically for easy recall) should be mastered. As noted, ability to think in terms of the structure of a lesson is particularly valuable.

As structuring a lesson involves a skill, practice is needed. Several classes might well be spent evaluating curricula, restructuring lessons in class, or developing and teaching a lesson of the student's own construction in class.

At this point the text moves from theory toward practice, and class sessions should reflect this shift.

Chapter 10 moves into the very heart (and the most misunderstood part) of the teaching-learning process. Research-and-assignment items 1-5 will help test your students' understanding of the major points made in the chapter. Additional readings on *transfer of learning* might prove helpful. Suggested are chapter 3 of Bayles, chapter 6 of Weber, chapter 5 of Eason, and chapter 2 of Frandsen (see Bibliography).

Again, since a skill is involved as well as a philosophy of approach, time should be given for students to evaluate and to work on lessons, to sharpen their approach to application.

Chapter 11 touches on motivation, a topic so important that it deserves an entire book. It breaks down the subject into two areas: personal factors in motivation and structural factors in motivation. You may wish to approach motivation as a whole. Helpful is Seagoe's suggestion to think in terms of conditions in which learning takes place. (See Appendix 1 of Seagoe, and LeBar.)

When looking at the personal aspects of motivation, a survey of "how to teach" books is informative—often in terms of what is left out! Many secular books deal with the nature and functioning of groups under various kinds of leadership. This, if you wish to develop it, is also helpful. Yet note the stress in chapter 11 on the basic Christian attitude of the teacher toward his students. This should characterize everyone ministering the Word.

Structural factors of motivation are widely disregarded in books on Christian education. A helpful project is to think through a unit of lessons on, say, the junior level, in terms of built-in motivation. Revising a set of such lessons to increase motivation provides for a review of lesson structuring skills; it forces use of ideas on motivation as well.

Chapter 12 should be touched on, lest the student get the idea that curricula are of little value. At the same time, a review of curricula on the market should help students discover for their future use the best materials available.

UNIT III

The material in this unit is provided to help teachers working on various age levels develop skill in planning learning activities.

The first section of three chapters (13-15) deals with preschoolers. The goal of preschool Christian education is spelled out first, then the kind of programs that facilitate effective communication on nursery and beginner levels is described.

The second section of five chapters (16-20) explores questions that have been raised about teaching the Bible to children, and demonstrates the structuring of children's lessons with learning activities designed to lead them through the processes described in chapters 6 through 12.

The third section of four chapters (21-24) explores learning activities suited to guiding youth and adults through the same process.

Preschoolers

Chapter 13 is the most heavily documented chapter in the book, for the simple reason that the ideas here are the most controversial. Conservatives simply do not have a stated and agreed upon philosophy of preschool Christian education.

The purpose of teaching preschoolers which is suggested here is a "hard line" one. It doesn't mix with older concepts of social development and adjustment. It stresses the communication of truths to help children formulate a biblical world view.

Note that this view does *not* exclude social development and adjustment emphases in classroom practice. It simply specifies that the *primary purpose* of teaching the Bible on this level is cognitive, and that this purpose should guide curriculum planning and teaching practices. The filmstrip *Sunbeam in Your Hand* (Scripture Press), on which the author worked and in which appear threes whom he taught for over a year, clearly demonstrates the kind of program and purpose chapter 13 advocates.

Chapter 14 looks at the structure of a nursery teaching program. The filmstrip just cited is helpful here, for it shows a group of threes going through an entire Sunday school hour, and it demonstrates principles suggested for interest-center time, etc. Its use is recommended.

Observation visits to nearby church nursery departments should be helpful too—and lead to discussion of what the purpose of nursery Christian education seems to be as presently conducted in our churches.

Chapter 15 first surveys the structure and activities of a beginner Sunday school hour and then touches briefly on curriculum.

Much work needs to be done in this last area. An exciting project, which can introduce your students to empirical research in Christian education, might be to develop, with the class, a sequence of questions to ask four- or five-year-olds, to discover (1) their level of Bible knowledge and (2) their awareness of the meaning of the known information. Factors such as time in Sunday school, whether or not a child is from a Christian home, etc., should be considered. From this a preliminary hypothesis might be worked out as to the Bible truths preschoolers can and should be taught.

Children, Youth and Adults

The rest of the text moves into skills and concepts needed to implement the teaching philosophy earlier developed on various age levels. Each chapter is quite complete, and each has a variety of recommended R & A activities which will guide in giving the students a practical command of the ideas and skills needed for creative teaching.

APPENDIX 2

Notes to Quotations Used in the Text

Chapter 1
1. Roy Zuck, "The Educational Pattern of Neo-Orthodox Christian Education," *Bibliotheca Sacra* (October 1962), pp. 348-49.

Chapter 2
1. Sara Little, *The Bible in Christian Education*, p. 11.
2. Lewis Sherrill, *The Gift of Power*, p. 69.
3. Iris Cully, *The Dynamics of Christian Education*, p. 86.
4. Sherrill, p. 69.
5. Ibid., p. 74.
6. Ibid.
7. Donald Butler, *Religious Education*, p. 150.
8. Little, p. 57.
9. Sherrill, p. 78.
10. Cully, p. 98.
11. Sherrill, p. 66.
12. Butler, p. 148.
13. Little, p. 5.
14. Ibid., p. 57.
15. Butler, p. 150.
16. Cully, p. 20.
17. Sherrill, p. 145.
18. David Hunter, *Christian Education as Engagement*, Introduction.

Chapter 3
1. Kendig B. Cully, *Westminster Dictionary of Christian Education*, p. 444.
2. Lewis Sherrill, *The Gift of Power*, pp. 135 f.
3. Randolph Crump Miller, *Education for Christian Living*, p. 156.
4. Harold L. DeWolf, *Teaching Our Faith in God*, p. 123.
5. G. C. Schreyer, *Christian Education in Theological Focus*, pp. 50-51.
6. Miller, p. 69.
7. Sara Little, *The Role of the Bible in Contemporary Christian Education*, p. 135.
8. James D. Smart, *The Creed in Christian Teaching*, p. 227.
9. Smart, p. 163.
10. Donald Butler, *Religious Education*, p. 148.
11. Roger L. Shinn, *Educational Mission of the Church*, p. 31.

Chapter 13
1. Annemarie Roper, past president, Preschool Assn., Detroit, *Childhood Education*, October 1959, pp. 3-9.
2. Phoebe M. Anderson, *Threes in the Christian Community*, p. 226.
3. Ibid., p. 233.

APPENDIX 3

BIBLIOGRAPHY

THESE BOOKS are selected from the great number available today. The listing is not an attempt to catalog all, or even most, of the resource material available. It rather catalogs those few books which are mentioned by title in the text or in Appendix 1, plus a few others which are of special value.

Inclusion of a book on this list should not be taken as endorsement of its contents by either the author or this publisher.

THE BIBLE WE TEACH

Butler, Donald. *Religious Education.* New York: Harper & Row, 1962.

Cully, Iris V. *The Dynamics of Christian Education.* Philadelphia: Westminster, 1958.

———. *Imparting the Word.* Philadelphia: Westminster, 1962.

Cully, Kendig B. *The Search for a Christian Education—Since 1940.* Philadelphia: Westminster, 1965.

———. *The Teaching Church.* Philadelphia: United Church, 1963.

———, ed. *Westminster Dictionary of Christian Education.* Philadelphia: Westminster, 1963.

Dendy, Marshall C. *Changing Patterns in Christian Education.* Richmond: Knox, 1964.

DeWolf, Harold L. *Teaching Our Faith in God.* Nashville: Abingdon, 1963.

Elliott, H. S. *Can Religious Education Be Christian?* New York: Macmillan, 1940.

Henry, Carl F. H. *Frontiers in Modern Theology.* Chicago: Moody, 1966.

Hyatt, Harold E. *Encountering Truth.* Nashville: Abingdon, 1966.

———. *How Encounter Yields Revelation.* Nashville: Abingdon, 1966.

Hunter, David. *Christian Education as Engagement.* New York: Seabury, 1963.

LeBar, Lois. *Education That Is Christian.* Westwood, N.J.: Revell, 1958.

Little, Sara. *The Bible in Christian Education.* Richmond: Knox, 1961.

Miller, Randolph C. *The Clue to Christian Education.* New York: Scribner, 1950.

———. *Education for Christian Living.* Englewood Cliffs, N.J.: Prentice-Hall, 1963.

Ramm, Bernard. *Protestant Biblical Interpretation.* Boston: Wilde, 1956.

Schreyer, G. C. *Christian Education in Theological Focus.*

Sherrill, Lewis. *The Gift of Power.* New York: Macmillan, 1955.

Shinn, Roger L. *Educational Mission of the Church.* Philadelphia: United Church, 1962.

Smart, James D. *The Creed in Christian Teaching.* Philadelphia: Westminster, 1962.

Smith, H. S. *Faith and Nurture.* New York: Scribner, 1941.

Vieth, Paul. *The Church and Christian Education.* St. Louis: Bethany, 1963.

Walvoord, John F., ed. *Inspiration and Interpretation.* Grand Rapids: Eerdmans, 1957.

Zuck, Roy B. *Spiritual Power in Your Teaching.* Chicago: Moody, 1972.

Teaching the Bible Creatively

Anderson, Phoebe M. *Threes in the Christian Community.* Philadelphia: United Church, n.d.

Bayles, E. F. *Democratic Educational Theory.* New York: Harper, 1960.

Eason, M. E. *Psychological Foundations of Education.* New York: Holt, Rinehart & Winston, 1964.

Edge, Findley. *Helping the Teacher.* Nashville: Broadman, 1959.

———. *Teaching for Results.* Nashville: Broadman, 1956.

Frandsen, Arden H. *Educational Psychology: The Principles of Learning in Teaching.* New York: McGraw-Hill, 1961.

Fritz, D. B. *Ways of Teaching.* Philadelphia: Westminster, 1965.

Gilbert, W. Kent. *As Christians Teach.* Philadelphia: Fortress, 1963.

Lobingier, John L. *If Teaching Is Your Job.* Boston: Pilgrim, 1956.

Lodge, R. C. *Philosophy of Education.* New York: Harper, 1947.

Morrison, E. S. and Foster, V. E. *Creative Teaching in the Church.* Englewood Cliffs, N. J.: Prentice-Hall, 1963.

Richards, Lawrence O., ed. *The Key to Sunday School Achievement.* Chicago: Moody, 1965.

Rolston, Holmes. *The Bible in Christian Teaching*. Richmond: Knox, 1966.

Rood, Wayne R. *The Art of Teaching Christianity*. Nashville: Abingdon, 1968.

Rozell, Ray. *Informal Talks on Sunday School Teaching*. Grand Rapids: International, 1956.

Seagoe, M. V. *A Teacher's Guide to the Learning Process*. Dubuque, Iowa: W. C. Brown, 1961.

Sisemore, John T. *Blueprint for Teaching*. Nashville: Broadman, 1964.

Swain, Dorothy G. *Teach Me to Teach*. Valley Forge, Pa.: Judson, 1964.

Weber, Christian O. *Basic Philosophies of Education*. New York: Rinehart, 1960.

DATE DUE
